COPING
WITH
UNCERTAINTY

COPING
WITH
UNCERTAINTY

Insights from the New Sciences
of Chaos, Self-Organization,
and Complexity

URI MERRY

Illustrations by Natali Kassavin

Westport, Connecticut
London

Library of Congress Cataloging-in-Publication Data

Merry, Uri.
    Coping with uncertainty : insights from the new sciences of chaos,
self-organization, and complexity / Uri Merry ; illustrations by
Natali Kassavin.
       p. cm.
    Includes bibliographical references (p.) and index.
    ISBN 0–275–94910–9 (alk. paper). —ISBN 0–275–95152–9 (pbk.)
    1. Uncertainty—Social aspects. 2. Complexity (Philosophy)
3. Social change. 4. Chaotic behavior in systems. I. Title.
HM291.M433 1995
301′.01′185—dc20   94–16996

British Library Cataloguing in Publication Data is available.

Library of Congress Catalog Card Number: 94–16996
ISBN: 0–275–94910–9
    0–275–95152–9 (pbk.)

First published in 1995

Praeger Publishers, 88 Post Road West, Westport, CT 06881
An imprint of Greenwood Publishing Group, Inc.

Printed in the United States of America

The paper used in this book complies with the
Permanent Paper Standard issued by the National
Information Standards Organization (Z39.48–1984).

10 9 8 7 6 5 4 3 2 1

Contents

Preface

We are living in a world that is becoming more and more complex. As individuals and as societies, people are finding it increasingly difficult to cope with a world that daily becomes more complex and uncertain. This is an endeavor to trace how and why this is happening, where it is leading, and to examine what options are open to people, as individuals and as societies, to find ways of coping with uncertainty. This will be done with the help of findings from the New Sciences of Chaos, Self-organization, Complexity, and new understandings of evolution. The New Sciences throw light on the intensification of complexity and chaos in the world at the turn of this century, and help to enhance understanding of its background and causes.

This book is about the intensification of uncertainty in people's lives. It is about what is happening to us, today and tomorrow, as we live through a very eventful, awesome, and chaotic period in human history. Based on the New Sciences, this is an attempt to describe the growing magnitude of uncertainty in the world, to trace how it has come about, and where it is leading.

All of this leads to the question of how people will be able to live in such an increasingly turbulent world, both as individuals and as societies, and what possibilities are open to them under these complex conditions. The final part of the book attempts to describe some ways of coping and functioning with the burgeoning uncertainty in the world and in people's lives.

A number of excellent books on the New Sciences have been published. These books brought the sciences of Chaos, Complexity, Self-organization, and evolution to the educated reader who was willing to devote time and concentration to the subject. This book is different. It is not a book about the New Sciences, but rather about these New Sciences as applied to human affairs in our times. It focuses on how they manifest themselves in the human world, ranging from cultures, societies, nations, institutions to families and personal lives. It analyzes why complexity, emergent novelty, and often chaos are becoming more and more prevalent and intense in people's lives, and describes some of the possible ways to cope with the growing uncertainty in the world.

It is impossible to deal with the New Sciences in human affairs without first having a basic understanding of what the sciences are all about. The first part of this book is therefore devoted to that purpose. It gives a short overview of the current findings in these sciences. Thereafter the bulk of the book applies the New Sciences to understand why uncertainty is intensifying and how to cope with complexity and uncertainty in the human realm.

The use of difficult concepts from mathematics, physics, chemistry and other exact sciences, has been cut to the necessary minimum. This is in line with one of the basic ways of coping with uncertainty and dealing with it--which is, to become conscious of and then understand the evolutionary processes that breed complexity and periods of chaos. From another perspective, as more and more people understand the chaotic developments raging in our world, humanity's chances of dealing with them and exploiting their advantages, whilst evading their more threatening consequences, become greater.

The book has three parts:

Part I THE NEW SCIENCES: This is an up-to-date, concise overview of the major findings of the New Sciences of Chaos, Self-organization, and Complexity. It applies the Nobel Prize-winning work of Ilya Prigogine, to understand how new order emerges out of chaos. It will assist in understanding the rest of the book.

Part II THE GROWTH OF UNCERTAINTY: This section analyzes why complexity is on the upsurge in the world, and why in these times in particular, human societies and individuals are experiencing such an intense period of uncertainty.

Part III COPING WITH UNCERTAINTY: Building on new knowledge of complex adaptive systems and evolution, this section surveys the major approaches of coping with uncertainty and chaotic transformations in society and in our personal lives.

This is a book for the thinking person who questions what is happening around him and to where it might lead. It is based on the studies, research, and theories of many of the finest scientific minds of our times. I have often quoted passages from their work, preferring the unique flavor of their words to a summary I could make. Nevertheless the final responsibility for this book is mine.

Thanks are due to many. Without the research and creative thinking of the scientists and writers whose works I built on and quoted from, this book would not have been written. Out of these I am especially indebted to Professors T.R. Young and J. Goldstein whose remarks, ideas and writings enriched me, and to Dr. S. J. Goerner whose writings stimulated me. The works of James Waldrop and Roger Lewin helped clarify my thinking on complexity. The writings of many others cited in the book also enriched me.

I owe a great debt to my editor James R. Dunton whose wise feedback to my first draft gave the book the form it has taken. I appreciate the work of Richard A. Sillett, the production editor, and M. Hammer, the copy editor, who improved my style. I wish to thank N. Kassavin for the illustrations, my institute for encouraging me, D. Atid for feedback on a first draft, my sister A. Abrahami for editing that draft, my son Nir for assisting throughout, Etai Leviathan, Arnie Lever, Norman Alabela, Irit Barnatan, Boaz Nishrai, Amitai Niv, and Ayah Atid for help in preparing the manuscript, and finally my wife, Ruth, for encouragement, help, and patience.

One final word on the illustrations. The cubelike figure of "order" always represents linear order. While the round, nobbly black (Mandelbrot) spot changes its identity throughout the book. Sometimes it represents chaos, sometimes complexity, sometimes self-organization, sometimes evolution, and sometimes all the New Sciences. That is left to the reader's imagination.

Uri Merry, Ph.D.

I
THE NEW SCIENCES

1
What Is Chaos?

GROWING UNCERTAINTY

The human world appears to be becoming more uncertain. Many people are becoming aware that growing complexity, periods of chaos, and fast changing novelty are having a mounting effect on their everyday lives. They have a vague feeling that these are important for them and that they are somehow gradually having more influence on the course of their lives. Many are feeling it more in various aspects of their existence. They may be going through chaotic periods in their personal lives. Family life may seem to be becoming more complex and having more chaotic episodes, and sometimes emerging in new forms, some of which carry the seeds of chaotic relationships within them.

Time honored institutions, with the values they exemplify, are being increasingly undermined by crises. Great cities are breaking down under the complexity of coping with a chaotic maelstrom of crime, pollution, strikes, racial tension, and traffic jams. New behaviors, styles, and novel developments surprise us daily.

The political governments of nations often face both complex and chaotic crises that they are incapable of dealing with. These manifest themselves in the economy, in the institutions dealing with education and health, in social services, in the plight of the poor and underprivileged, in relations with minorities, in conflicts between parties, in political corruption and in dealing with extremists.

On the international level these are times when one turbulent chaotic crisis follows another. From Vietnam, to Afghanistan, to trouble in South America, to tension in the Middle East, to the Gulf War, to the breakup of Eastern Europe, to the troubles in South Africa, to the riots in China, to the breakdown of the Soviet Union, Georgia, Yugoslavia, Somalia, Haiti--and so on and so on--one complex crisis after another. The complexity of new problems overwhelms us as situations emerge that were never faced before.

Do all these manifestations of intensifying complexity and chaotic periods in social living have anything in common with the "chaos," "complexity," and "self-organization" dealt with in the New Sciences of Chaos, Self-organization, and Complexity?

A Focus on Chaos

In this chapter we will focus on Chaos and leave Complexity and Self-organization for later treatment. In everyday usage, "chaos" has a meaning similar to abyss, from which the word chasm comes. Webster defines chaos as the "condition in which things are out of their normal place or relationships." Some of the synonyms given by the same source are: confusion, clutter, disarray, disorder, muddle, and snarl. The American College Dictionary speaks about "utter confusion or disorder wholly without organization or order." Chaos is sometimes described as turbulence. Some synonyms for turbulence are commotion, agitation, confusion, tumult and turmoil. These synonyms give a picture of a dynamic, active form of chaos.

Are these everyday definitions and descriptions of "chaos" compatible with the "chaos" studied by scientists in the behavior of pendulums or the patterns of changing weather systems? Is it possible to learn anything about the behavior of human beings and their societies from the New Sciences born from mathematics, physics, chemistry, and geometry? Is the "chaos" of political systems similar to the turbulence of the water in a waterfall? Can knowledge be gained about the behavior of civilizations, societies, organizations, families, and individuals by applying them to insights derived from the study of the New Sciences? These are some of the questions the book will attempt to answer. To do so it is first necessary to take a short look at the two kinds of chaos: the one of everyday life, and the chaos beginning to be heard about more frequently in science.

CHAOS IN SOCIETY

Donald A. Schon, an MIT social scientist, sees growing uncertainty as a loss of the stable state in human society: " . . . the attack on the stable state has passed beyond what our strategies of resistance can contain. Throughout our society we are experiencing the actual or threatened dissolution of stable organizations and institutions, anchors for personal identity and systems of values. Most important, the stable state itself is becoming less real" (1971:15).

Jeremy Rifkin (1981:3) describes a world of growing confusion and disorder in which nothing seems to work. Leaders are constantly lamenting and apologizing. Whenever we think we have found a way out of a crisis, something goes wrong. The solutions that are applied create more serious problems than those they were meant to solve. Accidents happen at nuclear power plants, inflation soars, people fear unemployment, mankind faces the danger of nuclear war, and "finally we want to roll down the window and scream in desperation, Why isn't something being done about all this!" Things about us accelerate, without getting anywhere. We and society are bogged down. Was Rifkin exaggerating? Here is a random collection of statements from the May 11, 1992, issue of *Newsweek*.

Los Angeles: Like bulletins from a war zone, the words and images came flying out of a city going up in smoke and flames. . . . Out of a city endlessly burning, out of the heart of Simi Valley and the soul of south-central Los Angeles, a verdict seen as a miscarriage of justice induced a convulsion of violence that left 44 dead, 2000 bleeding, and $1 billion in charred ruins. . . . The first few hours after the verdict were near chaos. . . . The sun came up on a city that had lost its center of gravity and was spinning out of orbit.

Germany: If there's one thing the Germans hate, it's *das chaos*. And suddenly, it seems it surrounds them. For the first time in almost 20 years, those legendary German trains stopped running on time last week; in fact many stopped running at all. So did buses and streetcars, leading to 100-kilometer traffic jams. . . . Mail went undelivered, and garbage piled up in the otherwise tidy streets of Frankfurt, Stuttgart and Hamburg. Opera and theater stages went dark. Zoos closed down.

Italy: The current German 'chaos' would be business as usual. In Bulgaria it would be paradise. There is chaos in Bosnia, in Armenia, in Los Angeles.

Philipines: no sane politician could hope to tackle the social and economic mess of the Philippines.

Moscow: On the streets chaos rules.

Uncertainty in Political Life

Citizens of a communist country have no doubt about what chaos in political life means. Michail Gorbachev spoke about the danger of chaos erupting in the former Soviet Union, and indeed it is emerging there in the new republics and expanding daily. Boris Yeltsin warned that if his new constitution was not approved chaos would reign. The constitution was approved, but will chaos disappear?

The image of Russia is one of anarchy. Competing political factions, splinter groups, religious and nationalistic extremists, national entities and national or cultural minorities all fighting for power, without a way in which the differences can be settled. For many years Lebanon was a tragic example of chaos at the political level. Somalia and Haiti are present-day examples. It appears as if neither government, democratic assembly, nor any other political entity has the authority or sufficient trust and power to bring about economic, national and political solutions that will be accepted by all involved.

Chaos is becoming more frequent in various countries throughout the world with turmoil and tumult being brought into people's homes every day by mass media. Turbulence and uncertainty also appear to be affecting political institutions more than they have in the past. Alvin Toffler (1981), author and social scientist, remarks that the system is out of control and asks if one can live in such a society. The problem is that not only technology has broken loose, but also many other social processes have begun to run wildly and are resisting our best efforts to guide them.

Political structures throughout the world are facing mounting chaos. Political parties of the industrial world as well as parliaments and presidencies and all the structures of government seem to be unable to perform their duties. Chaos is threatening not only representitive democracy, but all forms of government from communist regimes to social democracies to South American dictatorships. One of Webster's definitions for chaos is "absence of effective government or the resulting disorder."

The problems are not only in former communist countries. Chaos, in the form of crisis in the political institutions of democracy, is on the increase in the Western world as well. We are seeing a profound crisis not of a particular kind of government, but of democracy itself in all its various forms where political structures are breaking down. (Toffler 1981).

Being Caught between Two Systems

Deep chaos in society might manifest itself as a transition--a period of confusion--without ground rules and without a clear way to escape the mess. Such is the present predicament of Yugoslavia. This could be a time when there is an inability to create conditions under which different viewpoints will have the legitimacy to confront each other and find a way to pull the system out of the quagmire in which it is sinking. Such might be the situation in Haiti, Georgia, and Myanmar.

Deep chaos in political life might be a time of transition between orders; a temporary period of uncertainty, unpredictabilty, and disorder accompanied by great difficulty to end the uncertainty, disarray, confusion, tension, conflict and disruption. These conditions might be increasing in our times. Yugoslavia is in the midst of a period of intense chaos. A variety of political, ideological, national and cultural interests are engaging in battle without end. Some of the republics of the former USSR may be going the same way.

The republics of the former Soviet Union appear to be caught in between two systems. A large part of their population has said goodbye to the communist system and yet they are struggling with seemingly insurmountable difficulties to forge their way to a democratic market system. The situation may be similar in other countries such as Angola, Poland, Romania, and many other nations that appear as if entrapped between two worlds and are in varying degrees displaying symptoms of anarchy and the inability to rule themselves.

This may have relevance to chaos in human systems. Being caught between two systems, between two worlds, in the twilight land between two dimensions, might be one of the manifestations of deep chaos in human systems. Deep chaos might be found in the situation of systems, like societies, in transition between two basic ways of existence--belonging neither to one nor the other--and wandering in the no-man's land of inability to choose either one or the other.

Uncertainty in Organizations and Communities

Uncertainty is stalking organizations and institutions. These bastions of order, regularity, and stability are now under threat. The crises affecting the general level of society also affects institutions. Donald Schon (1971) says that currents of change are rolling through every domain of society, shaking the stable state. Today, there is no established institution in society that perceives itself as adequate to the challenges it faces.

The compounding of chaos in the world appears to engulf more organizations, institutions, communities and cities. Toffler (1971) eloquently describes how revolution shatters institutions and power relationships. This is happening in all the modern industrial nations. Universities are besieged with unrest. Riots rampage throughout ghettos. Great cities are hit by strikes, racial riots and breakdowns in essential services. There is a feeling that the whole system is getting out of control.

Deep chaos takes hold in organizations, institutions, and communities when crisis strikes. A period of deep chaos occurs in a stage of the development of a crisis when the organization enters what some call "the void," others call "the transition period," and still others call "the dark night of the soul." This is the twilight zone after crisis strikes an institution or community, when it is beginning to be clear that what was, will be no more. The new way of the future has not yet unfolded and can barely be discerned--and yet the past is finished. This is again the situation of being trapped between two worlds, without belonging to either. It is the wandering through the desert, having left Egypt behind while the promised land is not yet in sight. In a certain sense, this is being caught between two dimensions. This is something like the present predicament of Russia and the Eastern European countries. Being in a "fractal" dimension, in between two dimensions, is one of the scientific descriptions of chaos in physical systems.

Uncertainty in Families

In many modern cultures, families, which were regarded as bastions of continuity, security, regularity, order, assurance, and safety, are being besieged by uncertainty. The old familiar forms have broken down and the new forms have not yet matured. The institution of the family is caught in the intermittent period, when old forms are no longer relevant and new forms have not yet taken root. Uncertainty is everywhere.

Within the family itself life has become discontinuous and turbulent. The unpredictable, complex, diversified, turbulent world of today has an effect on personality and on the character of close relationships within the family and outside it. People are becoming more autonomous, complex, and internally fragmented and are bringing this into their family lives. Family members also bring many mutually incompatible realities from their myriad other activities and connections outside the family into the home. The intensity and variety of lifestyles, values, and priorities interact in close proximity and with much emotion in the family home.

Kenneth Gergen professor of psychology and the author of *The Saturated Self* (1991), describes how the technologies of social saturation such as the car, telephone, television and airplane have enabled members of the family to be in virtually any state of mind and/or motion at any time. The daily confluence of multiple lives within one home makes for a sense of fragmentation, as if the members of the family are being scattered by the centrifugal forces of modern life.

It is not by chance that so many families are marked by discontinuity, breakups, divorces, remarriages and disintegration. Gergen points out that chaos and discontinuity are only the most visible effects of the technologies of social saturation on family life. The form, structure, and boundaries of the modern family have become blurred and fuzzy.

In modern societies, the "regular" family of two parents, male and female, and their common children is already a minority among other forms of family alignment. Other forms of family life abound and have become the majority. These can be: a single parent of either sex with children; parents with their children from former marriages; a man and woman living together without an official marriage contract; communal marriages; homosexual marriages; and so on. The variety of forms is great.

Once there was no doubt who belonged to the family and who did not. Today this has changed and as Gergen describes it, the boundaries are blurred to such an extent that it is difficult to distinguish between family and not family. People belong to a floating family that consists of a relatively formless collection of relationships in a continuous state of flux.

Feeling Chaos Personally

Increasing uncertainty on many sides is touching people personally. The heightening breakdown and loss of predictability and certainty of many societies and institutions is affecting people as individuals. Human personality and individual identity which evolved into forms that could cope with a steady industrial environment are losing their bearings in the incalculable conditions of the twilight zone between eras, their new forms having not yet established themselves.

The greatest threat to the stability of institutions and anchors for identity is that people have lost their belief in the stable state itself. The old institutions appear inadequate to handle the problems facing them and people do not believe in the new institutions. People have lost their belief in the stability of social values and have no others to replace them. The loss of the stable state erodes the sources of support for personal security. People have those sources of support least where they are most needed (Schon 1971).

Personal security and identity are threatened as daily life becomes affected more by the fluctuations and turmoil around it. The complexity and uncertainty is internalized and becomes part of personality. Gergen (1991) vividly describes how we ingest multiple parts of others' being, for example, their values, attitudes, opinions or other aspects of their personalities, and incorporate them into our image of our self. As we mix the aspects of others with our own potentialities, we find it difficult to know who we are and what we want. We have collected so many parts of others to create ourselves that the pieces do not mix well and can be in conflict with each other. To look inward, is to risk seeing a maelstrom of partial beings in conflict.

Deep chaos at its most intense state is probably felt during periods of transition in life. It can happen to the adolescent caught between the world of a child and the beginning of maturity, and it can catch the forty year old reaching the peak of career and family growth and seeing the end in sight. It may come in the wake of losing a job and finding himself or herself without an occupation, or when emigrating to a new country, without roots in the new and having lost the old, or after losing a lifetime marriage partner. During such transitions, a person may feel life turning erratic uncertain, unpredictable and disordered. In this condition he or she may find him or herself in a state where all goes wild and nothing makes sense anymore. Everything seems to be happening at once and all is in disarray, disorder, confusion, and tumult.

Chaos creates stress in human life. When too many uncertainties engulf a person he or she may become stressed. There might be a feeling that matters are getting beyond control. A stress at work might be bearable. A combination of stress at work, in the family, illness and economic uncertainty--may be beyond one's ability to cope with. Uncertainty may come when a person loses his or her basic orientation to life. What made sense before has no meaning now. What was of importance yesterday has no value today. What was certain before is no longer certain. There may be a mixture of confusion, apprehension, helplessness, threat, and anxiety.

Toffler's (1971) version of the eruption of uncertainty in people's lives is called "future shock." He describes the way people react to it in different ways and how its symptoms can also vary according to the stage and intensity of the disease. Some of the symptoms are anxiety, hostility to authority, violence, physical illness, depression and apathy. Victims often manifest fluctuations in interest and lifestyle, and may turn inward and withdraw. Older people may feel this state more intensely. They may become dropouts, cutting off their contacts with the changing world around them and totally withdrawing.

CHAOS AS A NEW SCIENCE

Chaos did not exist in science until a few years ago. Only within the last thirty years and mainly in the last decade, have articles on chaos been published in scientific journals.

Chaos seemed to be in total contradiction to the fundamental basics of a scientific approach. It was therefore treated with suspicion and like many other cases, when something did not fit within the existing scientific worldview, was pushed underneath the carpet.

There are many different scientific definitions of chaos. This happens because chaos, like other complex phenomena, can be seen in various ways. The different definitions complement each other, with each one of them stressing another aspect of this complex concept. Possibly, for the reader without an advanced scientific background in the physical or mathematical sciences, chaos can be understood as the irregular, uncertain and unpredictable forms in which many things change, or in short, unpredictable change. When a system is in a chaotic state there is a particular patterned order in the way it changes as a whole, but the future behavior of its individual components is totally unpredictable. These uncertain and unpredictable forms of change are in contrast to the regular and predictable ways people expect and believe that most things around them do change. There is food for thought in this description. If periods of chaos in human systems have within them some hidden pattern of behavior of the total system, we may find ways to uncover the pattern, and thus be better able to deal with the situation.

Chaos Deals with a Way Things Change

Ian Stewart (1989) from Warwick's Nonlinear Systems Laboratory says that chaos is a dynamic phenomenon and it happens when the state of a system changes with time. The essence of chaos is change. Chaos is not a stable condition or a fixed state. It is a process, it is dynamic. It is more like the changing relationship between things than the things themselves. In a system, it is a form of changing behavior characterized by a pattern in the whole, and uncertainty and unpredictablity in the behavior of the components.

Chaos deals with the way many things change and regards all science as built on theories and propositions that they themselves will change. Professor T.R. Young from the Institute of Advanced Studies in Sociology in Michigan writes: "Where chaos begins, normal science ends. . . . Chaos Theory is the theory of postmodern society par excellence. In theory as in practice, there are no stable enduring clock-like systems; no eternal, fixed truths, no stable enduring theoretical relationships given by Nature or by God in the world we find when we look closely at it. In a chaos paradigm [worldview], all theory is, in the first instance change theory" (1991:5).

In *Scientific American*, J. P. Crutchfield et al. put it this way: "The larger framework that chaos emerges from is the so-called theory of dynamical systems. A dynamical system consists of two parts: the notions of a state (the essential information about a system) and a dynamic (a rule about how the state evolves with time)" (1986:49). The science of Chaos often deals with discontinuous forms of change. Discontinuous changes are those changes where something transforms itself completely. These changes occur when a system reaches a critical bifurcation point that leads either to disintegration or to radical change.

D. Loye and R. Eisler from the Institute for Futures Forecasting, Carmel, California, point out that: "What it offers at this critical evolutionary juncture is the first transdisciplinary understanding of bifurcational and transformational change. But to achieve this new understanding social scientists must understand natural scientific chaos theory, natural scientists must understand the social scientific potential, and must better understand how advancements at both levels relates to the overriding evolutionary challenge" (1987:54).

Chaos is the irregular, uncertain, discontinuous aspect of change within the confines of a patterned whole. While not understood or even recognized before, it suffuses and permeates everything of importance. If we were to pigeonhole Chaos anywhere, the most suitable place would be in the study of dynamics, that is, how things change in this world, not only how physical or living things change, or how the universe changes, but rather understanding the ways in which all things change.

The Everyday Relevance

The relevance of Chaos is not only for understanding the dynamics of change on the longtime evolutionary scale, but is also a key to understanding all kinds of change whether it be the flow of water through a tap, the fluctuations of the heartbeat, or the difficulties of perestroika.

Some of the areas in which the science of Chaos is developing knowledge and understanding are: the structure of galaxies, the evolution of the planets and of life, changes in chemical solutions, the flow of a river, the weather system, the flow of a current in electrical circuits, the behavior of convection currents in liquids, the functioning of the brain, epilepsy, how the heart beats, heart attacks, how societies change, what happens in organizational crisis, demographic changes in insect population, the traffic flow, how cities develop, how coastlines are created, the development of forest fires, the creation of an ant nest, the reproduction of bacteria, the development of the nervous system, the prevalence of crime, management science, and the list could continue!

Neuroscientist Paul Rapp declared that if there was a Holy Grail to neural functioning, chaos theory would help find it. Findings show that the brain functions normally, and even optimally, when it is in a chaotic state. When we are mentally challenged, the intervals between the electrical waves becomes more chaotic. This suggests, that chaos may be highly beneficial during problem solving (McAuliffe 1990).

Science appears to be only at the beginning on the road to understanding chaos and its implications, and from this to more understanding of the world we are living in.

Chaos Is Not a Negative Phenomenon

In the first section of this chapter, the intensification of chaos in human affairs was briefly described. People's natural reactions and associations to descriptions of this kind are that something negative is occurring. If things are becoming so chaotic, where are they leading, and what dangers are inherent in them? Many of the connotations of the concept of chaos are negative. Chaos is associated with turbulence, disorder, disarray, anarchy, lawlessness. Things are not in their normal state. All of these synonyms arouse stress and fears of loss of control, danger, and the unknown.

In dealing with the Science of Chaos it will be necessary to let go of negative reactions and begin to see chaos as a natural phenomenon. As a natural phenomenon, an aspect of how things change in this universe, chaos is neither good nor bad, it just is. Chaos and (lineal) order are like day and night, winter and summer. They are aspects of natural processes that are part of this world.

Under certain circumstances, too much order and regularity can be harmful to human societies. Similarly, an intensification of chaos beyond certain limits can cause great difficulties. But chaos as such is not bad for the world or for human beings.

There are problems of the intensification of chaos in human society in periods of transition. Along with this there is another "positive" side to the growth of chaos. Without the randomness of chaos, the rich variety and diversity of evolution would be stifled and throttled. Chaos is the rich soil from which creativity is born. Deep chaos is a natural, unescapable essential stage in the transformation of all life forms. Out of chaos come forth the fertile variety of forms of existence and life in this universe. Chaos is the father of innovation. Chaos is the basis of the ability of living matter to self-organize itself. Chaos breaks the bonds of a deterministic universe and grants humanity endless degrees of freedom in creating its own world. A mixture of order and chaos is the natural form of all living things. The edge of chaos is where complex systems are most adaptive.

APPLYING CHAOS TO HUMAN AFFAIRS

Chaos theory is beginning to revolutionize the understanding of social phenomena. The science of Chaos is shedding light on and helping to confront major problems facing humankind in these times. "As similarities between the 'chaos' being examined on the natural scientific level and potential chaos on the social problem level have become apparent, enthusiasm for applying the new theory to the global societal challenge has arisen . . . through informal networking many minds are already engaged in exploring this new territory for scientific and social advance" (Loye and Eisler 1987:56).

Aspects of the science of Chaos can throw light on contemporary problems. Much can be learned from chaos in dealing with current human affairs. Policy and action implications may be derived from advances in the application of the New Science to human and social systems.

It must constantly be kept in mind that science is only at the onset of this journey and on the brink of applying this New Science to human affairs. The bulk of the work and its application are still ahead. Some of what the trailblazers write and describe may later be found to not exactly be in focus, some may be completely off course, and some may only be pure speculation, as suggested by Young. At the same time some findings may be scientific breakthroughs of great consequence. Only time will tell.

The intensification of chaos and complexity in human society has raised many people's interest in the New Sciences. Their interdisciplinary character may also explain the wide interest in their findings. The great possibilities of utilizing the new sciences in so many different fields reaches out and appeals to many diverse people from a large variety of backgrounds and interests. At the same time, this also explains the difficulty of understanding the subject. Scientists from different disciplines use different languages and methodologies. Many intelligent people, including social scientists, began reading a book on chaos and gave up in despair.

The New Sciences are packed with unfamiliar concepts taken from an assortment of scientific disciplines. Explaining the concepts and using all of them will make this book very difficult reading. Doing completely without them is not feasible. So, if it is possible to avoid using a new concept, it will not be used. When necessary, unfamiliar concepts will be used and explained, hopefully in terms the reader will understand.

2
Order and Science

THE NEED FOR REGULARITY AND CERTAINTY

In former centuries people viewed the world as disordered and uncertain. In the middle ages, people beheld a world of spirits, works of the devil, and miracles. These influenced human fate and were responsible for the disorder, uncertainty, and unpredictability that were the lot of most people during their sojourn in this world.

For thousands of years most people felt they had little control of their fate. Their life course and destiny were in the hands of fickle gods, spirits, demons, and other such like supreme whimsical entities. People lived a short life of uncertainty in an unpredictable world governed by uncontrollable powers and forces. This view has changed in past centuries. Now many people see a world of order, certainty, and predictability around them. At school and at home and in interacting with others, they have been encouraged to see things through the lens of order. They have become used to seeing and understanding the world on the basis of a set of ideas that originated from the time of Newton. This

Newtonian worldview of modern science satisfies man's need for order and enhances the assuredness that indeed he or she does live in an orderly world.

It is a world that follows a set design or pattern. In this view of reality, the world is like a giant clockwork machine, that can be known and understood. If something is not yet understood with the advance of science and knowledge, it will be increasingly known and understood. This is a regulary structured world that can be understood by breaking it up into its parts and studying them objectively with great care and precision. The assumption is that the whole is the sum of its parts. By getting to know the parts it is possible to understand the whole. It is a world of lineal order in which there is proportion between cause and effect. The harder you kick the ball the farther it will roll.

Based on this approach, the more science progresses, the more man can apprehend the laws of nature. The more man understands the laws of nature, the more he can make generalizations that uncover the commonalties between things in this world. He can learn from one thing about another. From experience in the past, he can predict events in the future. The more man can make generalizations and predictions that are proven scientifically, the more he can control his life and the world around him. As science advances and continually expands its reach, the scientific basis of what he does not know today will, one day, be discovered.

As science advanced it would uncover more secrets of nature and discover its basic building blocks. With progress in all the exact sciences, humanity was getting closer to a grand unifying theory that would explain everything. One of the main goals of science was to seek after this grand unifying theory.

The modern scientific worldview, which has for centuries guided science has brought order, regularity, predictability, and control to the world. Where uncertainty, disorder, and irregularity were found, scientists thought that they stemmed from faulty methods or theory, and all that was needed was to improve and refine these methods or theories. This worldview of modern science was suited to the needs of the industrial era and met the needs of human beings and societies for a measure of order, stability, and certainty in the world they encountered.

People Expect Certainty in the World

For the past few hundred years--from about the time of Newton until the advent of the science of Chaos--mankind believed that it inhabited a world of lineal order, regularity and stability. People saw phenomena that repeated themselves in a regular manner, a universe of objects that displayed regularity and predictability in its behavior.

When the sky is overcast with dark clouds, rain will fall. The sun will rise tomorrow in the east and set in the west. It is possible to estimate quite correctly when it will become dark and when the morning sun will rise again. People build their daily schedules and routines on a measure of certainty about the regularity and order of their physical and human environment.

All these expectations of regularity and predictability are quite justified and apply to many things in this world that, within a certain time scale, have regular, repetitive patterns of behavior. On a practical level, many of the things people meet in their everyday life change in an orderly way in the sense that they behave similarly to the way they behaved beforehand. So generally people can expect a measure of order, regularity and certainty in their environment and in their daily lives. Societies can put their trust in the constancy, predictability, and stability of their world. The belief in the stable state of the world sees the regularity and constancy of central aspects of human life. It is ingrained deeply in our belief systems, our institutions, our identities, and our value systems. It is our major defense against the threat of uncertainty. It protects us from the threats of change. It gives us the illusion of maintaining stability in the face of unrelenting change. Uncertainty causes us anguish that grows as changes threaten the core of self-identity (Schon 1991).

Organizations as Bulwarks against Uncertainty

Order and regularity in the world give people a basic feeling of security, which is one of the primary needs of human beings. People, to a large degree, need to feel physically, psychologically, intellectually, emotionally, and socially secure. Take away their basic feeling of security and they feel lost and helpless. Many people like spontaneity and novelty, but these should be within a general context of certainty. Our feelings of intellectual security are so deeply anchored that we do not even see how they could be shaken. Nature around us is ordered and reasoned exactly as the human mind is. Our everyday activity implies a perfect confidence in the universality of the laws of nature.

Human beings create the structures of families, organizations, institutions and governments, not only for their declared purposes, but also to fulfil another latent function, to protect people from anxiety. Social organizations are a line of defense against the uncertainty of the chaotic elements in the world. People use the institutions to build walls around themselves as shelter from the uncertainty, unpredictability, and turbulence that is part of life.

People try to ensure regularity and predictability in the structures, routines, norms, rules, and roles of organizational life as a defense against uncertainty that might threaten them. Dr. Eric Miller (1992) of Tavistock Institute, London, says that organizations have to deal with predictability and unpredictability at the same time. Therefore, social systems can be seen as a defense against unconscious anxiety, engendered by the ever increasing uncertainty in human life. Miller also says that Chaos theory tells us that these environments are inherently unpredictable. We respond to the demand for order by advocating mission statements, strategic planning mechanisms, organizational structures and so forth as defenses against the anxiety of uncertainty.

Miller suggests that human enterprises import chaos from people who belong to them and export order to them. In other words the organizations, institutions, and other structures are created to serve as fortresses of routine, order, and certainty in a world that, to individuals, is becoming increasingly uncertain.

Daily Living and Production Need Certainty

It is not possible to breathe a lot for one hour and then not breathe the following hour. A person cannot gorge himself with food and drink for one month and then do without food and drink for the following month. Humans need order, regularity, certainty, stability and routine in these vital functions. Without a regular flow of oxygen, liquids, and food to ensure life's needs, humans would stop living.

Production itself necessitates a certain linear, regular order and routine in doing the work. Production demands coordination and order in all its activities. But these are difficult to maintain. Randomness and chaos break in. Kevin Dooley (1991), from Minnesota University's engineering department, says that in order to deliver a product that is consistent with customer expectations, it is necessary that the process which produces the product be consistent. Any given process would operate most economically if it followed a common routine. A break in the routine would result in economic loss. Dooley believes that if we had total knowledge of absolutely everything, output would be perfectly consistent. In reality, however, no matter how good a job we attempt to do in keeping up the routine, when we look at the output of our process, it's not consistent--it has variation. We find that it is random. In terms of chaos, a set of dynamic equations, unknown to us, is what creates this randomness. Daily living and production demand order, regularity, routine, stability and predictability. Generally, these are attained to a fair degree, and for a limited period of time until chaos pokes up its head and things become capricious, fluctuant, and haphazard.

A Stable Man-Made Environment

People seek the reliability and regularity of a permanent shelter from nature's irregularities of storms, lightning, cold, wind and heat. They need the assurance of privacy, a haven for belongings, and protection from the unpredictable behavior of others. People need the order and security of a home. Mark Michaels (1992), editor of the Chaos Network, says that the weather changes around us with no apparent order. This can harm our survival. Therefore, we examine the patterns of the weather for consistency, (i.e., seasons, rainfall, or humidity). With this knowledge we build houses that protect us from the weather's elements. It was the chaos of the weather that was the original catalyst for the development of the protective system. Out of the chaos came order. If the chaotic nature of the weather were to shift significantly, it would render the existing protective system meaningless.

In a society, if an industrial subsystem is out of balance, then the problem must be identified and rectified by a structure, or policy or program. The aim is to produce the same stability that existed before the problem. Michaels suggests that in reality, the community is an open system and the chaos in the environment has risen enough to force communities to reconsider the adoption of existing approaches to problem solving. In effect, the community was open and responsive to an environment that was far from orderly and stable.

In face of an environment that is disorderly and unstable people attempt to create for themselves an orderly, certain, stable man-made environment. Within this bastion of safety they build conditions of routine, regularity, and predictability that protect them from the fickleness, irregularity, and uncertainty of the world around. These chaotic elements, however, break through daily into people's homes in the news broadcasts of radio and television. Generally they are viewed from the safe haven and security of armchairs and family. But sometimes the uncertainty and chaos force themselves into people's personal, family, and work lives and disrupt them and the illusion that they can isolate themselves from the turbulence in the world.

Social Living Demands Order and Certainty

People live in families ensuring child care, intimate relationships, companionship, a home, and other functions. Without basic order, regularity, and a measure of certainty in the conduct of everyday affairs and in the behavior of the family members toward each other, it would be impossible to maintain this essential human institution.

Division of labor, property, and income all demand social and political order. Ensuring the safety of loved ones, of homes, and of property and belongings, all necessitate the enforcement of some kind of social and political order.

The sum of all this is that man is a social animal who needs to interrelate with others to work, produce, and ensure the necessities of life. To ensure these, man must maintain social relationships with others. To maintain these relationships there must be a measure of certainty, order, regularity, predictability, and some degree of stability and steadiness in the way people behave toward each other. Societies and individuals often try to ensure this through control and domination.

CONTROLLING THE WORLD

To ensure regularity, predictability, and routine, men also impose order around them. People are not only passive seekers after certitude, reliability, and predictability, they also actively impose these on the world around them. Where people cannot find order and regularity, they attempt to create them.

The language people use to communicate with one another is not only a tool of communication, it also enforces a certain lineal order, of man's own making, on the world he or she lives in. It is not an objective order of reality in the world, finding expression in language. It fixes boundaries that humans themselves create. People themseves create the concepts that differentiate between objects and in unlike cultures they have diverse ways of doing this.

People create order by conceptually breaking up the natural interconnectedness between things. In their minds they give different names to things, create boundaries around them, categorize them, and seek the certainties, constancies, and regularities in their relationships. The order people create in their minds imposes itself on the world of objects around them. Language is a filtering device through which we perceive information. In order to interpret information, we need conceptual frameworks that allow us to classify information and act upon it.

Beginning with international institutions, through the state and the government, on to cities, communities, organizations, and all the rich variety of forms that organize human lives, people create structures that foist order in their lives. Margeret J. Wheatley, of Brigham Young University, writes:

While we have lusted for order in organizations, we have failed to understand its true nature. We have seen order reflected in the structures we erect, whether they be bright mirror-glass buildings or plans started on paper napkins. These structures take so much time, creativity, and tinkering attention that it is hard not to want them to be permanent. It is hard to welcome disorder as a full partner in the search for order when we expended such effort to bar it from the gates. (1992:21-22)

Using Organizations to Control Others

Men believe that they can force order, certitude, and predictability on those they interact with by controlling them. They believe they can ensure regularity and assuredness in the behavior of others by having control and power over them--by dominating them. People, therefore, build hierarchic forms of social organizations, like that of the Catholic church, in which each higher level has control over the levels below it. This ensures that the members of the church will conduct themselves in the predictable, routine ways the edicts of the religion prescribe. Societies build armies with chains of command, from generals down to corporals and privates. This is done to completely ensure that each person, when fulfilling his military duties, will act in the way he is expected to act.

People create the nation-state to ensure order in the wider society.

In the modern paradigm since, say, the work of Thomas Hobbes, the operative question is how to ensure the triumph of order over disorder. The solution to such problems of order has been, in the hobbesian tradition, a strong state capable of enforcing its will on those lesser subjects who could not or did not see virtue in compliance with that which is necessary. That which was necessary was thought to be linear, monolithic and coherently connected to all other programs and policies of the state. (Young 1994: Ch.1, p.8)

People build industries around the frameworks of organizational charts, with executives on top, through layers of middle management, down to the shop-floor worker. These prescribe job and role descriptions, responsibilities, and duties to control the predictability of the behavior of people at work. Institutions and organizations elaborate a wide gamut of methods to ensure the control of behavior such as wages, salaries, bonuses, raises, promotions, fines, assembly-lines, and work quotas.

A REVOLUTION IN SCIENCE

The development of both modern science and its handmaiden technology, have played a major role in man's ability to control the world. No other factor has contributed more to our ability to ensure order and certainty in our environment. To attain this, science searches for and discovers relations of cause and effect between things. Crutchfield et al (1986) wrote that the great power of science was in its ability to relate cause and effect. For instance on the basis of the laws of gravitation, an eclipse can be predicted thousands of years beforehand. In the words of Stephen Hawking, a scientific genius of our time:

Laplace suggested that there should be a set of scientific laws that would allow us to predict everything that would happen in the universe, if only we knew the complete state of the universe at one time. For example, if we knew the positions and speeds of the sun and the planets at one time, then we could use Newton's laws to calculate the state of the Solar System at any other time. Determinism seems fairly obvious in this case, but Laplace went further to assume that there were similar laws governing everything else, including human behavior. (1988:57)

The very essence of modern science is to discover the order, and regularities in the world. The purpose of technology is to put this knowledge to use in the service of human needs. To quote Carl Murray of the University of London: "We can steer the Voyager 2 spacecraft nearly 5 billion kilometres on a 12-year journey from the Earth to an encounter with Neptune, so it arrives on schedule within kilometres of its target. We can accept unforeseen changes in our everyday lives and even come to terms with natural and man-made disasters yet we still have faith in the immutability of the orbits of the planets and the satellites" (1989:60).

Science creates order in the world by categorizing it into different objects. It arranges the world of things into neat drawers that allow people to differentiate and associate between them. It develops generalizations that allow people to describe the regularities of nature and therefore enable them to predict the effects of their behavior. Science develops laws and grand theories that organize these generalizations into neat bundles that create certainty and predictability in the universe.

Using the knowledge derived from science, man develops ever more sophisticated technologies to gain greater control of the environment. Science has been made into the handmaiden of human effort to control nature and impose order. And with every advance in science and technology it appears that humans are achieving greater control of their environment and encasing themselves in a bubble of order and certainty of their own making. That has been the picture of things until the advent of the New Sciences.

Modern Science Is Still Relevant

The New Sciences have brought about a revolution that undermines the monopoly of the basic tenets of modern science. Not that the fundamental outlook of modern science and its methods are wrong and should not continue to guide mankind. The New Sciences do not dispute the relevance and applicability of the modern scientific approach to many real-world phenomena. The contribution of modern science to humanity is also not challenged.

Linear order, certainty, regularity, reliability, predictability, similarity, replicability do exist in this world and they can advance our understanding of it. As before man can continue discovering the regularities of the universe and from them enrich our knowledge.

Within certain time scales and under certain conditions many phenomena do change in an orderly, linear way. From their behavior in the past people can predict how they will behave in the not-to-distant future. Their components maintain a proportion between them when they change; they do not behave randomly.

Often, small causes have small effects and large causes have large effects. Two similar things under the same conditions will often develop in the same way. In many circumstances, small errors in measurements will cancel each other out and are negligible in predicting outcomes. From the way something changed in the past, it is often possible to predict how it will change in the future.

The methodology of science tests the truth of statements by research and experiments, examining if they are replicable, discarding them if they are falsified, generalizing from them when they prove that they repeat themselves, developing theories to explain their universal features and all of these methods, in many circumstances, are still relevant. The New Sciences have however shown that all of the above statements apply to part of the phenomena in this world, within certain circumstances. They have also clarified that when they do apply, it is within limited time scales.

Enter the Science of Chaos

Newtonian science ignored nonlinear phenomena that did not behave in a predictable manner. It pushed them under the carpet and tried to deal only with the regular linear aspects of reality. When nonlinear phenomena poked their heads into scientific findings they were treated as approximate linearities. Otherwise they were seen as strange features of reality that would one day be explained as scientific knowledge advanced.

Chaos shows that along with the world of order, certainty, predictability, and regularity there exists and intertwines a nonlinear deterministic world of randomness, uncertainty, unpredictability, and irregularity. These features are ingrained in reality and will not disappear with the advance of human knowledge. It is not that science has yet to uncover the secrets and display the regularitity, linearity, and order in these phenomena. Uncertainty, unpredictability, complexity, and chaos are a natural, legitimate, necessary, inescapable aspect of reality and will never go away.

The New Sciences have clarified that the basic tenets, approaches and methodologies of modern science apply only to linear, simple phenomena. Yet humanity inhabits a world teeming with nonlinear, complex phenomena. These nonlinear phenomena--like the turbulent flow of fluid through a tap, termites building a nest, or the events in Yugoslavia--do not follow linear paths and cannot be addressed by a science based on linearity. The advent of the New Sciences has proved beyond a doubt that order and chaos intertwine inextricably, and that alongside the linear world of regular predictable order, their exists a nonlinear world with strange patterns of unpredictable order.

A Different Way of Seeing the World

Chaos shows and explains how many phenomena change in an unpredictable nonlinear way. Their behavior in the future cannot be predicted by their behavior in the past. Their components do not change proportionately and they do have an element of randomness in them.

Small causes can have gigantic effects and enormous causes can have negligible effects. Small errors in measurement may not cancel each other out and can have enormous effects in predicting outcomes.

Two similar things under the same conditions can have completely different developmental paths. A system in one phase of its development may behave in an orderly manner and in another phase it can behave chaotically.

Many systems in their development go through discontinuous changes to more complex forms and pass through a chaotic transition stage.

Under many circumstances the basic methodologies of modern science are inappropriate. Replication, falsification, and generalization cannot always be applied as scientific criteria in many nonlinear chaotic conditions.

The New Sciences are creating a new paradigm in science. This paradigm is not discarding the paradigm of modern science, but is relegating it to its rightful place as dealing with part of reality. The New Sciences recognize the great contribution of modern science to humanity's development. But they point out that for further advances the nonlinear, complex, chaotic and self-organizing aspects of reality need also to be recognized. The social and behavioral sciences, both theoretical and applied, are at the beginning of the road of applying the insights of the New Sciences to their fields of study and practice.

3

The New Science of Chaos

SENSITIVE DEPENDENCE ON INITIAL CONDITIONS

When a person plants a flower garden, he or she may add fertilizer to enhance growth. In some cases, insignificant differences in the amount of fertilizer used may not make any difference on the later growth of the the flowers. In this particular case small differences in initial conditions are of little consequence. In many cases, if fertilizer is not given to the plants, it will probably affect their growth. If too large quantities of fertilizer are given, this might kill the flowers. But tiny differences in the quantity of fertiliizer, like small differences in the distance between the plants, may sometimes have no effect.

Many of the systems men deal with as in the above example, act in a linear way. They can absorb small differences without it affecting their behavior. Giving them a slight nudge is not going to affect their course. Linear systems are, as a whole, generally insensitive to tiny differences in their initial conditions. Some of the systems humans deal with are of this kind; they are almost linear systems. Their output is proportional to their input.

Tiny, insignificant differences in initial conditions or in measurements will not have major effects later. Small differences, or changes have small effects, and large differences and changes will have larger effects. People can plan things and live their lives with a measure of certainty when objects they deal with are insensitive to small differences in their initial conditions. Because of this insensitivity to small differences in initial conditions, many objects will generally develop in a linear way. They will change in the future as they did in the past. They will not be affected by slight differences in circumstances. Little differences will generally cancel each other out. When changes take place, it is possible to know what the outcomes will be. This is a case of dealing with orderly linear change; change that can be predicted.

Science built itself on this principle of insensitivity to small differences. James Gleick describes it thus:

This assumption lay at the philosophical heart of science. As one theoretician liked to tell his students: "The basic idea of Western science is that you don't have to take into account the falling of a leaf on some planet in another galaxy when you're trying to account for the motion of a billiard ball on a pool table on earth. Very small influences can be neglected. There's a convergence in the way things work, and arbitrarily small influences don't blow up to have arbitrarily large effects." Classically, the belief in approximation and convergence was well justified. It worked. A tiny error in fixing the position of Comet Halley in 1910 would only cause a tiny error in predicting its arrival in 1986, and the error would stay small for millions of years to come. Computers rely on the same assumptions in guiding spacecraft: approximately accurate input gives approximately accurate output. (1987:15)

Many Phenomena Are Sensitive to Initial Small Differences

Insensitivity to small differences is not always the case. "In principle the future is determined by the past, but in practice small uncertainties are amplified, so that even though the behaviour is predictable in the short term, it is unpredictable in the long term" (Crutchfield et al. 1986:46).

Attempting to make a weather forecast, Edward Lorenz, the MIT meteorologist, was working on his primitive computer to solve a number of equations that modeled the earth's atmosphere. He took a coffee break in the middle of his calculations and repeated them again after. Once, before coffee, he did them with six decimal points accuracy and after coffee, with three decimal point's accuracy. The results were not only far from each other, but completely different forecasts. The tiny differences of three numbers after the decimal point had by repetitive calculations resulted in completely different solutions. If you assume that small input differences only yield small output differences, why should this small difference matter? Why should the second run, after the coffee break, be more than just a trifle different from the first run before the coffee break? What had been discovered by Lorenz was that there are phenomena in this world that do not change in a linear way. When they change they are extremely sensitive to tiny initial differences, which in the process of repetitive change are blown up beyond all proportion.

People have known that chains of events can have far-reaching consequences like Boris Yeltsin's stand on the tank, or losing the nail in the horseshoe in the well-known saying. But Lorenz had demonstrated that sensitive dependence on initial conditions, which is in effect, the enhancing of small differences that could not be measured accurately to enormous effects beyond prediction, develops naturally in many systems.

When they began looking, scientists found that there were many things that behaved this way. There are many systems in the world that are affected by small differences, not unlike the proverbial straw that broke the camel's back. In fact, the nonlinear world includes many of the changes in the living, the human, the social, and the individual's world. There are many things that either cannot be measured exactly, or if they can be measured, the slightest initial difference, if amplified repeatedly, may lead to unpredictable behavior.

Initial Conditions in Human Terms

In very simple terms all of this leads to a startling conclusion: in a nonlinear system, starting points that are almost the same may evolve into completely different ending points. Two neighbouring nations with almost identical beginning conditions can evolve into completely different national cultures. Two identical twins, with very similar beginning conditions can develop completely different personalities.

Two young brothers born and brought up in the same crime- and drug-infested slum, although influenced by almost similar starting conditions, may each go his own way. One may end up as a reputed scientist and the second may spend his days in prison. You may therefore expect that small inexactitudes or discrepancies in the measurement of a system in its initial state may be blown beyond all proportion at later stages of its development.

The world is full of objects that can never be measured exactly and the universe abounds in discontinuous events such as explosions, breaks in a material substance, eruptions, transformations, and so on. The world teems with systems that change in a nonlinear way, with feedback from one change affecting the following change. When science can model these changes, it can do so only by nonlinear equations. These equations contain within them the seed of randomness and unpredictability.

In seeing regularity and order everywhere people have tended to ignore all the phenomena in the real world around them that do not change in an linear, orderly manner, but rather in a chaotic way. This discovery throws new light on changes in human systems of all kinds. Relationships between people are nonlinear. The behavior of a person, a group, an organization or a nation always affects other systems of its kind and is affected by the reaction in a long link of repetitive, mutually affecting relationships. The same holds true for the relationships between subsystems of an individual, such as body and mind.

This leads to the sobering conclusion that human systems, in interdependence with other human systems, interact nonlinearily. When such interactions are iterative and combined with a sensitivity to small differences, the conditions have been created for the appearance of varying degrees of chaotic episodes, in the functioning or relationships of those systems. The important insights stemming from this understanding are just now being revealed and researched in psychology, sociology, political science, economics and so on.

Enhancing the Differences

Systems that are sensitive to initial conditions do not always display chaotic change. The change becomes chaotic only when the initial tiny errors, differences and inexactitudes are blown up by repetitive amplification. Randomness and unpredictability set in when the initial differences are repeatedly magnified.

In describing the case of billiard balls Crutchfield et al. write: "The large growth in uncertainty comes about because the balls are curved, and small differences at the point of impact are amplified at each collision. The amplification is exponential: it is compounded at every collision, like the successive reproduction of bacteria with unlimited space and food. Any effect, no matter how small, quickly reaches macroscopic proportions. That is one of the basic properties of chaos!" (1986:9).

This phenomena of repetitive amplification is called iteration. Iteration describes situations where something changes repetitively, in a way that each following change is effected by the change that preceded it. The results of one change are fed back to the system and serve as the basis for the next change. Exponential amplification by repetition enhances the initial small difference.

Iteration can be illustrated by the metaphor of the "baker transformation." One can visualize a picture of a baker kneading dough to prepare it to be baked into bread. The dough is repeatedly stretched and folded back onto itself. If at the beginning of the kneading you were to mark with color two points on the dough that were close to each other, within a minute they might be far apart. The stretching and folding make each new location unforeseeable. Following their movements, you would see that their locations on the dough would appear to be unpredictable. In fact, they are acting chaotically.

Interdependence between Systems

The repeated stretching and folding of the dough, simulates the amplification of small, initial differences in phenomena that are in relationship with each other. Nonlinearity and sensitive dependence alone are not enough to create chaotic conditions in systems. When it isolates them, modern physics is able to deal with nonlinear independent systems. Calculus can solve many nonlinear problems of isolated systems.

Chaos develops in nonlinear systems that are interdependent with each other. Nonlinearity is not the same thing as interdependence. Nonlinearity deals with proportionality. It expresses a disproportion between cause and effect; small causes may lead to large effects and large causes may have small effects. Interdependence is another matter; it deals with the *relationships between things* and the way they affect one another. Members of a family or an organization are interdependent. Their behaviors mutually affect one another. Our body and components of our personality maintain a relationship in which they constantly affect each other.

Modern science attempted to deal with systems in a manner that isolated them from all that was around them. Newton's equations worked with isolated objects or dealt with the effect of the massive body of the sun on a small planet. In his research, at the beginning of this century, the famous French scientist Henri Poincare added to a two-body system the influence of a third body, another planet or moon. His calculations showed that in some orbits a planet might begin to wobble and the system could begin to exhibit chaotic behavior (Briggs and Peat, 1990).

Sally J. Goerner (1992) of the Triangle Center for the Study of Complex Systems writes that the nonlinear revolution's most crucial insight comes from nonlinear *interdependent* systems. Phenomenon of chaos (sensitive dependence) itself occur only in nonlinear interdependent systems. Nonlinearity itself is not sufficient. In this world there are in effect no absolutely independent systems. There are different degrees of mutual effect and interdependence between systems, but never absolute isolation. Goerner points out that independent systems are idealizations. In this world there are no truly linear systems as there are no truly independent systems.

When a human system changes, it affects other systems around it. When a member of a family changes he or she affects the other members of the family. When family members react to the change, their reactions may feed back on that person and affect how he or she continues affecting the people he or she interacts with. When you shout at your son, he reacts and this affects how you continue to behave. When changes in Angola affect the UN forces, they react and their reaction affects the Angolans whose reaction again affects the behavior of the UN forces, and so and so on.

In human and social systems of all kinds, when feedback cycles like these continue to occur interdependence develops. In this way repetitive cycles of changes between interdependent human systems that are affecting one another may contribute to the development of chaos. The interdependence of people within organizations is necessary and it also has the potential to enable the organization to pass through chaotic episodes.

Chaos in a certain sense reveals the unity of the universe and the hidden tie between one thing and another. When people cut up this indivisible unity and isolate things into compartmentalized boxes, chaos pokes its head up to remind them that they are living in a holistic, indivisible world. Interdependence alone does not create chaos but its combination with nonlinear conditions of sensitivity to initial conditions increases the probability of chaotic conditions arising.

Increasing connections, interactions and interdependence between nonlinear systems (such as in human societies) are an inevitable aspect of evolution. Simultaneously they create the fertile soil for the proliferation of chaotic states. As complexity involves growing interdependence, burgeoning complexity may increase the possibility of an intensification in the rate of chaotic states. The following section of this book will deal with the chaotic ramfications of growing complexity in the human world.

THE BUTTERFLY EFFECT

The inescapable conclusion is reached that man is living in a world in which, under certain conditions, tiny causes can have enormous effects. This is called the butterfly effect. In certain circumstances, because of sensitivity to initial conditions, a slight difference or initial uncertainty can be blown up by iteration and amplified beyond all proportions. The butterfly effect is in sharp contrast to the behavior of linear systems. Give a ball a slight nudge and it moves slightly. Give it a hearty kick and it will fly far away. The very essence of linearity is the proportionate relationship between cause and effect.

In nonlinear, chaotic systems the story is different. Ten aspirins do not reduce the headache tenfold. The flapping of the wings of a butterfly in Hong Kong can affect the course of a tornado in Texas. This phenomenon of the butterfly effect is one of the hallmarks of chaos. Dr. Jeffrey Goldstein of Adelphi University writes:

Sensitivity to initial conditions demonstrates that one would need infinite precision of initial conditions to predict the future state of a nonlinear dynamical system since errors in the measurement of the initial conditions, no matter how seemingly small and insignificant, would soon be amplified from their microscopic effect to a macroscopic influence on the system's evolution. . . . The key to the amplification of the uncertainties or fluctuations in initial conditions hinges on the nonlinearity showing up in Lorenz's equations. Nonlinearity introduces the possibility of exponential relationships between variables in a system, so that a small change in one variable may result in a large change in another variable. (1991:6-7)

The butterfly effect raises deep doubts about when it is feasible to invest in national ten-year plans, or to commit oneself to long-term strategic planning in organizations, or to place too much trust in "planned change" in families or organizations and other human systems, or to be tied to long-term policy guidelines.

On a worldwide scale, the realization that small causes *can* have gigantic effects may be seen from two viewpoints. A pessimistic view would point out that a slight error in judgment of a national leader or a miscalculation in the building of a nuclear plant could lead to a nuclear catastrophe. An optimistic look at the butterfly effect would note the openness of evolution to human action. This allows for a small group of enlightened individuals to propagate their views affecting, exponentially, the outlook of people throughout the world and ushering in a more humane, caring, and responsible era in human history.

FAR-FROM-EQUILIBRIUM STATES

The physical sciences generally tended to concentrate on systems that were in equilibrium or close to equilibrium. These systems behaved in a predictable, linear fashion that the sciences knew how to deal with. They always returned to their same predictable selves. Touch a clock's pendulum and after some time it will return to its original oscillation. Far-from-equilibrium systems do not return to their regular state, they never repeat themselves and they are nonlinear. They were unpredictable systems and for many years the physical sciences did not understand them and chose not to deal with them.

The basic outlook of science, as dealing *only* with near-to-equilibrium systems, was changed by the work of Ilya Prigogine. Prigogine's studies will be dealt with at length in later chapters. Suffice at this point to state that Prigogine demonstrated how many kinds of open systems--such as chemical, biological, and social systems--operated at far-from-equilibrium conditions.

A far-from-equilibrium system does not return to some fixed stable state. It is forever in a continuous flux of change; never being the same, always becoming something else. A far-from-equilibrium system is never being the same, it is always becoming. Prigogine spoke about his theory as "from being to becoming." A far-from-equilibrium system is like the flame of a candle or a whirlpool in a river. Its wholeness, structure, and form can only be maintained by the endless flow through it. Its existence depends on its flux. In the face of relentless change, the system is using a lot of energy to maintain itself as being whole and coherent. The constant flow of energy through it enables it occasionally to take a quantum leap in which it transforms itself and reorganizes itself into a new basic order.

Systems such as these do not always dampen changes and fluctuations but sometimes amplify them so that the fluctuations invade and agitate the system. At a certain point the fluctuations pass a critical threshold and then, following a transitional stage of chaotic fluctuations, completely reorganize the entire system. In fact the nonlinear interactions in far-from-equilibrium open systems allow the system to pass from one basic state to another in discontinuous transitions. As the transitions are discontinuous, the forms they will take, like that of the star-shaped crack in a window, cannot be foretold.

In the preceding sections of this chapter the basis of chaos in nonlinear conditions was discussed. Now we are noting the circumstances in which nonlinear conditions develop. When a system moves from an equilibrium mode of functioning to a far-from-equilibrium functioning, its nonlinearity is revealed.

Social Science Deals with Equilibrium Systems

Behavioral and social sciences are built on a model that regards all human systems as equilibrium seeking. Human systems have certain levels of functioning that they try to maintain. When this equilibrium is disturbed by the effects of some change, the system will after some time return to functioning at its equilibrium state. This is called *homeostasis*. From this viewpoint, when something happens to a family, or an organization to change its regular relationships, the system will do everything possible to eliminate the disturbance and return to its regular way of behaving and relating. Resistance to change is regarded as the system seeking to maintain its equilibrium and return to homeostasis. Equilibrium is the balance of forces pushing for change, and of forces trying to maintain the system's cohesion and inertia. The stability and regularity of the functioning of social systems is ensured by their seeking to return to equilibrium and maintaining homeostasis.

People often ignore the fact that the constancies they find, such as homeostatic mechanisms, are features of their own creation and need for order. People punctuate reality around themselves so that it shows regularity, order, and constancy. As Paul Dell, from the University of Texas, put it:

To attend to the constancy is to see it as being apart from the rest of the system. The last point tends to upset people because they insist that constancy is there regardless of any theoretical mumbo-jumbo; it is objectively there. But the point is that the constancy or redundant pattern is "there" in precisely the same sense that the homestatic mechanism is "there". Such regularities of systemic functioning are not features of the operative system, but of our description. There exists an infinity of apparent "features of the system" and each one is defined by a way of describing the system. Such descriptions are not of the system; they are something we bring to it. (1982:26)

Equilibrium systems are regarded as displaying regularity, constancy, and predictability. They are linear systems. Nations, societies, institutions, families, and individuals-behave in this way; their behavior is regular and orderly and can be predicted. Social change is the gradual transition from one state of equilibrium to another state of equilibrium. Order, regularity, and predictability are maintained in the system by its tendency to continue functioning in the same way as before-that is, near its equilibrium.

This approach ignores states of disequilibrium in the human world. It cannot account for discontinuous change, for evolution, for self-organization, and for emergence. It gives only half of the picture and ignores the other half. The human world, like the nonhuman world, is not only one of lineal order and continuity, but also of nonlinearity and discontinuity.

Far-From-Equilibrium as the Basis of Life and Evolution

Far-from-equilibrium behaviors are more meaningful than these former examples might convey. Far-from-equilibrium means that something is always changing itself and it is never exactly repeating its former behavior. Man needs to be in a far-from-equilibrium state in order to be alive.

Life means self-organization, self-creation, and emergence of novelty and these necessitate far-from-equilibrium conditions. Life is built on the basis of far-from-equilibrium change. Individual growth and development is on a far-from-equilibrium basis. This theme will be returned to and made more understandable later on. It will also be seen how evolution itself evolves on a far-from-equilibrium principle.

The social systems--national states, institutions, organizations, teams, family units--that humans create to organize their lives, need to constantly cooperate and coordinate their actions and change them according to changed circumstances. These systems and their components must regularly adjust their behavior to that of their changing environment. The only way social systems can continue to exist under these circumstances is behavior based on far-from-equilibrium structures.

Far-from-equilibrium in nonlinear interdependent systems is both the source of chaos and of renewal. Living and social systems that are by their very nature nonlinear, far-from-equilibrium and interdependent are in a permanent flux that includes a phase of chaos, self-organization, and renewal. Let us summarize what has been said so far:

- CHAOS DEVELOPS IN NONLINEAR, INTERDEPENDENT SYSTEMS. NONLINEAR MEANS THAT INPUT IS NOT PROPORTIONAL TO OUTPUT. INTERDEPENDENT MEANS THAT THE SYSTEMS MUTUALLY AFFECT ONE ANOTHER.

- WITH THESE CONDITIONS SMALL DIFFERENCES IN INITIAL CONDITIONS MAY BE BLOWN UP BY REPETITIVE AMPLIFICATION LEADING TO COMPLETELY DIFFERENT UNPREDICTABLE OUTCOMES.

- THE NONLINEARITY OF A SYSTEM TENDS TO COME OUT WHEN IT IS IN A FAR-FROM-EQUILIBRIUM STATE. FAR-FROM-EQUILIBRIUM MEANS THAT THE SYSTEM IS CONSTANTLY CHANGING AND NOT RETURNING TO SOME PREFIXED STATE.

- HUMAN AND SOCIAL SYSTEMS ARE FAR-FROM-EQUILIBRIUM, NONLINEAR, INTERDEPENDENT SYSTEMS.

ATTRACTORS--DIFFERENT STATES OF DYNAMIC SYSTEMS

When you open a tap and let the water flow, you can see that there are different kinds of flows. Depending on the pressure in the pipe and how much you open the tap, the water will pour forth in different forms and intensity. For example, the water can flow smoothly and steadily; it can gush forth pulsating with spurts; or it can burst through agitatively in an irregular turbulent flow. The various flows represent different patterns the flow can be "attracted" to.

A free-swinging pendulum, if disturbed swings sometime from side to side and then comes to rest at a certain point. It is as if the pendulum is attracted to that point. Scientists call this kind of movement a *point attractor,* depicting how the system is attracted to the same fixed point. It is as if the system has no degree of freedom in its choice of movement. It is caged in the same regular flow. The term "attractor" is used because a system appears to be pulled toward a definitive point or region during its cycles or periods.

A different movement may be discerned in a clock's pendulum when the clock's mechanism gives the pendulum a periodic kick. The pendulum now oscillates in its movement between two points. It is not attracted to a fixed point but moves in a cyclic path. Scientists call this form of movement a *limit cycle.* The pendulum, if disturbed, will return to the same original rhythm. It is as if it is attracted to the same limit cycle; in fact it has a limit cycle attractor. The system is still caged, but the cage is slightly larger. Systems that oscillate like this, with periodic fluctuations, are, for example, electrical circuits and economic cycles. In a certain sense, a system like this has no sense of time because it keeps returning to the same attractor. Ian Stewart describes the two attractors treated thus so far:

What do attractors look like? . . . The great majority of answers fall into two classes: steady-state behavior (nothing happens) and periodic (the same thing repeats over and over again forever). It is chastening to realize that from the qualitative viewpoint these myriad calculations reveal the presence of just two distinct forms of attractor. One is a single point; the other is a closed loop, corresponding to a periodic motion. These are rather simple ingredients from which to cook up our mad Universe. Is there anything else? (1989:45)

Although we try to create them in the work processes in industry, both single point and limit cycle behaviors are not typical of the living and the human world. In the world of life, even when something seemingly repeats itself, it is never exactly the same. Each repetitive cycle does not copy in exact detail the form of former cycles. Therefore, while some may use these kinds of behavior as metaphors for rigid human and social behavior which seemingly repeats itself with little degree of freedom, one must be careful in stretching this analogy.

Similar Behavior

The behavior of human beings never repeats itself exactly. Although it may look exactly the same as before, that is never so. Even when similar, it is always at least slightly different than former behavior. Much human and social behavior is nonlinear and can be typified more by the patterns of a *torus attractor*. This type of behavior can be illustrated in the form of traveling in a vertical direction around something that looks like a doughnut, with a hole inside it. Each circle around the doughnut is like an oscillation, or a limit cycle, although each circle behaves as if it is attracted to the surface, each circle is not exactly the same as the one that preceded it. Behavior varies in each new periodic circle it makes. It never repeats itself, there is always some variation. It is "quasiperiodical." Systems behaving like this are predictable, but just beginning to enter a region of nonlinearity. "This shape describes motion made up of two independent oscillations, sometimes called quasi-periodic motion. . . . The important feature of quasi-periodic motion is that in spite of its complexity it is predictable" (Crutchfield 1986:50). Thus while the orbit never exactly repeats itself, the motion of the system stays regular. Orbits that begin close to one another remain close to each other, and thus long-term predictability is ensured.

Periodic-and monotonous-limit cyclic behaviors are necessary for machines. They reflect locked periodic behavior. They do not allow a slight change in the range of rhythms, such as that needed under certain conditions. Torus-like behavior is exemplified by the way you brush your teeth; every time slightly differently. Life and social living necessitate systems that can handle constant, small changes within them and around them which never allow them to be the same as before. These adjustments are small and predictable and are suitable for describing the kinds of orderly changes that take place in human behavior. They are found in all living things that go through processes of gradual change, never once returning to what they once were. The behavior is similar but never exactly the same; like tying your shoelaces in the morning.

Describing the three kinds of attractors dealt with so far, John Briggs and David Peat write: "At this point we notice that the kind of nature described so far by attractors is quite regular. Systems decay gently to fixed point attractors or oscillate in well-behaved limit cycle attractors around tori shapes. It is a classical world where scientists can predict the behavior of even complicated systems for long periods ahead" (1989:41).

STRANGE ATTRACTORS

To describe nonlinear, unpredictable behavior, scientists had to discover a new kind of attractor. They called it a *strange attractor*. And strange indeed it was. Although one would expect it to take the form of a scattered random blurb, surprisingly enough it appeared to have some kind of patterned order and boundary. This is a stable, nonperiodic pattern that is confined to a finite range. Paths leading from two nearby points rapidly diverge. The chaotic pattern needs an infinite line as it never goes through the same point twice but continues indefinitely within a bounded area. This peculiar pattern is called a strange attractor.

There is some kind of patterned order within chaos. To meet the requirements of never repeating itself, the changing behavior has to be in the form of a line that is drawn in a limited space, never repeating itself, never crossing itself, never following the same path, and infinitely long.

Epidemiologist William Schaffer found the occurrence of measles among children varied according to a strange attractor. Studies have begun of chaos in in the human heart, cell growth and cancer, the effect of antidepressants, respiratory disorders and white cell regulation.

The search for strange attractors spread to astronomy to understanding Jupiter, to recessions in economics, and to epilepsy and heart attacks. Scientists have developed a computer program that allows one to discern if there is a strange attractor representing the hidden patterns behind seemingly random data depicting nonlinear dynamic change in a complex system.

Universal Transition Points

In 1975 Mitchell Feigenbaum of the Los Alamos National Laboratory made a breakthrough that proved universality existed in the transition points of different kinds of systems on their way from lineal order to deep chaotic states. While working on completely different systems, the same numbers came out. Feigenbaum had discovered constants that did not depend on the systems and were universal in entirely different systems.

Feigenbaum calculated the transition points on the route of a system to deep chaos. He showed that, irrespective of the kind of open dynamical system one was dealing with, it is possible to use the same universal numbers and calculate the transition points of the system on its way to chaos. These universal numbers, which are ratios, are now named after their discoverer and called the *Feigenbaum numbers*. After the fourth bifurcation, when the key parameters reach about 3.7 (called the Feigenbaum Point) all systems cascade into total deep chaos, where infinite choices create a situation in which freedom has no more meaning.

The Feigenbaum numbers showed that systems of a completely different nature would behave in a similar manner when turning chaotic. They allowed scientists from a variety of disciplines to predict the onset of turbulence in the real world systems they were studying. The Feigenbaum numbers were applied and found to predict the transition points on the route to chaos in phenomena as wide apart as optical systems and business cycles, electrical circuits and population growth, or the flow of gases and human learning. Medical researchers are studying the implications of these findings on their ability to be prewarned of the forthcoming occurrence of certain heart attacks. *Newsweek* reported in its May 25, 1992, issue that Michael Sheridan of the State University of New York used the model to predict avalanches on Colima volcano in Mexico.

Social and behavioral scientists have begun working on the implications of these findings for forecasting basic transitions in human systems. It is probably a matter of time before the Feigenbaum numbers will be used to prewarn of oncoming chaotic states in human and social systems. In the Santa Fe Institute for the Study of Complex Systems, work is in progress in applying these findings to understanding fluctuations and chaotic crises in the stock market.

Different Modes of Behavior

Four kinds of attractors that define and prescribe different basic modes of behavior in systems have been described so far. It is possible to group together the point and limit cycle attractors as they both depict fixed linear modes of behavior and change. The different modes describe systems on a continuum from linearity and predictability through stages of an intermix of linearity and nonlinearity, to an increase in unpredictability, and into total deep chaos where complete randomness reigns. These modes of behavior may also be regarded as different ways a human system--an individual, an organization, or a nation--can behave.

Some scientists prefer dividing behaviors into: equilibrium; close to equilibrium; far-from equilibrium; and deep chaos (Mark Michaels 1992). T.R. Young divides behaviors into four kinds: (1) Linear behavior (point and cycle) where there is little space for human agency. (2) Torus-like behaviors, with one outcome basin, having a limited room for human agency. (3) Butterfly-like behaviors swayed by strange attractors with two up to sixteen outcome basins, where potentials for human agency increase. (4) Deep chaos, beyond sixteen outcome basins, where freedom overwhelms human agency and entirely new forms of order emerge. These kinds of behavior can be described as:

A. Repeating former behavior in the same way.
B. Varying behavior slightly and predictably.
C. Adapting new behaviors (butterfly-like).
D. Chaotic behavior leading to (E), a new more complex mode.

A human system probably never does something in exactly the same point or cyclic way (A). Sometimes in industrial repetitive tasks attempts are made to attain this kind of behavior. Some individual and social behavior can be described as varying behavior slightly and predictably (B) for example shaving. New behaviors intermixing linearity and nonlinearity (C) may also be adapted, as when immigrating to a new country. Individual and social behavior can sometimes also go through phases of almost total chaos (D), as in Russia today, out of which new, more complex orders (E) are born.

There may be circumstances, where each of these different kinds of behavior are appropriate. There are times when behaving in one of these modes and not the other would be problematic. Behaving predictably but slightly different each time or adapting new behaviors with different degrees of linearity and nonlinearity, or functioning chaotically are as much a natural and necessary form of behavior as the other forms.

As will be explained in a later chapter, scientists at the Santa Fe Institute of Complexity, have found that complex adaptive systems (e.g., individuals, families, organizations, and nations) are able to survive and adapt more effectively in turbulent environments, when they are functioning in a mode that is described as "the edge of chaos." This probably describes behavior somewhere within the nonlinear, far-from-equilibrium category C--the butterfly intermix of predictability and unpredictability. Finding out what this precisely means and entails in practice in human systems, could become a major thrust of research and application for social and behavioral scientists.

FRACTALS AND CHAOS

Benoit Mandelbrot, a geometer from Belgium, was working at IBM on the problem of noises in the form of static bursts that interfered with hearing on telephone lines. Confronting the problem, Mandelbrot found that whatever time scale he used--hours, minutes or seconds--he always found the same ratio of noise to noise-free transmissions. The behavior of the static was always the same on any scale.

Mandelbrot had discovered similar degrees of irregularity (static bursts) across different scales. He was used to thinking in terms of figures and shapes and he began to create geometric forms to represent the characteristics of these transmissions. The forms he drew had the property of self-similarity across scales. They maintained a similar proportion of disorder (irregularity) to order (regular transmissions) on whatever scale they were measured. Mandelbrot named these forms *fractals* from fractus meaning broken or to break. A new geometry was born. It was not the regular Euclidean geometry of straight lines and perfect circles. But it was a geometry that could depict the natural forms of nature such as clouds, mountain ranges, and coastlines and the forms of life such as trees and the nervous system.

The Universality of Fractal Forms

From fractal forms it was not far to accept a fractal dimension, which represented the degree of irregularity of an object. It can also be seen as the measure of the relative degree of complexity of an object and the degree to which it fills up the space at its disposal. The degree of irregularity corresponds to the efficiency of an object in taking up the space it occupies. When you could compare the degrees of irregularity of one object to another, you had their fractal dimensions. A tire's irregularity could be matched with the irregularity of the roads it would travel.

Mandelbrot began looking for data on systems that could be measured by the self-similarity of fractals. He searched for recursion of form and repetitiveness of patterns inside patterns. He found this self-similarity in the ebbs and flows of rivers such as the Nile, on which there are data for hundreds of years. He found the repetitive patterns within patterns displaying both persistence and discontinuity in the prices of commodities.

Mandelbrot (1983) wrote that mathematicians would be delighted to find that fractal forms were not exceptional, they were the rule; that forms that appeared pathological should devolop naturally from very concrete problems, and that the study of forms in nature could help solve old problems and simultaneously yield many new forms.

Other scientists from different disciplines found fractal forms and patterns in their fields. Fractals could be used to describe the appearances and properties of a variety of materials such as metal fractures and polymers. Doctors began using fractals to study heart attacks. In addition, the wake of an airplane, the study of an earthquake, the seeping of oil, some problems of nuclear reactors could be better understood using fractals.

Natural objects, other than man-made objects, seldom fill their available space. They may appear to be solid, but in effect they are not so. The measure of their fractality is the degree to which they occupy the region available to them. If an object does not fill all of its available space it leaves the possibility of other objects coexisting in the same space. For example, a person can simultaneously be both a scientist and a father. Counting the number of "father" behaviors during a day can give that fractal dimension.

Fractals and Chaos

Close examination of a variety of strange attractors showed that they all had a number of common characteristics. They did have a stable form of some kind that could be depicted within a limited space. Strange attractors all exhibit a characteristic of self similarity on descending scales, although never exactly repeating themselves. They are like a set of wooden Russian dolls, each containing a smaller replica of itself within.

The self-similarity of the strange attractor never ended. It was infinite. You could go on and on as much as you were able to magnify and always find another even smaller replica. These are the characteristics of fractals. The forms of strange attractors were fractals. A strange attractor is an object that reveals more detail as it is increasingly magnified.

A system in deep chaos seems to be caught between different worlds, different dimensions--belonging to neither of them. It is in a no-man's land wandering between the dimensions, unable to return to the former and not yet in the other. It is in a fractal dimension between them. In human terms the fractal form of chaos depicts a transition state between basic orders. Chaos is an expression of being between social orders, different worlds, disparate systems, and changing eras.

Deep chaos is an indication of important transition points in the history of a human system. It is the way the system behaves when it has to make a jump from one order to another, from one phase to another. It is the turbulent phase out of which the novelty of the new order is born.

Deep chaos lies in the no-man's-land between ways of being in the world. It is found at the turning points in the history of human and social systems' development. It is the crack between two orders, being neither the order of the past nor that of the future. It is not belonging to either here or there--the "dark night of the soul," the wandering through the desert.

Deep chaos is the state in which Russia is attempting to leave its past regime and create a new order. It is the condition of an organization in deep crisis that cannot continue the way of the past and needs to transform itself completely. It is the chaotic time of transition between the industrial era and the coming era.

The Alternation of Order and Chaos

In human and social systems both linear order and chaos intertwine in varying degrees and alternate throughout the life history of the system. A period of relative order is followed by a period of chaos, which in its turn brings forth a new order. The period of deep chaos is a natural and necessary part of the development of every living and social system. It comes at the bifurcation point of discontinuous change. The conditions that are the fertile ground for the creation of the new order are born out of the turbulence of chaos.

Complex systems at some stage in their history reach a point at which they must go through a total restructuring to continue functioning. At this bifurcation junction they go through a chaotic transition to enable themselves to give birth and self-organize into their new form. To understand how this happens it is necessary to take a look at the science of Self-organization. That is the subject of the following chapter.

4
The Science of Self-Organization

BRIDGING THE GAP

As the Nobel committee put it, Ilya Prigogine's research into thermodynamics had not only fundamentally transformed and revised that science, it had given it new relevance and created theories to bridge the gap between biological and social scientific fields of enquiry. Describing Ilya Prigogine, the receiver of that acclamation, Mary Lukas writes:

The stocky little man who stood that day at the pinnacle of Nobel recognition was himself the product of a striking series of historical anomalies, of cruel chance and unexpected change. The second son of a Russian factory owner and a romantic, gently bred young woman who had studied at Moscow's conservatory of music, Ilya Prigogine was born the same year as the Russian Revolution.

When the Soviets restricted private enterprise, his family fled to the West. . . . his mother, clinging to aesthetic memories of her girlhood, strove to bring her two sons up with grace. She taught them music, and according to her recollections, Ilya could read piano scores before he could read books. . . . he was an oddity, a little Jewish boy from somewhere in the East, fallen into homogeneously bourgeois Catholic Belgium, handicapped by a thick German accent.

. . . Inside his head, he made a world where he could be comfortable. He read voraciously, devouring the classics and books on archaelogy, philosophy, and literature. His music was a refuge. He played Bach, Mozart, and Debussy; He even dreamed of a career as a concert pianist.

the chemical . . . [wanting to know what makes a criminal] the first volume his hand fell on was a study of makeup of the brain. He found it fascinating. He changed his prospective speciality to chemistry.(1980:85-86)

Like the chaotic trail of the metal balls in a pinball machine, one chance event led to another. A body of research and scientific theory that has developed within the last two decades, has played a major role in the understanding of how order develops out of chaos. This research was developed in chemistry and physics by Ilya Prigogine but in effect it has become the bridge between the sciences that deal with inanimate matter and the sciences that deal with the living. In 1978, Ilya Prigogine, the physical chemist from Brussels (now also at the University of Texas), received the Nobel Prize in recognition of his work on how random, chaotic changes in systems can lead to new patterns of order and stability.

The Wide Applicability of the Theory

Prigogine's theory could be applied to chemical solutions, to termites building nests, to traffic jams, and to the growth of cities. It could describe and explain transformations in a person's belief system, in organizations, in cultures, in political systems, and in historical eras. In all of these systems new patterns of order emerged out of chaos. In all of these, the same phenomena took place. A major transformation occurred that was triggered by instabilities and fluctuations that led to a quantum leap into a completely different order of things.

Prigogine's theory of order through fluctuations has far-reaching implications. More of these are becoming clear as time goes by. The theory has been found applicable in a wide range of areas, from the behavior of chemical reactions to brain research, to changes in states of consciousness and the evolution of mental processes to organizational transformation.

Prigogine's ideas started out in the areas of chemistry and physics. They developed into a theory of how living things change and evolve. They are now being used in technology, sociology, economics, psychotherapy, organizational change, medicine, psychology, astronomy, evolutionary theory, and elsewhere. The ramfications spread to art, the humanities, and philosophy. A book on Self-organization science, called *Time, Rhythms, and Chaos in the New Dialogue with Nature,* (Scott 1991) contains studies and research reports on the application of Self-organization science to human society, literature, art and communication, and philosophy.

How It Happens in Boiling Liquid

A pan of boiling liquid can illustrate the entire process of how new order develops out of chaos. A pan of liquid is heated on gas. As the pan heats up, the lower part of the liquid nearest the heat becomes hotter than the upper surface of the liquid, which is at a greater distance from the heat. When this happens the heat flows in a regular manner from the lower part of the liquid to the surface liquid. The liquid is in a near-equilibrium condition and the heat flows in a smooth and regular manner from the bottom to the top by a process of conduction.

After some time, with continued heating, a change takes place in the state of the liquid. A far-from-equilibrium state takes over. In this state the liquid's flow becomes increasingly disordered, with eddies and whorls. The increasing difference in temperature, between the upper and lower layers, changes the form of the flow. Molecules from the lighter, heated fluid at the bottom flow upward. Simultaneously, molecules of the cooler and more dense upper layer of the liquid are being pulled down by gravity. The water has moved into a different state, a state which is far-from-equilibrium. With continued heating the flow becomes more and more turbulent. The movement of the eddies and whorls in the liquid becomes increasingly agitated. The system, after some time, reaches a state of complete disorder. The liquid has moved into a state of chaos.

At a certain stage another critical bifurcation point is reached. The heat cannot disperse fast enough. The flow of the liquid changes into what is called convection currents, which can carry the increase in the rate of the flow and quantity of heat. When this happens, orderly, neatly arranged "hexagonal cells" begin to form and cover the surface of the liquid. The system has moved into a new order; order has emerged out of chaos.

There were five scenes in this story. In the first scene the liquid was in a regular steady equilibrium state. The second scene of the story is when heating caused an energy gradient and the liquid changed to a far-from-equilibrium state; it had become a "dissipative structure." It dissipated energy to its surroundings in order to maintain its coherence. In the third scene the liquid is agitated by fluctuations. The far-from-equilibrium, dissipative system is reaching a bifurcation point. With the growing fluctuations the liquid reaches a bifurcation point where the flow cannot be contained in the present structure.

Around the bifurcation point, with the increased agitation of the fluctuations, the far-from-equilibrium dissipative structure moves into a chaotic state. In the fifth scene the liquid transforms itself into a new order. It self-organizes itself into a completely new structure, of hexagonal cells. Prigogine and Stengers say that a new molecular order has been produced spontaneously. This new order corresponds to a giant fluctuation stabilized through energy exchanges with the outside world.

IN HUMAN AND SOCIAL SYSTEMS

All human and social systems are open, far from equilibrium systems. Biological and social systems are open, which means that trying to understand them in mechanistic terms is doomed to failure. This suggests, that most of human and social reality instead of being orderly, stable equilibrial, is "seething and bubbling with change, disorder and process" (Toffler 1981).

The former Soviet Union was unable to dampen its internal fluctuations indefinitely. It could not contain the growing internal fluctuations of economic, social, and national unrest. It broke up into national entities, each of which is being forced to self-organize into a new economic, social, and national order.

The Middle East may be going through a similar experience. The proliferation of nonconventional weapons may be making, the commomplace fluctuations of unrest, terrorism, and war both dangerous and unfeasible. The countries of that troubled area may be forced to restructure their relations into a new order. The other alternative of another major war with non-conventional weapons is so terrifying that, hopefully, it will be averted.

As with the chemical dissipative structure, so too all living systems and societies are in a never ending process of change, which creates new orders through internal fluctuations. As far-from-equilibrium open systems, they are in an intensive exchange of energy, matter, and information, with their ever-changing environment. They are constantly dissipating energy to maintain their wholeness and integrity. The systems are in a steadfast flux with never-ending internal fluctuations. The fluctuations are dampened as long as the society is able to contain them. But at some point, when an energy gradient becomes increasingly difficult to contain, the fluctuations reach a critical size that perturbs the system. Discontinuous change nucleates around one fluctuation. This leads to a period of great disorder, instability, insecurity, and chaos that finally ends in one of two ways. The society, organization, family, or personality breaks down and disintegrates, or it self-organizes itself into a new, more complex order.

George Scott (1991) writes "there is something truly new and remarkable in this comparison between the laboratory behavior of a chemical solution and human historical behavior." We can now apply the models derived from chemical solutions to human behavior. "Thus when we talk of societies dominated by critical events we may be thinking of the acts of George Washington at Yorktown and Robert E. Lee at Gettysburg, and we may be comparing them to critical behavior change in model oscillating physiochemical systems such as the famous BZ (Belousov-Zhabotinsky) reaction" (pp. 6-7).

The Catalyst of Transformation

The heating of the boiling liquid intensified the energy gradient, increased the disequilibrium, and led to fluctuations that changed the water's state. In analyzing the analagous factors in social systems, Professor J. Goldstein (1991) suggests that gradience in the environment leads to gradience within organizational systems and this activates the nonlinear potential for change. Goldstein suggests that the increasing internal gradience of the organizational system can also be seen as the increase of information in the system.

T. R. Young (1994) proposes that a small change in a societal parameter, such as raising the interest rate or a tax (e.g., the famous tea tax) may have a butterfly effect by triggering a bifurcation of some polarity within or between societies. At a social level, such a polarity may be in the accessibility of resources such as power, status or money. This may ignite a surge of fluctuations that will finally catalyze the society into transforming itself and self-organizing into a new order.

Possibly, in our times, schisms in or between societies are intensified by the abundant flow of information (newspaper, radio, television, fax, travel) that sometimes aggravates and polarizes the schisms by leading to growing awareness of the differences when these are extreme. This may bring out increasing fluctuations and a beginning of self-organization into a new order. It would be illuminating to make a historical analysis of the disintegration of the communist regimes based on this model. This may be the case also in the threatening schism between the technologically advanced Western countries and the very extreme poverty in under-developed countries with uncurbed population growth. The fanatic perturbations of Muslim fundamentalism may be signals of such a growing danger.

Energy Gradients in Societies

The catalyst of transformation in the heating liquid was the growing energy gradient between the lower and higher layers of the liquid. Young's (1994) theory proposes that the analogy to energy gradients in human societies is the widening schism between different nations or between sections of a society in terms of control of resources such as force, status, or income. Young sees the

Feigenbaum Points as indexes of degrees of gradient in control of resources
between sectors of a society. He suggests that it is to be expected and quite
normal that there will be such gradients within a society. The society will
continue to function without disruptions approximately up to the fourth
Feigenbaum bifurcation (i.e., with a range of difference in control of resources
up to a ratio of one to sixteen) meaning the rich sector of the population will not
be more than sixteen times as rich as the bulk of the lower income populace.

Young writes that: "Income differences which are greater than 16-1 (four
bifurcations), given similarity in market prices and similarity in levels of desire,
might well propel some firms and some private individuals into new ways to
generate income, some of which are decidedly harmful to the human condition
(for examples: theft, pollution, unnecessary surgery, fraud, extortion,
prostitution)." Beyond a certain point: "The resources required for social control
balloon as bifurcations accumulate" (1992). Deprived sectors will resort to
nonlinear behaviors to redistribute wealth outside the linear rationality of the
market place. In these terms, the flow of illegal immigrants from Mexico and
Cuba to the United States, or from Eastern Europe, Africa, and North Africa to
Europe, may be understood in terms of a widening resource gradient leading to
nonlinear solutions.

Within a society, Young regards crime as nonlinear behavior within the
linear framework of the system of distribution of wealth. He sees many forms of
crime as nonlinear feedback loops in which wealth is redistributed outside the
rationality of the marketplace. When a thief steals a television, that theft is
nonlinear in terms of a market dynamics. If a bank teller embezzles funds from
the bank, the transfer of resources is nonlinear in terms of a linear wage policy
that is based on a linear wage scale. The more hours worked, the higher the
income.

In Young's eyes crime is a nonlinear system of distribution which, tends to
amplify disorder by adding to the uncertainties of its victims. Street crime in
particular is a vicious expression of nonlinear distribution, since its victims
generally are those already living in great uncertainty with regard to their
income, health, housing, family, and racial relations. Organized crime resorts to
fictitious solutions such as gambling, drugs and commodity sex.

If we want to maintain the integrity of a market economy with its many advantages, then
their must be such forms of nonlinear response with which to defeat the transformation of
the torus which describes, say, the frequency of entry into the market itself for essential
goods and services. If not, the market itself may split into 2 or more attractors: one
oriented to those with discretionary income and those without. As income inequalities
between ethnic groups, economic classes or nations grow, more and more capital is
attracted to the basin of production allocated to luxury goods and less and less to the
production basin [in] which essential goods are produced. . . . At some point, low wage
owners will begin to seek alternative ways to increase income or to reduce costs in order
to stay in the market place. (Young 1992:11)

Young's view of the alleviation of crime is not accomplished by increased law enforcement, larger police forces, and stiffer punishments. He suggests that one of the major roots of crime lies in the polarized extremities of resource distribution. He suggests a more humanistic approach of moving from a strategy of control of the deviant to the empowerment and enabling of all persons in society.

Trying to Remain the Same

South Africa tried as long as it could to delay abolishing its racial policies. Quite often a system will prolong its present state after its situation demanded a major change. This can often be seen in social systems doing their utmost to postpone major changes. The system will continue to dampen the fluctuations, control, repress and contain them, not allowing them to undermine the foundations of the existing order.

The difficulties of moving to a new free market order in Eastern Europe, exemplify this situation. This phenomenon is called *metastability*. It is the dampening of changes found in chemical reaction systems and in living and human systems.

It often seems as if social systems resist change by delaying major upheavals and dampening all needed changes. When the fluctuations can no longer be dampened, the system reaches a point of instability where it cannot continue. This happened in Albania and, if policies do not change, it may happen in the Western world with problems of racial minorities. The system either breaks down, decomposes and disintegrates, or self-organizes itself into a new order.

Resilience

Delayed change should not be seen in a negative light. The ties between the parts of a system may be sufficiently flexible, and they may be fast enough in their adjustments so that they can absorb the fluctuations without the immediate need for a major transformation.

Resilience can be viewed as delayed evolution. The system is constantly changing itself while delaying the need for a major reordering. The flexible, but dense, coupling among its parts (subsystems) and the sensitive, fast mutual adjustment between them, allow the system to continue functioning and changing for a long time without going through a major restructuring.

The slow, difficult, sometimes delayed but steady move in Western Europe toward a European common market, might be viewed as a case of resilience.

In a resilient system when the fluctuations finally necessitate a transformation into a higher, more complex order, opportunities are greatest with a wide variety of possibilities open to the new order into which the system will self-organize itself. On the other hand, in a metastable system that has resisted change far too long, the danger is greater that the system will disintegrate through a major upheaval that it will be unable to restrain and control (Jantsch 1980). This is happening today in the former Soviet Union and Yugoslavia.

At this moment in history mankind, on a worldwide scale, is facing such a situation. Many factors, including the growth of technology with its blessings and dangers, society's reluctance to move to alternative sources of energy, and the efforts to maintain domination and control, might be delaying the shift to a new era. The dangers to humankind in the form of an ecological disaster, another Chernobyl, a major war, or the use of nuclear weapons, might increase with every decade of delay in the shift to a new era.

Crossroads of Choice

On the road throughout life people are often faced with basic decisions that have major implications for their life courses. On its way to a new order, a living system passes through a period of great instability. It is faced with decision points on which its future will depend. A variety of different paths are opened up before the system. Which particular road it will choose at each of these forks will determine the possibilities open to it in the future. Prigogine named these points of choice bifurcations, that is, points of forking or branching. When a system reaches a bifurcation point it is faced with the possibility of choosing from different paths. Each path may lead in a completely different direction and open the possibility for entirely different ways of self-organizing itself.

Briggs and Peat say that at its bifurcation points the changing system is, in effect, being offered a choice of orders. In some cases the system is constrained by its circumstances and the choices are few, either this or that. On other occasions there are infinite degrees of freedom, which in effect means that the system has become chaotic.

Yugoslavia can restructure itself into a new system as a federation of autonomous states or as separate independent national states. Each major decision on the way, increases the possibility of either one of these, or other ways, of resolving the fluctuating dangerous present situation now bordering on chaos.

In *The Age of Bifurcation* (1991) Dr. Errvin Laszlo of the Vienna International Academy, describes our changing world in terms of being at the bifurcation point between two eras. Laszlo surveys the choices facing humanity at this crucial bifurcation point.

Unpredictability at the Crossroads

Mankind does not know what regime will develop in Russia. You can trace a system's bifurcation points backward into the past. But before the bifurcation point, you can never predict a system's path into the future. Which path the system will choose is randomly determined by the particular fluctuation that is amplified at the bifurcation point.

The human race does not know what will develop as a result of the proliferation of nuclear weapons. The behavior of a far-from-equilibrium system becomes highly specific. There is no longer any universally valid law from which the overall behavior of the system can be deduced. Each system is a separate case (Prigogine and Stengers 1988).

Humanity does not know what will happen with the spread of AIDS. In a far-from-equilibrium situation it is impossible to predict the system's further behavior. Prigogine and Stengers say that when a bifurcation point is reached, deterministic description breaks down. Humanity cannot foresee the results of the world's exponential growth of population. No one knows what fluctuation will bring the downfall of Saddam Hussein's regime in Iraq.

Mony Elkaim (1981), who has applied Prigogine's theories to psychotherapy, writes that the same general laws that could describe a system at or close to equilibrium, do not apply in the same way when far from equilibrium. In terms of the therapeutic process, at the same point different choices are available and it is impossible to know which one of the fluctuations will transform the person's state.

Jantsch (1980) suggests that the future evolution of such a system cannot be predicted in an absolute way. It is like a decision tree with truly free decision at each branching point.

In the instability conditions, close to a bifurcation point, fluctuations that might appear to be small, may have an enormous effect. Others that appear of major importance have little effect, as that of the Kurd's rebellion on Saddam Hussein's regime. The butterfly effect reappears here in the far-from-equilibrium conditions.

When a system is near to a bifurcation point, it is relatively unstable. Therefore small, chance fluctuations which are always in the system, can be decisive in pushing it in one direction rather than another. Human history is made up of successive stages of relatively predictable stability and development along a particular path, separated by periods of instability during which the future of the system is decided by small, chance events which push it into one or another path. George Scott describes a bifurcation point in American history:

In our mind's eye we can picture the scene at the infamous "bloody angle" on the Gettysberg battlefield at the crucial moment when General Pickett's gray wave of confederate soldiers were stopped by the blue wall of union soldiers and turned back southward. Four months later on the same field Abraham Lincoln proclaimed that "a new nation conceived in liberty and dedicated to the proposition that all men are created equal" and moreover "any nation so conceived and so dedicated" could endure in the space and time of the earth's biosphere. In other words he proclaimed that humanity had passed a critical bifurcation point. (1991:8-9)

All this leads to the sobering conclusion that, in a human or social system undergoing transformation, the selection of the future path cannot be controlled.

Applying this to family therapy, P. F. Dell from the University of Texas and H. A. Goolishian from Galveston Family Institute, said: "One can intervene into such systems and push them toward the point of instability, but one cannot control precisely when they reorganize, nor can one control in what fashion they reorganize" (1981:104).

This point is of extreme importance for political leaders, commentators, therapists, organizational consultants, and other change leaders or consultants who are attempting to control future developments or manage a social system transforming itself. There are limits both to predicting and controlling what will happen to nations, organizations, families, and individuals. The events in Somalia and the recent elections in Russia have shown this. Design and guidance to some degree appear to be possible, but not control. It is impossible to predict precisely when a transformation will take place and what exact form it will take.

Taking the Most Ordered Path

While the new path the system will take cannot be predicted and controlled, there are theories as to the general direction the system will take when it proceeds to transform itself. If behavioral and social systems are guided by the same basic laws as physical and chemical systems, they will first favor changing directions with a capacity to allow their energy to flow at a maximum rate. Such directions are generally the most ordered ones. A system in a far-from-equilibrium state going through intensifying fluctuations will use all the possibilities open to it. Nevertheless, like the molecules in the boiling liquid, flow paths that will allow the maximum flow rate will be those chosen. Professor R. Swenson (1989) suggests that, in physical and chemical systems, the path the system will choose will be that path in which the energy flow has the fastest rate. As energy flows faster in an ordered flow, that is the path it will choose.

When more orderly fluctuations have a sufficient amount of energy poured into them, they develop into self-sustaining ordered flows. The emergence of order is a competition between flow efficiencies. A fluctuation gets the energy it needs to develop into a self-organizing flow because it is sufficiently more efficient than other flow paths (Goerner 1993). Sally Goerner points out that ordered flows allow energy to flow faster than disordered flows. The pressure to go as fast as possible will lead the system to support order whenever it possibly can. It will do this by pouring energy into more orderly fluctuations. And as Goerner suggests this is what amplifies the fluctuations into novel forms of order.

An example given by Goerner is that of the flow of heat from a warm bathroom. The heat will flow first through an open door before infiltrating outside through the bathroom walls or tiny cracks in the window frame. The selection of the most efficient flow channel leads to change first taking the most ordered channel to flow through. If such a channel exists it will be preferred.

A later chapter will deal with the principle of "the economizing of flexibility" as a guiding principle of transformative changes taking place in human systems. This means that a human system will choose a less drastic, stability-maintaining change path before embarking on a more far-reaching and destabilizing one. This may be the behavioral and social analogy to the most orderly efficient channel in physical systems.

The author's personal experience with many organizations, corporations, and communities going through a basic transformation is that generally the organization will first choose the path that appears to be the less threatening and easiest to put into practice. In other words even if a path of change will be seen to have more far-reaching results, if it will be seen to cause major upheaval, it will not be chosen first. Possibly the ordered energy flows, given priority in human systems are those that appear easier to put into practice, with less resistance and commotion and minimal upheaval (Levy and Merry 1986).

Transformation to a New More Complex Order

Water reaches a boiling point. A marriage careening toward a breakdown, reaches the divorce court. The racial tension in Los Angeles reaches a stage where it erupts after the decision in the trial of police officers charged with assaulting a black driver. The increasing intensity of the fluctuations within a system reaches a critical stage. At this point, the system in its present form can no longer contain the heightening fluctuations. The system and its components have been so shaken that they are unable to continue functioning in the former order. The system has passed a threshold from which there is no return. The system is driven into a new regime or it dissolves as a whole system as, for example when the Soviet Union broke up into independent republics.

When machines break down, if someone does not repair them, they stop functioning. Living and social systems need not disintegrate they may transform to a different order. The new order established is one of greater complexity. That means that there are greater differences among the parts, more intricate ties among them and higher energy flow through. The society has changed. There is greater differentiation among its inhabitants, and at the same time a more intricate pattern of relationships among the people.

Jeremy Rifkin (1981) describes how the reorganization always tends toward a higher order of complexity, integration, connectedness, and greater energy flow through. After each transformative reordering, because it is more complex than the one preceding it, the system is even more vulnerable to fluctuations and restructuring. Complexity creates the condition for greater reordering and speed up of evolutionary development and energy flow through.

Chaos can develop in nonlinear interdependent systems, those that are mutually connected and interactively affecting each other. This means that if complexity is increasing the interdependency and the rate of energy flow through of nonlinear systems, it might also be increasing their vulnerability to chaotic dynamics. If complexity is growing on a worldwide scale it may be ripening the conditions for the proliferation and rate of transformations and increasing uncertainty in the human world.

Self-Organization in the World

Europe is self-organizing itself into a common market. Some of the limits of the former structures are being overcome by the ability of the system to evolve and self-organize itself into a new structure. The widened limits of the new structure will possibly be able to contain within them and deal with the gradients that were the sources of instability and fluctuation that disrupted the former structure.

The new system that might develop in Russia, or Armenia, will, hopefully in time, be able to contain and inhibit the fluctuations that are at present creating chaos in those countries. This does not mean that only one new order is possible. There often are a variety of possibilities for a new structure available for the transformation of the old structure.

Throughout history humanity has made the change from one era to another through self-organization. Mankind has made quantum leaps that completely transformed civilization. Jantsch (1980) wrote that in the past the evolution of mankind generally took the form of self-reinforcement of fluctuations and spontaneous structuration of total sociocultural systems.

Far-from-equilibrium systems in nature as well as all living and social systems differ from machines in that far-from-equilibrium systems are able to spontaneously self-organize themselves into new orders. Margeret Wertheim gives some examples from nature:

A whirlpool is a fine example. A stream flowing over rocks suddenly forms stable vortexes. Some last only a few seconds, some may last for minutes. They aren't eternal, but while they last, they are complex, well defined forms, which have arisen out of apparent disorder. Again, the vortex is an open relationship with the stream. Water flows in and out, yet the vortex stays stable. Clouds are another example. They're just vaporised water molecules, yet they can form spectacular patterns across the sky. (1990:54)

Self-Organization in Science

Self-organization is not only the principle underlying the emergence of a rich world of forms manifest in physical, chemical, biological, ecological, social, and cultural structures. It is also a unifying principle connecting the sciences of the physical world and the world of the living. Self-organization dynamics are the link between the realms of the animate and the inanimate. Life is no more a thin superstructure over a lifeless physical reality, but a basic principle of the dynamics of the universe.

Dr. L. Meyer (1991), professor of philosophy at the University of South Dakota, says that self-organization science contributes to scientific unification in a number of ways. It deals with phenomena at all levels from microscopic to macroscopic. It deals with different disciplines such as natural and social sciences. And finally it unifies scientists working together in interdisciplinary research.

Prigogine's work on how order develops out of chaos led to the understanding that at a far-from-equilibrium state, matter becomes active and has the potential to spontaneously and unpredictably develop new forms and structures by itself. As Wertheim suggests, this: "brings back into the realm of science the notion of ongoing creation. It suggests that the universe is constantly in the process of creating new things, and that this process will always be going on." (1990:54). The implications of the increasingly complex human world will be discussed in chapter 13 of this book.

Continuous processes of self-organization mean that the world as a whole and the human world are growing ever more complex. Growing complexity is leading to an intensification of uncertainty and difficulties of adaptation. The coming section will deal with this subject.

5
The Science of Complexity

Complexity is on the cutting edge of science. Physicist Heinz Pagels put it this way: "I am convinced that the societies that master the new sciences of complexity and can convert that knowledge into new products and forms of social organization will become the cultural, economic, and military superpowers of the next century" (1989:53).

The center and birthplace of the study of the New Science of Complexity is in the Santa Fe Institute. Writing about this institute in *The Wall Street Journal*, B. Wysocki reports:

Even in this city of artists, New Agers and freethinkers, the Santa Fe Institute ranks as an oddity. The headquarters of this private think tank is a converted convent built of adobe. Inside are Ph.D.s with ponytails who wander the halls talking about Boolean algebra and artificial life. Biologists rub shoulders with computer jocks. Economists argue with physicists. . . . Yet the Santa Fe Institute isn't just another kooky little outfit. To begin with, four Nobel Laureates in physics and economics are actively involved in what goes

on here. . . . The president of the organization is the noted scientist, George Cowan, from
Los Alamos National Laboratory.
Unlocking the secrets of complex phenomena is the stated purpose of the handful of full-
timers, as well as the hundreds of transient thinkers who are here for a week or a month
or a year. Some of the work falls into the scientifically fashionable category of "chaos
theory," which holds that certain events are neither strictly predictable nor random.
(1990)

Through understanding complexity, the institute hopes to offer in the future a
new understanding of the world's economy and the body's immune system,
which may work in similar ways. What is common to all the systems studied at
the institute (and other institutes that have sprung up in its wake) is the study of
complexity and adaptive complexity. The subject of this chapter is the New
Science of Complexity and, in particular some of its implications for behavioral
and social systems, which are complex systems. The following chapter will deal
with "the complexity spiral," that is, the growth of complexity in the world and
the human world in particular. In the last section of the book we will return to
complex adaptive systems.

WHAT IS COMPLEXITY?

The groundwork for understanding complexity was laid down in the
preceding chapter that dealt with the science of Self-organization. It was shown
that complex systems self-organize themselves into states of greater complexity.
But what is complexity? An overview of the Santa Fe Institute says that complex
behaviors may emerge from a number of basic rules controlling parts of the
system. That behavior is not predictable from knowledge of the individual
elements, no matter how much we know about them. But it can be discovered by
studying how these elements interact and how the system adapts and changes
throughout time. This new, emergent behavior of the system is important for
understanding how nature operates on the macroscopic level. What looks chaotic
at first may be predictable from an understanding of the patterns and rules of
complex behavior.

The organization of simultaneous interaction of many components of a
system create complexity. Stephen Wolfran of the Institute for Advanced Study
in England says that complicated systems most often are built up out of basic
components and laws that are quite simple, "the complexity arises because you
have a great many of these simple components interacting simultaneously. The
complexity is actually in the organization--the myriad possible ways that the
components of the system can interact" (Waldrop 1992:86).

Complex systems are in effect "dissipative systems" discussed in the
preceding chapter. Physics divides dynamical systems into two major categories:
classical conservative systems that are in effect closed systems that conserve

their energy; and dissipative systems that are open systems that maintain their coherence by energy flow through.

Dissipative systems are the more ubiquitous "complex" systems. Energy in dissipative systems is in constant exchange with the environment; it dissipates. They are "open" or exchanging systems versus the conservative closed or containable systems. Rather than clear crisp causality their parts interact, they reciprocally affect each other. In dissipative systems, as many psychological studies attest, "interaction effects" are often the major effects. Dissipative charateristics define the heart of what we experience as complexity. I will use the term complexity to refer to the dissipative side of the dynamical systems tree. (Goerner 1991:8)

Goerner describes some of the characteristics of complex dissipative systems as being unpredictable in theory not just practice; showing forms of qualitative transformation; and, the behavior of their whole as not an extrapolation of the behavior of the smallest parts, but as governed by global relationships. Professor Daniel L. Stein of Santa Fe Institute, writes that "Complexity is almost a theological concept; many people talk about it but nobody knows what 'it' really is." Stein suggests that the following are features that distinguish complex systems:

Nonreducibility. The complex system cannot be understood by reducing it to its parts. "The behavior we are interested in evaporates when we try to reduce the system to a simpler, better-understood one."

Emergent behavior. Complex systems "all show surprising and unexpected behavior that somehow seems to be a property of the system as a whole." At the level of complex systems "emergent behavior", as it is called, appears and it is a property of the whole system.

Unpredictability and regularity. There is unpredictability with patterns of regularity in the behavior of the whole system. Stein writes that "there is an inherent unpredictability to many of these systems, not because of our lack of sophistication, but for more fundamental reasons. . . . However, even though the behavior of the system is unpredictable in detail, surprising regularities nevertheless exist; for many diverse systems, the transition from regular to chaotic behavior shows certain universal features, independent of the details of the system." One cannot predict the outcome of an experiment with such a system "a given experiment may have many outcomes a given problem may have many solutions, all nearly equivalent, near optimal, with none much better than the rest. . . . In all cases, extreme sensitivity to initial boundary conditions or historical path makes detailed prediction impossible; nevertheless, important regularities occur." (Stein 1989:xiii-xv)

The interplays between order and disorder, predictability and unpredictability, regularity and chaos, are characteristics of complex systems. Complex systems abound in the real world, and they reflect the world's inherent irregularity. The real world is a world of complexity, of messiness, of change, flow and process and cannot be pinned down to the simple, solid, unchanging objects people like to cut out of it.

Human and Social Systems as Complex Systems

All of the features Stein describes as properties of complex systems are also features of behavioral and social systems. The elder people in a workplace retire and young people join. Some people leave to move to other vicinities, some change their occupations. There is constant movement, with new people coming in and others going out. Living and social systems are complex processes of pattern and organization.

Human and social systems cannot be understand by reducing them to the sum of their ever-changing parts. The system has many outcomes; an evolving population may radiate into many species. Their wholes show emergent behavior; there is an inherent unpredictability in them. The transition from regular to chaotic behavior shows universal features; their extreme sensitivity to initial conditions makes prediction impossible. The interplay between order and disorder, regularity and chaos, predictability and unpredictability characterize them.

Human Systems as Process Structures

The water in a whirlpool or the water flowing through a tap are not solid structures, but process structures. The flow of the water through the tap may assume many structures, depending on how much the tap is opened. It may be a regular flow of drops or a random flow, it may be a laminar flow or a turbulent one. The drops of water are ever-moving and creating the structure in their dynamic movement. What is seen as solid has no solidity in it. It is not composed of the same components but changing ones in different relationships. Every drop of water is passing through a dynamic regime, which differs with every change in the structure of the flow.

Understanding living systems necessitates a change in the way the living, behavioral, and social worlds are seen. People need to move from a way of seeing human systems mainly in terms of substance and matter to seeing them in terms of complex patterns and organization. Living things and social systems are complex process systems whose components are always changing and are in constant need to readjust themselves and their relationships to these changes. The cells in human bodies are always being replaced. People come and go and the organization transforms itself. Generations pass away and the nation lives on.

This view of behavioral and social systems is more process oriented in contrast to systems that are seen in terms of solid components and the structures they form. Human systems cannot be understood by breaking them into their parts and studying the parts. The parts are constantly changing. The whole is different from the sum of its parts.

Human systems have the property of self-creation. Social system too are never the same, but ever-changing. Parts are always being renewed and replaced, relations between components are in a never-ending flux of readjustment. The system has the property of self-organization allowing it to renew itself in discontinuous jumps into new orders and forms.

Jantsch (1980) points out that the notion of system is not tied to a specific spatial structure nor to a particular changing configuration of components, nor to certain sets of internal or external relations. A system is a set of coherent, evolving, interactive processes which manifest themselves temporarily in globally stable structures that have nothing to do with equilibrium and the solidity of technological structure.

The caterpillar and the butterfly are examples of this. The form is different; the relations between parts are changed; the relationship with the environment is not the same. They are two temporarily stabilized complex structures.

CONNECTIVITY

A basic characteristic of complex systems is connectivity. In a world of complex systems everything is connected to everything else. An example from Laszlo illustrates the point:

Urban concentrations, industrial complexes, misused or inappropriate technologies, and unsuitable forms of energy create pollution, cause deforestation, trigger climate change, and reduce world agriculture. Combined with unrelenting growth in human numbers, they produce an unsustainable load on the environment. While per capita load is higher the more affluent the population, the load imposed by extreme poverty also creates serious, and often irreversible degradation. (1991:23)

A world of complex nonlinear systems is a world of butterfly effects. Events in one place can cause major repercussions throughout the world. The uncertainties before the Gulf War affected stock markets and the lives of people throughout the world.

Complex systems cannot exist in isolation. By their very nature they are tied to and connected to other systems, thus creating a dense web of connections between complex systems throughout the world. Affecting one system has repercussions in countless other systems.

Coupling and Emergence

Complex systems couple together to create higher order systems. The evolution of life is the history of the coupling together of simpler systems into more complex systems, which in turn couple together to create even more complex systems. That is the story of how single-celled creatures coupled to create multicellular creatures. These multicellular creatures, in turn, coupled to create more complex organisms and so on up to social systems and the worldwide socioeconomic global society.

Out of the coupling together of systems emerge new systems of a higher order with properties that were not existent in the systems that created them. Writing about the workshops at Santa Fe Institute, Waldrop points out how the discussions focused on systems comprised of many agents. What was common to them was that they were all the time reorganizing themselves into larger structures through clashes of mutual accommodation and rivalry.

This property of joining together to create new systems at a more complex level can be found throughout nature and society. Atoms join to create molecules, molecules join together to create cells, cells couple to create organs and so and so on, from individuals that join together to create families and companies that then join to create an economy.

At each new level a new form emerges. The new form at the higher level is greater than its parts and it has novel properties and behaviors that cannot be be found in its components. Complexity is the science that deals with the emergence of new, more complex forms from the joining together of components.

Doyne Farmer of the Santa Fe Institute says that while it may seem to us like magic, it is happening at all levels, with organisms interacting and coevolving to become an ecosystem, atoms bonding to become molecules and people interacting to become families and cultures. "Somehow, by constantly seeking mutual accommodation and self-consistency, groups of agents manage to transcend themselves and become something more" (Waldrop 1992:88).

Roger Lewin (1992) summarizes that emergence is the central feature of the New Science of Complexity. It appears in the evolutionary models and in models of coevolving systems, in the unfolding of morphological form in embryological development, in the properties of ecosystems, in food-web structures, in the persistence of communities, and in global control. It appears in the different levels of complexity in human societies, from bands up through to the state. In chapter 13 we will return to emergence and search for insights it can give us in coping with uncertainty.

Emergence provides a new viewpoint through which we can understand evolution. Evolution of the new and novel is no more only the blind result of the survival of the fit, but develops naturally out of the self-organizing properties of complex systems.

Functioning at the Edge of Chaos

Complexity arises as a natural development when a system reaches a certain level of variety and diversity. Internal processes of autocatalysis feed the system leading it to self-organize into a more complex level of functioning. This occurs only at a certain level of internal complexity; thereafter, complexity breeds ever more complexity. Referring to autocatylytic sets, Stuart Kauffman a leading biologist at the Santa Fe Institute says that if their chemistry is too simple and the complexity of the interactions is very low, nothing will occur. A system of this kind is "subcritical." If the complexity of the interactions is rich enough then the system is "supercritical." The autocatalyctic process would be inevitable, and the order we would get would be for free (Lewin 1992).

A country with a subsistence level of production of one crop, such as tea, may not have reached the phase transition point to allow it to take off into a higher, more complex regime. Investing more in tea plantations is not going to change this. A system needs a certain level of complexity in order to evolve into higher levels of complexity. Below a certain level of complexity the system will not evolve and it will have difficulties if at a higher level its state becomes too chaotic. It can adapt best at the intermediate level between order and chaos. This point should arouse interest in small companies and small communities, that have not reached sufficient complexity to allow them to take off.

Complex systems evolve themselves to the edge of chaos. This is the state where the system needs to balance itself so as not to fall into too much chaos on the one hand (as in the present state of the former Soviet Union), and too much order on the other hand (as in the centralized, totalitarian Stalinist regime). In many coevolving complex systems, the systems attain the state of being at the edge of chaos by adjusting their degree of coupling. Systems reach the edge of complexity by tuning their ties to other systems.

Stuart Kauffman says that "By selecting an appropriate strategy, organisms tune their coupling to their environment to whatever value suits them best. And if they adjust the coupling to their own advantage, they will reach the boundary between order and randomness--the regime of peak average fitness. The bold hypothesis is that complex adaptive systems adapt to and on the edge of chaos." He also says that "It now begins to appear that systems in the complex regime can carry out and coordinate the most complex behavior and adapt most readily and can build the most useful models of their environments" (Ruthen 1993:117).

Systems on the edge of chaos are stable enough to receive and keep information, while they are also able to transmit it. They can do complex computations, they are able to react to the world, to be both spontaneous in adapting to their environment, and be alive. They adjust themselves to a point where their computational ability is maximized. This is also the point where they attain their highest level of fitness and adaptibility (Waldrop 1992).

Research at Santa Fe Institute raises the following possibilities: the edge of chaos is where complex systems are best able to function adaptively. It is where they get better at evolving and have the highest fitness. The edge of chaos is where complex adaptive systems show lifelike behavior and can best perform complex computations. This is where they acquire the basic evolutionary competence of developing internal models of the environment.

The edge of chaos is where complex adaptive systems have the widest range of behaviors to choose from. This gives them an advantage of being able to function effectively in a varied and fast changing environment. They have a rich choice of alternatives they can pick from when dealing with a turbulent environment.

The behavioral and social sciences have a lot of research ahead of them to understand how the systems they deal with adjust and tune their couplings to their environments to attain a regime of peak average fitness at the edge of chaos. Biological species do this by tuning the degree of interdependence/autonomy of their components and between themselves as a whole and other systems. The way human systems tune themselves to the edge of chaos needs thorough research.

THE COMPLEXITY SPIRAL

Evolution is going in the direction of ever-increasing complexity. There is direction to the arrow of time. That direction is pointing to the continual evolvement of systems to ever-higher levels of complexity. Every transformation of a complex system moves it either to disintegration or to a higher level of complexity. In his book Laszlo describes how "evolution moves from the simpler to the more complex, and from the lower to the next higher level of organization," and that "there is an observed probability that bifurcations lead to increasingly complex systems progressively further from thermodynamic equilibrium" (1991:113, 116).

Roger Lewin (1992) comments that the Darwinian view of complexity is based only on natural selection, which is a blind nondirectional force. In the Darwinian view there is no growth of complexity. In the New Science of Complexity there is a combination of both internal and external forces.

Increased complexity is a fundamental property of complex dynamical systems. Doyne Farmer, of Santa Fe Institute, remarks that: "evolution is constantly coming up with things that are more complicated, more sophisticated, more structured than the ones that came before." He traces how all later systems whether in nature or society--as in the economy, in cities, and in technology--are more structured than their counterparts that preceded them in time. Thus learning and evolution move systems along the edge of chaos in the direction of greater and greater complexity.

Complexity and Stability

Does increasing complexity in a system lead to a growth of instability in the system? A stable system is a robust system. It is a system that maintains its pattern of behavior despite disturbances. Does the growth of complexity in a system disrupt this ability? For a system to continue functioning and developing it needs to be able to maintain its stability. Goerner writes:

Stability (i.e. robustness, in the face of perturbation) is very important in real-world systems because the real world is full of disturbances large and small. Systems that do not retain their coherence in the face of disturbances will tend not to exist. For instance a pencil standing on its point is very sensitive to small disturbances and thus we do not commonly observe pencil-on-its point systems. Systems that we generally observe have structural stability, the ability to exist in the face of the world's many disturbances. (1991: 25)

Stability is not the same as constancy. Goerner points out that stable behavior is not necessarily constant behavior. A system may have many stable patterns of behavior. Even "infinitely unique and locally erratic chaotic behavior can have a stable robust global pattern." Nonlinearity contributes to stability because some of its forms will tend to dampen out disturbance effects.

As the stability of complex systems is strengthened by nonlinear feedback, complex nonlinear systems may be more robust than linear systems. While there is local unpredictability, the behavior of the system as a whole is stable. Goerner suggests that the unique behavior, found during chaos is stable in that it returns to former behavior despite small differences in initial conditions.

While a complex system may be robust, such a system is increasingly sensitive to internal and external fluctuations. Prigogine and Stengers wrote that the more complex a system is, the more numerous are the types of fluctuations that threaten its stability. The more complex a system is the more sensitive and vulnerable to fluctuations it becomes. The more vulnerable the system becomes, the more energy the system needs to maintain its coherence. In other words, in human systems, the more awareness, attention, and care it will have to devote to maintaining its internal ties and communication networks. The more the modern family or organization becomes complex and vulnerable, the greater its need to become aware of and devote communication, information resources, and interaction skills to maintain its internal processes. Prigogine and Stengers describe this as a competition between communication and fluctuations: "There is competition between stabilization through communication and instability through fluctuations. The outcome of that competition determines the threshold of stability" (Prigogine and Stengers:189).

On one hand, the more complex a human society, the more robust it becomes. On the other hand, the more numerous are the fluctuations that threaten the society's stability. To maintain its wholeness--its coherence through transformative discontinuous changes--it has to invest in more meaningful communication and effective relationships between its component parts and between itself and its environment.

At this state of knowledge it appears that when a human system takes care of its communication systems it can maintain its resilience and robust stability. If it does not do so, increasing complexity may entail breakdowns and faster rates of discontinuous transformations. Discussing biological systems, Stuart Kauffman says that such systems cannot avoid complexity; it emerges in them spontaneously. This complexity does appear to increase over time. But there is a price to pay for becoming more complex. The price is that the system is more likely to break (Lewin 1992).

In social systems growing complexity necessitates a parallel investment of resources to maintain the resilience and coherence of the system as a whole. When this lags the society may face a future of greater discontinuities.

As the global society changes, grows, develops and becomes more complex the more vulnerable it and its component societies become to fluctuations, such as the Gulf War, the plight of Somalia, the events in Haiti and the wars in Yugoslavia, the instabilities in the Middle East, and in the republics of the former Soviet Union. To maintain its stability and robustness, such a global order needs to develop novel ways to maintain its resilience and coherence. The more it needs to invest in different forms of information, communication, and means to coordinate the interaction between its nation parts, the more it might need to develop suitable forms of global intervention to deal with trouble spots and alleviate unbearable discrepancies in the quality of life among societies. A policy of isolationism does not work in such a richly connected and sensitive complex global society.

It seems that if global society does not understand and act in accord with its growing complexity, it will face times of growing turbulence. These chaotic transitions, hopefully, will enable the system to self-organize and transform itself into a higher order of greater responsibility, cooperation, mutual aid, and support between its societies. Briggs and Peat ask if the breakup of order into turbulence is a sign of the system's deep interconnectedness and its wholenes. Strange as it may seem, there is evidence that points in this direction.

LEARNING FROM THE NEW SCIENCES

Before entering into the next section of the book it is now possible to attempt to answer the questions raised in the first chapter. Let us recapitulate.

1. Have all the manifestations of chaos in people's lives and social living, anything in common with the "chaos" dealt with in the New Science of Chaos? Are these everyday definitions and descriptions of "chaos" compatible with the

"chaos" studied by scientists in the behavior of pendulums or the patterns of changing weather systems?

2. Is it possible to learn anything about the behavior of human beings and their societies from the New Sciences? Can knowledge be gained about the behavior of civilizations, societies, organizations, families and individuals by applying to them insights derived from the study of turbulence in inanimate systems?

It seems that the answer to the first question is no and yes. The answer is no if chaos in behavioral and social systems is understood only in the dictionary sense of disorder and turbulence. The term "chaos" as used in the New Sciences entails a certain global pattern of order beneath the uncertainty and unpredictability in the behavior of the components. The everyday usage of the word "chaos" does not convey and is not associated with a pattern within the behavior of the whole system beneath the seeming disarray and turbulence. However, if manifestations of chaos in behavioral and social systems are examined in the light of Chaos and Self-organization theories, many of the human manifestations of chaos will be found to replicate in their characteristics and behavior the "chaos" of the New Sciences. In that sense the answer to the first question is yes.

As to the second question, this book and other works of a similar vein are living evidence as to how much it is possible to learn about human beings and their societies from the New Sciences. We have only begun to scratch the surface of the rich mine of knowledge that can be dug up using insights derived from the New Sciences. The insights range from understanding how individuals and societies change to a new understanding of events taking place in our times. Similarities between the chaos of science and chaos of everyday and global social problem are easily apparent. The behavioral and social sciences have much to learn from the New Sciences.

The following section examines the manifestations of growing complexity and uncertainty in the human world.

II
THE GROWTH OF UNCERTAINTY

6
The Complexity Spiral

The chapters in this section will describe four interrelated complexes, each of which contributes to the growth of uncertainty in our times. Each complex increases uncertainty and their mutual interaction intensifies it even more. Understandings born out of the New Sciences clarify why this is happening.

This chapter describes a process of growing complexity in the human world at all levels up to global society. The underlying assumption is that increasing complexity breeds growing uncertainty. Chapter 7 deals with our attempts to control growing uncertainty by using more present-day technology. This misfires as the technological proliferation only enhances complexity. The transition between eras is covered in chapter 8. Major areas of human functioning have reached bifurcation points pushing global society into the uncertainties of a chaotic transition stage between two epochs. Finally chapter 9 outlines the uncertainties stemming from the adaptation crisis humanity is going through, as a result of the interaction of the three complexes described in the three previous chapters.

GROWING COMPLEXITY IN THE HUMAN WORLD

At the end of this century, humanity is facing a world that is spiraling into ever-growing complexity. The human world and its ecosystems are growing more complex. There is a spiral of change that is leading to an acceleration in the rate of complexity and with it growing uncertainty, as nonlinearities and chaotic phases abound. The connection between burgeoning complexity and growing uncertainty will be explained in chapter 9.

The growth of complexity in the human realm can be understood from a number of approaches. The first approach is Self-organization theory. Chapter 4 on Self-organization dealt with the inevitable growth of complexity as a result of systems transforming themselves to orders of greater complexity. It was pointed out that this process is taking place in the living and human world together with growing entropy in the nonliving world.

Human systems, like all complex adaptive systems are constantly evolving in the direction of even-greater complexity. If left to themselves they become more complex. This is in contrast to the behavior of conservative nonliving systems, that if left to themselves turn to entropy, to random dispersal of energy, to an ultimate equilibrium, as described in the second law of thermodynamics. Each time a human system, at any level, is transformed and makes a qualitative jump to a new order it becomes more intricate and complex. Behavioral and social systems are constantly organizing themselves into orders of higher complexity.

The second approach to growing complexity is from the point of view of evolution theory. Chapter 5 began telling how evolution is moving in the direction of ever-growing complexity; "increased complexity is to be expected as a fundamental property of complex dynamical systems." (Lewin 1992:149). There are many scientists who equate evolution with growing complexity. Will Provine of Cornell University speaks about "the irreducible lovely properties of evolution going higher and higher, getting more and more complex" (Lewin: 181). Doyne Farmer of Santa Fe Institute says that "evolution is constantly coming up with things that are more complicated, more structured than the ones that came before" (Waldrop: 295). Laszlo writes: "In the science of nonequilibrium thermodynamics the evolution of complex systems is always irreversible because the only alternatives available to the system are those of increasing complexity, or else total extinction" (1991:5).

A third approach to growing complexity is to observe indicators of complexity growth. But how is it possible to estimate or compare degrees of complexity? Different methods have been proposed to estimate the degree of complexity of a system. It has been suggested that complexity be measured by the length of the program necessary to descibe the system. Another approach in dealing with complex problems is how long it will take a computer to solve the problem.

Degree of diversity and organization have been suggested as measures of degree of complexity of systems (Pagels 1981). This means that if they are becoming more diverse and more organized they are becoming more complex. The indicators of complexity growth can be the degree of differentiation and degree of organization in terms of intricacy of connectedness. The energy flow through needed to maintain the differentiation and organization can be added as an indicator of growth of complexity. This approach will be used here.

DIFFERENTIATION AND COHERENCE IN THE HUMAN WORLD

Behavioral and social systems are not only complex systems, but they are complex systems that are becoming more complex as they become more differentiated, more intricately connected, and organized internally and externally. They are changing more rapidly and consuming more energy to maintain their differentiation, organization, and coherence.

The human world as a whole is becoming more differentiated with ever-increasing variety among people, nations, and cultures. At the same time it is becoming a "global village," with people, nations and cultures becoming more related and dependent on each other. To maintain their growing intricacy, connectedness, organization and coherence, these human systems are devouring more of the natural energy resources of the world. In the former Soviet Union, the Baltic states, Moldavia, and other nations sought independence. Each republic attempted to differentiate itself from the Soviet Union. Within each new republic, ethnic minorities--Azers, Armenians and others--seek to differentiate and separate themselves from the larger ethnic majority. In a society, differentiation means that there is an increase in variety in many forms. People as individuals, as groups, and as segments of the population become increasingly dissimilar from each other. They differ more in their occupations, their loyalties, their interests, their education, their views, their motivation, and their life styles.

In organizations people become more specialized in their activities. Simultaneously they become more intricately connected, related, and dependent on each other. Toffler (1991) quotes Lehman confessing to his colleagues in the Pentagon that so many specialized cubbyhole units had sprung up that it was impossible for anyone to accurately describe the system they operated. Companies grow to enormous size and reach the limits of organizational specialization. In company after company, the cubbyhole system is breaking down under its own weight.

Modern society is in a phase of diversification or differentiation. Eighty years ago mankind could be classified into blue-collar workers, white-collar workers, professionals, and sometimes remnants of aristocracy. Now there is a diversity of lifestyles and class identifications. Toffler extensively documents the growing processes of differentiation in all aspects of human living. He describes how society is honeycombed with colorful groupings: "hippies and hot-rodders, theosophists and flying saucer fans, skin-divers, homosexuals, computerniks, vegetarians, bodybuilders and Black Muslims." The impact of the coming era is splintering society. "We are multiplying these social enclaves, tribes and mini-cults among us almost as fast as we are multiplying automative options" (Toffler 1971:260). The forces that are increasing individual choice in all areas of life are also creating more differentiation in social structures. This is behind the proliferation, emergence, and disbanding of all kinds of cults and fads.

The new era is creating not identical mass men, but people richly unlike one another, individuals, not robots. Humanity is not being flattened into conformity; rather it is becoming more diverse than it ever was before. The new society, which is now beginning to develop, will encourage "a crazy-quilt pattern of evanescent life styles" (Toffler 1971:275). Similar processes of differentiation are taking place in the family, with its innumerable new forms, types, constellations, and life styles. Differentiation and diversity are rife at all levels of human systems.

Deepening Interdependence

When two people start to perform different parts of a whole job that one of them did before, they begin to be more connected to each other and depend more on each other. When people become differentiated from each other, much more must be invested to satisfy their growing connections and different needs and tendencies. Increasing variety and burgeoning specialization necessitate greater interdependence, organization, and more intricate communication.

The European system of nations is becoming elaborately connected internally. Notwithstanding backlashes of national extremists, European nations are doing away with borders, abolishing customs, allowing free travel across borders, and encouraging unrestrained flow of money, capital, and labor. They are creating a single, central bank and currency, a common political policy.

While societies become more differentiated, they also become more braided. When they transform to higher orders of complexity, human systems become more connected to each other in many ways and at many points. The leap to a higher level of diversity, speed and variety demands a corresponding leap to higher, more sophisticated forms of integration, for example, the North American nations become more interdependent on each other and seek to break down economic barriers.

Toffler describes that as we emerge from the industrial era, we become a more diversified society. The old smokestack economy serviced a mass society. The post-modern economy services a demassified society. Everything from lifestyles and products to technologies and the communications media is growing more heterogenous. And all this new diversity brings with it increasing complexity.

Human systems of all kinds are constantly shuffling themselves and their parts to readjust to changes. All this is happening in dynamic complex systems that are in constant flux. Change and never-ending adjustment is continually taking place in the relations between the parts of these systems, which are constantly exchanging energy and matter with the environment.

The more complex an organization becomes, the more it has to invest to maintain this ever-increasing complexity. The more varied and intricate the connections and the information flow, the more coherence is needed to maintain this ever-growing intermeshed changing braidedness.

The Greater Energy Flow Through

Most people's electric and fuel bills are much higher than those of people a generation before. In everyday terms the more civilized societies become, the more energy they use. Modern industries devour far more energy than their early-century predecessors. Jeremy Rifkin writes that with only 6 percent of the world's population, the United States consumes over one-third of the world's energy. In "Haiti the energy consumption is equivalent to 68 pounds of coal per year, while the per capita consumption in the United States is equivalent to 23,000 pounds per year" (1981:99).

The more energy a system needs to maintain its increasing dynamic complexity, the more energy it needs to extract from its environment and the greater the energy flow within the system. The history of human civilization is a history of increasing use of energy. The movement from one major era to another is also a quantum leap in the use and flow of energy in the new society. It also means a change in the major source of energy, as the former source becomes insufficient to satisfy the growing needs.

The move from a hunting society to an agricultural society entailed an increase in the use of energy. The transformation of Europe from a predominantly agricultural society, based on energy extracted from burning wood, to an industrial society was intertwined with the discovery and exploitation of new sources of energy, coal, and oil needed to satisfy the growing needs. Half of all the energy used by man in the past 2,000 years has been used in the last one hundred years.

ONE INTRICATELY CONNECTED WORLD

The growth of complexity has reached global wide proportions. Two seemingly conflicting trends are developing on a worldwide scale: diversity and coherence. This planet is gradually becoming a world of compounding variety and diversity that is perpetually becoming more networked by endless ties, connections, couplings, and interdependencies. The Global Village, as it has been named has become a reality that can no longer be denied. Every area of human life is riddled with intricate connections to the rest of the world. The three-day Russian coup sent the stock markets of the world reeling. The real-time broadcasts of every development in the coup were followed by millions of listeners throughout the world. The sigh of relief at the end of the Gulf War could be heard echoing throughout the planet.

The world-wide market has created an exchange network that covers every corner of the globe. Goods of growing variety are being exchanged between more people in the world. The number of transactions taking place are beyond calculation. The complexity of managing these transactions involves development, production, transportation, marketing, distribution, accounting, insurance, patenting, payments, and instructions throughout the world.

The production of one single product can involve many countries. The idea for a product may have been developed in England; the technical development may be done in France; based on scientific technology developed jointly between Belgium and the Netherlands. The capital may have come from Japan and the United States; the first factory may be in South Korea, with parts coming from Switzerland, Austria and Israel, and the company may be registered in Luxembourg. The Insurance may be based in England and the transport to many countries throughout the world by Scandinavian ships.

There is one worldwide market that ties people throughout the world together. It is almost impossible for people to live outside this market as the tragic dash for freedom of the Albanians to the Italian ports so sadly illustrated. Labor, finance and capital break their national boundaries. The growing interdependence of the world capital market is dramatized now and then by huge swings and stock market crashes and recoveries.

The very notion of national autonomy is losing its meaning as the world becomes complex and interrelated. The power of states over their territory and their ability to attain national goals and purposes is steadily diminishing with the growing world wide intermeshedness of production, communication, science, and other catalyzers of the Global Village. By interrelating billions of people to one another, the market has created a world in which no nation has complete autonomy and control of its future.

The Globalization of Science and Culture

Science, like in the New Sciences of Chaos, Self-organization and Complexity, is an international effort that no nation can sustain on its own. Kenneth H. Keller (1990) points out that megascience has now reached such a scale that it is beyond the capability of any nation to support independently. This can be seen today in the war against AIDS and space research and, as Keller suggests, international, cooperative scientific research is becoming even more critical.

Sharing the fruits of science among nations has become an issue that cannot be evaded. Writing about physics displacement from its leading role in science by the biosciences, Keller notes that what distinguishes these technological developments from earlier ones that came from physics, is their affinity to agriculture and health, areas of great political sensitivity and social importance. International technology transfer in the biological fields is a matter of sharing the means of survival.

The new trends in the development of the biosciences, information technologies, the growth of multidisciplinary research "big science", and large-scale high-cost technology, are reaching a scale that is beyond the means of any single nation to support independently. Keller points out that these new trends in scientific development have consequences such as limitations on the ability of a nation to exercise governing authority over its territory and people. It is becoming impractical for nations to try to control the international spread of technological information as a means of improving their competitive advantage.

Morever national boundaries are becoming less meaningful as improved remote sensing by satellites allows nations to see what is going on behind other borders. In Keller's view, the autonomy to make decisions within those borders-- on various issues that concern others, such as trade barriers or pollution--is greatly reduced, not only by the constraints of a common global environment, but also by the growing interdependence of nations which has been created by international markets in economies driven by science and technology.

In every area of human living people are living in one intricately, interrelated, interdependent, intermeshed world. This holds true in most areas of human existence including the market economy, capital and finance, production, services, consumption, science, technology, ecology, health, religion, politics, art, literature, and entertainment.

COMPLEXITY AND UNCERTAINTY

Professor C. H. Waddington notes the implications of increasing connectedness with the growth of complexity and the interrelation of human problems within the growing complexity:

At the deeper level, we find that most aspects of life and its interactions with its surroundings are interconnected into complexes. No powerful action can be expected to have only one consequence, confined to the thing it was primarily directed at. It is almost bound to affect lots of other things as well. We have found ourselves faced by a series of problems--atomic warfare, the population explosion, the food problem, energy, natural resources, pollution and so on--each complex enough in itself, but then it turns out that each of these is only one aspect of, as it were a Total Problem, in which all aspects of the world's workings are inter-related. (1977:xii)

Complexity intensifies at all levels of human functioning. It is tying the human world into one interconnected system of diverse, interacting and interdependent elements. This growth of complexity is one of the factors feeding the intensification of uncertainty in our times.

Why should increasing interdependence and interconnectivity intensify uncertainty? The hypothesis is that increased interdependence intensifies uncertainty if the quality of the relationships does not match the degree of inerdependence.

Stuart Kauffman gives an example of two coevolving species, frog and flies. He says that the dynamics of their joint system depends greatly on how they interact. "If the frogs do not find the flies tasty at all, then the fitness of the frog population will be independent of the fitness of the flies." The situation changes when the frogs depend on the flies as their food source. "If the coupling is very strong any slight change in strategy is likely to change the character of the whole fitness surface. No frog or fly can adjust to the rapidly changing system. . . . The frog fly system is in a random, dynamic supercritical state" (Ruthens 1993:117). In the case of the frogs and the flies they will need to adjust the degree of their coupling to a state at the edge of chaos, where the interdependence is neither too weak nor too tight. If they do not do this their coevolving systems will disintegrate.

Human beings also have these choices. When they coevolve with each other they can adjust the degree of their interdependence. When a married couple cannot get on together, they attempt to adjust the quality of their relationship to the degree of their interdependence. They try to deal with the quality of their relationship on their own or sometimes go to a family therapist. But if they cannot change the quality of their relationship to a more cooperative, mutually responsible and empathetic one, it will not match the level of their interdependence. The alternative remains then to break up their interdependence by divorce.

But what happens when evolution pushes human societies and the human global system to ever-greater complexity that entails increasing interconnectedness and interdependence? Like the frogs and flies, people, organizations and societies need to adjust their relationships to the edge of chaos. The hypothesis suggested here is that they need to match the quality of their relationship to the measure of their braidedness and interconnectedness.

When human and social systems lag in matching the quality of their relationship to the degree of complexity of these relationships they are in for a period of great uncertainty in terms of conflict, crisis, and chaos. Increasing complexity in systems breeds growing uncertainty when it is not matched with a parallel change in the quality of relationships. This holds true for the components of a system like the members of a work team, and for the relationships between larger systems as with the relationships between nations.

In this way human evolution and growing complexity become tied to human culture and relationships. Growing interdependence will not hold for long in a culture that encourages only domination, control and unbridled competition among people. The growing connections and interdependence between people, in families, organizations, nations and the global society, necessitate a parallel evolution of worldview and cultures. These should match the increasing connectedness with a quality of relationship that also encourages cooperation, mutual aid and responsibility, and awareness and consciousness of their evolutionary cointerdependence.

7
The Technological Catalyst

A CYCLE THAT INTENSIFIES COMPLEXITY

The preceding chapter dealt with how human systems and civilization as a whole are caught in a spiral of growing complexity. Building on Self-organization and evolutionary theory, the chapter spelled out the story of how these systems become more complex. Growing complexity took the form of increased differentiation, interdependence, and connectivity. When these were not matched with a parallel change in the quality of relationships they led to growing uncertainty. This chapter examines a cycle that is intensifying and augmenting the complexity spiral. Toward the end of the industrial era, a number of factors are caught in a self-sustaining cycle that is feeding the complexity spiral and intensifying the burgeoning growth of uncertainty. The escalating development of modern technology acts as a catalyst leading to an acceleration in the rate of change coupled with an exponential growth in the size of human populations. These feed into the complexity spiral by adding to the already growing increase of complexity in the world. This intensifies uncertainty in the world.

The flourishing of transportation, communication, and information technologies is making the human world into one intricate unitary web of interdependent parts. These parts are becoming so intermeshed that the world is turning increasingly sensitive and vulnerable to differences in and among its parts. This is occurring without a sufficient parallel development in the quality of cooperation and mutually supportive relationships among societies. The conditions under which the rate of transformational crisis and chaos increase are growing more dominant.

The cycle described is self-sustaining and feeds itself. At the end of the century, the difficulties societies are having adapting to a world of growing complexity is leading to the increasing prevalence of crisis in behavioral and social systems of all kinds together with growing uncertainty. Fired by the industrial era's culture of domination, humanity tries even more to use technology to regain control. Thus the cycle reinforces itself (see chapter 9).

Modern technology is not the culprit. It alone would not create the present predicament. We need not smash the machines. Modern technology is the accelerator in a vicious circle that feeds itself. It plays its part only in combination with the other factors, such as a culture in which people attempt to dominate others and control conditions.

The Technological Accelerator

Technology is the ways and means society has of transforming matter energy and information in the service of human needs. It is the hammer, the computer, the airplane, the test tube, the way to plant orange groves, how to make a computer chip, the ship, the fax, open heart surgery, the production line, the tractor, the drilling of gas, the electric battery, the spaceship, the particle accelerator, the gas pump, the car and splicing genes.

The driving force of the cycle is the never ending exponential growth of modern technology. Not only is technology growing but it appears to be expanding at an increasing rate from year to year. This means that the more technology society has, the faster it breeds. Technology might be the catalyst that feeds the circle. It feeds the other elements in the circle and they feed back to it. When they feed back to it, it grows exponentially, which means that the rate and the magnitude of its growth jumps higher every time it cycles.

Schon writes that technological change is now reaching a level of pervasiveness and frequency that is threatening of the stable state. Writing about systems breakdowns related to chaos in the contemporary world, David Loye and Rianne Eisler suggest that changing technologies are driving these discontinuities and crises. Orenstein and Ehrlich write that each triumph of technology contains new kinds of threats.

Ervin Laszlo recognizes the part technology plays but he does not lay on it the ultimate responsibility for the world's problems. But he does write that the indiscriminate use of modern technology is behind mind-boggling waste and pollution. New technologies have destabilized social and economic systems and created unsustainable environments.

The Speedup of Technology

The U.S. National Academy of Engineering describes the most important engineering achievements of the the last 25 years. These include, among others, the Apollo moon landing, satellites, microprocessors, lasers, jumbo jets, and genetically engineered products. Some of these products have revolutionized the lives of human beings.

Production of goods and services in modern societies doubles itself every 15 years and the doubling time is on the decrease. Although it has now slowed down, for a long period Japan produced about 8 to 10 percent more than it produced the year before.

One hundred years ago it took about 60 percent of the workforce of the United States to supply its agricultural food needs. Today about 3 percent of the workforce easily supplies all of the far greater agricultural food needs of a much larger population and has abundant surpluses to export to the rest of the world. About 15 percent of the United States workforce supplies the far larger quantities of industrial output to the United States and the whole world than about 50 percent of the workforce did about 60 years ago. The exponential growth is not only in quantity but also in variety of goods. Today it has become a problem to choose between the rich variety of options offered in every kind of good or service.

The time it takes for a new invention to spread and diffuse becomes shorter and shorter. Research on this showed that from the turn of the century, it takes about 60 percent less time for a major scientific discovery to be translated into a technical application. A similar shortening in time takes place in the spread of the technology in the market. The time required for the diffusion of the steam engine was about 150 to 200 years and the transistor took about 15 years.

The time required for the diffusion of major technological innovations is approaching zero as a limit! There is probably an even greater slashing of duration in the lifetime of a technology before it is supplanted by an even newer one. The revolution in technological acceleration is also breaching boundaries between sciences and many of the breakthroughs are in interdisciplinary sciences. Technological change has become increasingly widespread. Changes whose impacts in the past might have been contained in particular industries, regions or particular aspects of life, now spread to all industries, all regions, and all of life (Schon).

Technology feeds on itself; technology makes more technology possible. Each new invention and innovation when diffused spawns endless new inventions in countless other fields. The steam engine revolutionized industrial production, mining, agriculture, and transportation. Technology breeds technology at ever greater speed and variety.

Ornstein and Ehrlich write: "Many people who are alive today were born when the automobile was a curiosity and there were no freeways, airplanes, refrigerators, dryers, paperbacks, computers, antibiotics, credit cards, lasers, satellites, or nuclear weapons" (1990: 63). It is possible to add innumerable items to the list such as robots in industry, automatization in offices, space travel, atomic energy, open heart surgery, and genetic manipulations. In all of these and the other manifestations of the explosion of technology the advances are mind-boggling and almost incomprehensible to most people. Even a specialist in any of these particular fields finds it impossible to keep up with the innovations, inventions, and advances in his or her particular field

Transportation, Communication, and Information

Besides the exponential growth of all kinds of technology in industrial production, agriculture, and services, it is worthwhile to pay particular attention to the growth of technology in three major fields. Schon points out that while all new technology is more or less disruptive, the implosiveness of the type of technology developed in the last half century has made it uniquely disruptive.

The development of transportation, communication, and information technology has revolutionized the world and has had enormous consequences on every aspect of life. These technologies have played a major role in the increase of complexity in our world. The developments in these particular fields, in the last half of this century, have had an exponential catalyzing effect on the growth of science and technology in other fields and unforeseen wide-ranging consequences on every aspect of human life.

A great part of the new technology is infrastructure technology. This technology governs "the flow of goods, people, money and information." The new electronic technologies of communication have made the world into one in which there is "instantaneous confrontation of every part of society with every other part. As a result social inequities leap to universal attention." The new technologies exacerbate differences and conflicts. Conflicts that did not break out because of separation "escape the bounds that had confined them, as new societies come into contact, new conflicts emerge" (Schon 1971:26).

The Effects of Technological Development

The enormous advances in the technologies of transportation, communication, and information probably are the catalyst that aggravate the complexity spiral. They do a number of things simultaneously that, directly or indirectly, intensify the growth of complexity, the rate of transformative chaos and the intensification of uncertainty.

- As infrastructure technologies their growth has stimulated the growth of all other technologies. They have created the conditions that allow the other technologies to grow and flourish.

- The thriving development of technology has quickened the rate of change and novelty. The speed of change has risen exponentially and unrelenting ceaseless novelty has become a mark of modern civilization. The rate of change and novelty is testing the limits of man's adaptive capabilities.

- The flourishing of technology in all fields and especially in food production, medicine, and health care has lead to exponential population growth. The growth of the world's population is possibly reaching the limits of this planet's carrying capacity.

- By their very nature transportation, communication, and information have played a major role in making the human world a global village. They have created the means by which different parts of the world are closely tied and braided together. They have been a major factor in creating the intricate web of inter-dependencies between all parts of the human world.

- This network of increasingly interwoven ties and connections has increased the sensitivity to differences in the global system. The after effects of something happening in one part of the world reverberate throughout the global network. This iterated sensitivity to differences is the breeding ground of chaos and uncertainty.

Transportation

A few thousand years ago the fastest transportation was a camel caravan that did about eight miles per hour. About 1,500 years ago the chariot raised the speed to 20 miles per hour. Only at the end of the nineteenth century was there a jump to maximum one hundred miles per hour with the locomotive. Another 80 years brought the speed of airplanes up to far over 4,000 mph. And about ten years later the speed of space vehicles reached about 18,000 mph.

Never in human history have so many people traveled so much from country to country. The authorities of Venice, Bath, Westminster, and other places are trying to find a way to close themselves to the droves of tourists as they threaten the places they visit with their breath and footprints.

Never in human history have so many people migrated temporarily or permanently to other places in their country or to other countries in search of better living conditions. The richer countries of Western Europe and the United States are not succeeding in facing problems of stemming this flow.

Communication

The speed of communication technology has so revolutionized itself that it affects revolutions. As people were watching the Russian coup play itself out in real life on the radio and television, the democrats gathered in the Russian Kremlin were sending messages to their countrymen and the world through radio, telephone and fax. These were factors affecting the outcome of the coup itself. The knowledge that extremely bloody use of brute force would be reported, televised, and transmitted throughout the world affected the decisions of the coup leaders.

Satellites, telephones, radio, fax, computer networks, television and stations like CNN, Star, and other worldwide media have made the globe into one interlocked world. They have in times of crisis tied up the lines of communication that cause stock market crashes on the same day all over the world. They have created one intricately connected undivisible world.

Television has broken down national, regional, cultural, and class boundaries to a far greater degree than any other media. Television has contributed to national, social, and geographic mobility, to mass immigrations and the movement of temporary workers from country to country. It has shown people in the poorer countries how more, advantaged populations live their lives.

Information

The Information Age is a term used by many writers to describe the times we are beginnning to live in. The exponential growth of information technology is affecting people's lives as never before. Kenneth E. Keller (1990) writes that information technology, which includes the gathering (through sensors, imaging techniques, telephotography), processing and storage (in computers), and transmission (via communication networks and broadcasting) of information, is affecting our lives and our society more intimately and more ubiquitously than any other field.

Never in history have human beings been constantly bombarded with so much information on so many subjects. This can often lead to a breakdown called information overload. A person can reach a state that he or she is so overloaded with new information that both physically and mentally the person is unable to deal with it and literally breaks down.

Toffler (1971) describes how radio, television, newspapers, magazines, and novels have swept through society. There is an acceleration in the pace at which image producing messages are presented to the individual. The flood of new information begins to overwhelm his senses and receptive ability. There is so much new information in every field that it is simply impossible to keep up with it. A subject studied in a university about ten years ago is already stale today. Specialists in most professions spend about half their time keeping up with new developments in their field. The changes in modern societies are so swift and relentless that yesterday's fact is today's fiction.

The Scientific Eruption

While technology can be seen as a frenzied machine, science can be viewed as the fuel that drives it. And the power of this fuel is enabling it to double itself at faster and faster rates. The ever-expanding know-how flowing from the explosion of scientific knowledge is impelling technology at dizzying rates.

There is not a single area of human knowledge that has not been revolutionized within the last century. The very foundations of all scientific knowledge have passed through major revolutions in the last few centuries, and at present are going through another major upheaval. At the rate at which knowledge is now growing, by the time a child born today graduates from college, the amount of knowledge in the world will be four times as great as it is today. When that same child is 50 years old, it will be 32 times as great, and 97 percent of all the knowledge known in the world will have been learned since the time of his birth (Toffler 1991).

There are many times more scientists living today than in all the ages of human history put together. The rate at which scientific knowledge grows accelerates itself exponentially. People's ability to store knowledge in journals, books, and computers boggles the imagination. It reaches a point that if a scientist has not read the scientific journals of his profession in the last two years he may have fallen aeons behind. The number of scientific journals doubles about every 15 years. The average elementary school child of today probably has more scientific knowledge of the world than university scholars of the seventeenth century.

Humanity's ability to create knowledge has increased exponentially by its growing know-how about the knowledge process. This is what is called second order learning, which is learning about learning itself. In every area knowledge is changing rapidly "in studies of nonequilibrium, chaos and dissipative structures, the knowledge base is being revolutionized. And even as this occurs, competing researchers in fields like neural networks and artificial intelligence are providing new knowledge itself" (Toffler 1991:385).

The computer has revolutionized civilization's ability to increase knowledge and to store it. With its ever increasing speed of calculations it can solve, in seconds, problems that would before have taken centuries. The computer has penetrated every area of human knowledge and technology and revolutionized knowledge in almost every area.

Computers have grown so powerful and cost-effective that they can be found nearly everywhere doing nearly everything. Supercomputers, manipulating billions of commands per second, forecast the weather and analyse complex medical images. Sensory computers respond to spoken sentences and visually recognize parts on assembly lines. Robotic computers turn those parts into full products. Like the telescope and microscope, computers are opening up new realms for scientists by simulating everything from astronomical collisions to molecular reactions. Fifty million personal computers along with thousands of varieties of software packages help people at work and at home. And millions of computers disappear every year into the cars, microwave ovens, telephones and television sets that they control.
At the same time, the reach and speed of networks have increased by equally awesome strides: millions of miles of glass fibres handle most longhaul communications and are capable of relaying data at speeds of up to a billion bits (gigabits) per second. (Dertouzos 1991:31).

Before 1500, Europe was publishing 1,000 books a year. Today the number is hundreds of thousands. On a worldwide scale scientific and technical literature grows at a rate of about 60 million pages a year. Today knowledge accumulates not only in books, but also in computers, videos, films, micro-tapes, and television texts. The flowering of education for all ages, from schools to universities, is revolutionizing the standard of education of the populace of developed countries. This evolution in human knowledge in all fields of science and knowledge is the fuel that is feeding the expansion and growth of the technology engine and propelling it forward at ever accelerating rates of growth and expansion.

TECHNOLOGY ACCELERATES CHANGE AND GROWTH

This is an epoch of human history in which change has accelerated at an exponential rate. Societies have not yet acclimatized to one change before a new change replaces it. The proportion between confirmation and novelty has changed. There are far shorter periods of confirmation interspersed between increasing periods of novelty.

Robert Oppenheimer, the father of the atomic bomb, said that there is a change in the quality of change itself. It is not only more change, or greater change, it is a different kind of change. The rate of change has accelerated so much that society is dealing with a qualitatively different kind of change.

Major changes do not take generations. Within a lifetime almost everything has changed unbelievably. A person born 400 years ago would end his days in a world that was the same as the world into which he was born. Today the world changes weekly in front of people's eyes. Momentous events that change the course of history happen in a day. The Russian coup and the fall of communism in Russia took place wihin a few days.

Fifty years ago a majority of the countries that are today in the UN did not exist. Seventy-five years ago there "had not been a world war, electricity and pasteurization were rarities, and one in three babies died in infancy" (Ornstein and Ehrlich 1990:63). Today the map makers and globe designers have a problem of keeping up with events. The newspaper printed last night is already outdated by morning. Events develop at such a rate that even television is sometimes behind the happenings and only a radio transmitter can keep up with the unfolding events. The rate of change is increasing rapidly and humanity is transforming the world so quickly that each decade's world and environment is very different from that of the preceding decade. The accelerated rate of change fed by the growth of technology and fueled by science, affects every aspect of human life and creates novelty--from transience, to the pace of life, to throw-away consumerism and fads, to mobility and short term relationships, to new forms of organizations and family structure.

The explosion in the rate of development of communication, transportion, and information have revolutionized the speed of transfer of products, innovations, new ideas, lifestyles, cultures, scientific inventions, and technologies. They have completely changed the rate at which things change. They have created a metachange in the speed of change itself.

Social systems such as organizations and other institutions are reeling under the impact of the rate of change. Their knowledge bases and skills lose their relevance a short time after they are acquired. Firms have increasing difficulty keeping up with the innovations in their area of speciality. The speedup of change makes knowledge concerning consumer preferences, markets, suppliers, technology, interest rates, and all other business preferences shortlived.

A firm's entire inventory of data, skills, and knowledge is thus in a constant state of decay and regeneration with faster turnover. This means that some of the old bins into which knowledge has has been stuffed begin to break into parts. Others are crammed to overload. Still others become useless as the information in them becomes obsolete or irrelevant.

Exponential Population Growth

Increased production capacity made possible by science and technology, together with the blessings of medical care, added to the runaway character of population growth, are boosting the world's population on an exponential curve. Seventy-five years ago one in every three babies died in infancy. In one month the world population increases more than the number of people that lived on the earth 100,000 years ago. In four years more people will be added to our planet than covered the entire planet about 2000 years ago. About 15,000 years ago, before the advent of agriculture there were about 5 million people on the earth. We are now reaching the 5 billion mark.

Rifkin points out the staggering statistics: It took about 2 million years for the human population to reach the 1 billion mark. The second billion took a hundred years. The third billion was reached after thirty years, between the years 1930 and 1960. The fourth billion took only fifteen years. At the present growth rate of 1.7 percent, the world's human population will reach 8 billion by the year 2015 and 16 billion by the year 2055.

Writing about the accelerated exponential growth rates of population numbers and power consumption, C. H. Waddington states that today, many people are fearful that the situation "may be getting out of hand, and soon may run away with itself, and us, into some sort of chaos" (1977:115). The drain on the world's food resources, energy capacity, mineral deposits, and living space have already passed what some call the world's carrying capacity. Ornstein and Ehrlich write that the world's population "at today's level of affluence and using today's technologies, is far above earth's long-term carrying capacity." They believe that the long-term carrying capacity of the earth is below 5 billion people (1990:245).

The dangers of uncurbed population growth to the world's ecology have been discussed so much that it is futile to repeat them. The danger marks are already visible in some cities in Europe that are planning to curb the daily influx of people. Uncurbed population growth also contributes to the greenhouse effect, the depletion of the ozone layer and the ruining of the world's ecology. Most of the worlds great cities, such as New York City, Mexico City, and London, are reaching such a size that the complexity of managing them is beyond human ability and the willingness to live in them decreases each year.

The complexity of dealing with sheer numbers of unmanageable magnitude is of itself a factor that is beginning to defy human resourcefulness. This can be seen in African famines, in soccer-crowd tragedies, in daily traffic jams in and out of major cities, in the dangers of over-crowded airports, in the filthy rivers and oceans, the regional acid rains, the global carbon monoxide buildup, in the dying forests of Europe, in the changing world climate and other ecolological menaces to mankind.

FEEDING THE COMPLEXITY SPIRAL

As we move toward the end of the industrial era, there is a mixture of factors that is pushing the human world to the brink of complexity. The interplay of the different factors has created a world of such complexity and transformative periods of chaotic crisis and uncertainty, that human beings and societies are facing ever-increasing uncertainty.

In this chapter additional elements have been added that intensify the complexity spiral. These affect the braidedness, interdependence, and sensitivity to small differences of the intricately connected, complex world. The world is becoming more and more complex from day to day and at an ever-increasing rate. At this bifurcation point, the mutual reinforcement of the factors is creating a world of complexity chaotic crises, and uncertainty, that human systems are having difficulty joining onto it, adapting to it, and perhaps surviving in it.

At this major junction in history, human adaptive capabilities face a momentous challenge. Complex modern civilization, growing exponentially more complex, is in the turbulent throes of the chaotic transition stage of a shift in eras. The following chapter will explicate this.

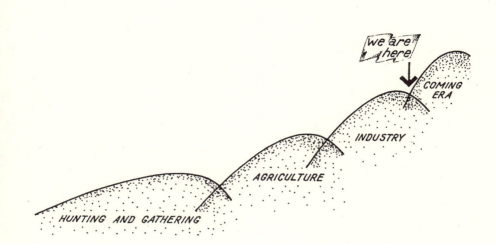

8
The Shifting Eras

CAUGHT IN A SEAM OF HISTORY

Like the giant tectonic layers of the planet shifting and shaking the earth beneath, humanity is going through an extensive shift in the foundations of civilization. The present generations are experiencing a chaotic transition and turning point in human history. These are turbulent times in which human civilization shifts from the third to the fourth era in its development. The human race is caught in a turbulent seam of history from which there is no escape. The present generations are living in eventful, critical and tumultuous times.

George Leonard called this period The Transformation. Fritjof Capra called it The Turning Point. Marilyn Ferguson described it as The Acquarian Conspiracy. Willis Harman named it Global Mind Change. Ervin Laszlo called it The Age of Bifurcation.

Alvin Toffler, who named it The Third Wave, wrote about the powerful tide surging across the world in which much, in all walks of human life, is going topsy-turvy, breaking down, and splintering. A new world is emerging which challenges old assumptions, ways of thinking, ideologies, values, and political relationships.

So profoundly revolutionary is the new civilization that it challenges all our old assumptions. Old ways of thinking, old formulas, dogmas, and ideologies, no matter how cherished or how useful in the past, no longer fit the facts. The world that is now emerging from the clash of new values and technologies, new geo-political relationships, new lifestyles and modes of communication, demands wholly new ideas and analogies, classifications and concepts. (1981:15-16)

Leonard (1972) was one of the first to sum up the current period when he wrote that it represents the beginning of the most far reaching change in human existence since the birth of civilized states some five thousand years ago. The term "transformation" stood for both the process and the period during which the process was taking place.

Capra said that we find ourselves in a state of profound, worldwide, multidimensional crisis whose facets touch every aspect of our lives, from health and livelihood to economy, technology, and politics. This is a crisis of intellectual, moral, and spiritual dimensions of a scale and urgency unprecedented in human history. Capra ends his book thus:

The Democratic and Republican parties, as well as the traditional Right and Left in most European countries, the Chrysler Corporation, the Moral Majority, and most of our academic institutions are part of the declining culture. They are in the process of disintegration. . . . While the transformation is taking place, the declining culture refuses to change, clinging evermore rigidly to its outdated ideas, nor will the dominant social institutions hand over their leading roles to the new cultural forces. But they will inevitably go on to decline and disintegrate while the rising culture will continue to rise, and will eventually assume its leading role. (1983:418-19)

Prigogine said that we were at a very exciting moment in history, perhaps a turning point. Marilyn Ferguson (1980) wrote that the transformation was also the ascendence of a startling worldview that gathers into its framework breakthrough science and insights from earliest recorded thought. Harman (1988) said that without a fundamental change, industrial society appears unable to resolve the sociopolitical and ecological dilemmas that trouble it. Each decade seems to be more problem-laden than the one before, and the problems seem more intertwined, with the tradeoffs getting less and less favorable. The change that is needed is not a shift from one kind of industrial society to another, but rather a major transformation in the basic assumptions underlying the different versions of industrial society.

Human Concerns at Bifurcation Points

Complexes of interrelated problematic areas that are important to mankind are at a point where they must undergo a basic transformation. Writing about such bifurcation points in "the complex landscape of a nonlinear system," David Peat says: "Close to a normal attractor, we can perturb a system and have it always return to its limit cycle or limit point. But push it too far up a mountain, and it may reach a ridge or a peak, a critical region in which the system faces a decision: It can either fall back to its limit cycle or roll down the other side of the mountain into some qualitatively new region of behavior." Peat points out that nature abounds in such bifurcation points, where the smallest force can decide which way a system will go. "Its systems can move very quickly from stability to instability, from order to chaos, from oscillation to wild fluctuation, from self-correction to infinite sensitivity" (1991: 201).

Ervin Laszlo (1991) notes that bifurcations occur when systems are destabilized in their environments and stressed out of states in which they are functioning. A number of connected, interacting areas of major human concern are close to a transformative bifurcation point. Within the structures of the present industrial era, these human concerns cannot continue as before and they are in dire need of a deep change of quantum proportions. The agitative fluctuations within these areas are bringing them close to a critical chaotic region in which they will have to face the necessity of major restructuring.

In this region of instability they will confront the choice of making a transformative leap to another order or be threatened by the possibility of breakdown and disintegration. Humanity is now deeply feeling the agitation, disruption, turbulence, and instability that accompanies such turning points in history.

The social, economic, political systems in which we live are complex and unstable; sooner or later their evolutionary paths must bifurcate. Our world, no less than the world of nature is subject to phase changes. Bifurcations are more visible, more frequent, and more dramatic when the systems that exhibit them are close to their thresholds of stability--when they live "dangerously." This is just the behavior our complex societies are exhibiting in the late twentieth century. (Laszlo 1991:7)

At the end of the century, major areas of human concern are moving from order to chaos, from stability to instability, and from oscillation to wild fluctuation. They confront the need of self-correction through an extensive transformative restructuring. Toffler caught the essence: "These and many other seemingly unrelated events or trends are interconnected. They are in fact, parts of a much larger phenomenon: the death of industrialism and the rise of a new civilization" (1981:16).

THE WAVES OF SHIFTING ERAS

This is not the first change in eras humanity has gone through. Laszlo writes how in the context of the New Sciences, societies are particular kinds of complex systems developing in the constant flow of energy in the biosphere. Their evolution follows the path of many bifurcations between times of relative stability and times of instability. Beneath all this one can discern the nonlinear process of evolution. "There is a period of chaos as new orders take shape. But new orders do arise, and history sets forth its jagged course from the Stone Age to the Modern Age--and then beyond" (1991:49).

The hunting and gathering nomadic period of human civilization lasted for tens of thousands of years without any major change. It was a very simple civilization involving sparse populations spread out in areas that could supply a source of food. It lasted seemingly almost forever without a major transformation of the way of life, work, energy source, and culture.

The next major form of civilization was one of farming. People settled down in fixed habitations and began tilling the soil. This form of society was more complex, demanding division of land, water and labour. The population of these settled places increased considerably because of man's greater ability to achieve regular sources of food for his existence. It necessitated a greater energy flow and a source of energy (such as wood and animal power), different from that of the nomadic hunter (gatherers). This civilization lasted about six thousand years.

The following era was the industrial age. It was exceedingly more complex, with populations exploding to a degree that makes life almost intolerable in most great cities. This era has created increasingly complex societies, with gargantuan production capabilities and with multiplying differentiation and variety. The societies are braided together by intricate webs of interdependence, interaction and communication. The energy needs of this complex society have jumped exponentially. The enormous thirst for energy created by the Industrial Revolution is being satiated mainly by the depletable fossil fuels of coal and oil. In advanced economies, this era has already passed its peak and is on the wane, with the coming era some time ahead of us. It is worth noting that the rate at which humanity is moving from one major era of human civilization to another is accelerating with shorter time intervals between each era.

AREAS AT A BIFURCATION POINT

Now at the end of the industrial age we face another bifurcation point. The industrial era has reached a point where it is no longer sustainable. A number of major areas of human concern are fluctuating agitatedly near their bifurcation points. These areas of concern are in need of a transformative qualitative change as they have reached the limits of their present form.

They are not separate entities but complexes connected to and affecting each other. They are like nodes of flashing red lights in a closely intermeshed network. The areas of concern are described separately in the following section, but in effect in the real world, they cannot be isolated from each other.

The problematic areas are braided together into complexes that interact with one another and mutually stress each other. They in their mutual interactions are bringing the contemporary era closer to a bifurcation point that has all the hallmarks of a chaotic transition to a new era. Some of the symptomatic expressions of the end of an era can be summarized as follows:

- The depletion of natural energy and material resources
- Reaching the brink in man's relations with the world environment
- The end of the reigning scientific paradigm
- The collapse of the paradigm of man controlling the world
- The widening gap between developed and underdeveloped societies
- The decline in autonomy of the nation state
- The deteriorating ability to govern societies and organizations
- The lost individual

Natural Resources

The present forms of production and consumption by the advanced industrial nations, are rapidly depleting the finite sources of nonrenewable energy and minerals.

Water energy and wind energy are renewable. The wind keeps blowing and the water falling. But the deposits of oil created millions of years ago by decaying animals and plants are nonrenewable. Various studies show that within the foreseeable future resources will fail to meet the increasing demands for oil. Two factors aggravate this situation. The first is the overwhelming, accelerating consumption of oil in the industrial nations. The United States, which has about 6 per cent of the world's population, consumes more than a third of the world's energy.

The second factor is the exponential growth of the world population, which is multiplying the use of energy. The world's population is doubling itself within shorter and shorter periods. It took two million years to reach the first billion. The second billion took only a hundred years. The third billion took only 30 years. Eight billion will be reached by 2055.

In the last ten years of this century, the energy needs are expected to quadruple. The energy needs of mankind are rampaging at a rate that will soon deplete the natural resources. After Chernobyl, the difficulties and real dangers of replacing natural resources with nuclear fuel are obvious. The same fate awaits other nonrenewable mineral resources. It is estimated that America uses about 40,000 pounds of new mineral supplies per person each year, for various needs from homes to machines. The United States gobbles up most of the nonrenewable materials of the world with Japan following closely. For the rest of the world to catch up with the American standard of living, it would need to consume 200 times the present output of these materials.

Rifkin writes that within 75 years the planet's economies will have used up the known recoverable reserves of perhaps half the world's now useful materials. By 2050 the United States will run out of "tin, commercial asbestos, columbium, fluorite, sheet mica, high grade phosphorus, strontium, mercury, chromium and nickel" (1981: 113-14).

The great achievements of this era were only possible because of man's ability to multiply the exploitation of the natural resources. The decline in these resources coincides with the breakdown of the industrial base that was built on them. The end of the age of mechanical-based industries is interlocked with the depletion of nonrenewable natural energy and material deposits.

Mankind is reaching the limits and is finding it harder to find sources of available energy and difficult to find places to get rid of energy wastes. Humanity is closely approching a turning point in its relations with the extractable non-renewable resources of the planet. Man is beginning to feel the chaotic tremors of these approaching cataclysms in the energy crisis, the oil embargo, the Gulf War, the wars in the Congo and in other nations that own resources.

The Ecology

A BBC television broadcast reports that flocks of sheep in South America are developing serious eye afflictions. These are attributed to dangerous radiation resulting from the depletion of the ozone layer. The dangers of this radiation are no longer a threat in the distant future to penguins in the antarctic. The dangers are here and now threatening people in heavily populated regions and it is estimated that it is too late now to prevent the damage.

The disaster at Chernobyl has already taken place. Society has seen its terrible consequences in human suffering, death, devastation of a city and large surrounding area and pollution of crops and poisoning of livestock in countries as far away as England. Russia and Eastern Europe abound with many other potential Chernobyls.

An American government report warns that it has found a direct correlation between the spread of disease and environmental pollution. It says that the environment may be a major cause of death in the United States. Cancer, heart, and lung disease, accounting for 12 percent of deaths in 1900 and 38 percent in 1940, were the cause of 39 percent of all deaths in 1976. The forests of Germany are dying from exposure to the pollution of too many cars. The depletion of the rain forests in Brazil which endangers the entire balance of the world's climate, is going on unabated. The results of the Greenhouse effect are affecting the world's climate and are estimated to be steadily progressing.

Rifkin notes that in New York City taxi drivers have such a high level of carbon monoxide in their blood that it often is unsuitable for use in blood transfusions. Breast milk contains more and more pesticides, residues, and other carcinogens. Sixty to 90 percent of all types of cancers in the United States are caused by human-made environmental factors such as food additives and chemical substances.

Civilization has reached the end of an era in which the emmisions of energy resources, industrial waste, and disregard of nature's delicate balance continue unabated. Humanity's interrelation with the environment has reached a bifurcation point. This bifurcation point at the ecological brink signals the end of the industrial era.

The Modern Scientific Paradigm

Society has reached the end of a scientific era and is now in the transition period of searching for and attempting to create a new scientific era. The sciences of Chaos, Self-organization, Complexity and evolution are part of the revolution which is taking place in science.

In *The Structure of Scientific Revolutions*, Thomas Kuhn (1970) describes the process of the replacement of all embracing scientific worldviews by new ones. Kuhn uses the word "paradigm" to describe such a total, all encompassing worldview. It is a basic way of perceiving and understanding reality, an all enfolding belief system. Kuhn contends that in each period of scientific history a specific paradigm reigns. An example of such a paradigm could be the Newtonian paradigm, which was the basic foundation of science for a number of centuries.

Scientific work, research, and discovery proceeds within the framework and basic tenets of the reigning paradigm. Science progresses and research is advanced on the basis of the foundation of the governing paradigm. If a research result or scientific discovery does not fit within the basic paradigm, it is pushed under the carpet, ignored, or not acknowledged. Under the paradigm existing in his day, Galileo's findings that the earth was not the center of the universe were regarded as heresy.

This state of affairs continues for quite a time, until contradictory evidence from many findings can no longer be ignored. At a certain point, a scientific revolution takes place and the reigning paradigm is replaced with a new paradigm. The new paradigm can deal with and explain the contradictions that undermined the former paradigm. The new paradigm now becomes the basis and framework of all scientific endeavors. It prevails within the scientific world, until in its turn it too is replaced. The Copernican paradigm replaced the Aristotelan paradigm, which had ruled scientific thinking for many centuries. In such a manner the Newtonian paradigm replaced the paradigm of Kepler and Galileo and dominated the world of science for many generations.

The human race is now going through another paradigm revolution in science. The reigning linear, objectivistic, mechanistic paradigm of the machine age is breaking down and is in the process of being replaced. Under the combined onslaught of the findings of quantum theory; Heisenberg's uncertainty principle; Godel's theorem; the discoveries of the sciences of Chaos, Complexity, Self-organization, evolution, autopoiesis in living systems, and other breakthroughs in science, the mechanistic paradigm that has ruled science for generations is falling down.

The machine model of reality, which was the reigning paradigm in science, was the natural offspring of the industrial era. With the crisis and breakdown in industrial civilization comes the crisis and breakdown of the scientific paradigm that expressed and represented this era. The breakdown of the Newtonian scientific paradigm is part and parcel of the end of the industrial age. The paradigm built on Prigogine's ideas might be heralding the new scientific worldview; The breakdown of the industrial era might be seen as a civilization bifurcation from which will be born a new differentiated, society. This may be regarded "as a leap to a new 'dissipative structure' on a world scale. And if we accept this analogy, might we not look upon the leap from Newtonianism to Prigoginianism in the same way?" (Toffler in Prigogine and Stengers 1988:xxvi).

Here are some of the basic assumptions of the reigning paradigm that are now being questioned:

- Science can learn about things and understand them by breaking them into their parts.
- Scientists can study things objectively by separating themselves from the object of study.
- There is a clear demarcation between the objective world and man's subjective experience of it. Objective, value-free truth statements may be made.
- Science can measure things exactly, and on that basis make predictions about their behavior in the future.
- All qualitative properties are ultimately reducible to quantitative ones.
- The world is generally linear, with clear direct lines of cause and effect and regular proportion between the dimensions of the cause and the effect.
- The mission of science is the discovery of universal and eternally valid laws of nature.
- It is always possible to make predictions regarding a single case from the general laws pertaining to it.

- Science studies discrete objects whose boundaries can be clearly defined.
- Objects should generally be studied by operationalizing them and this is done by quantification of their parameters.
- Inconsistent axioms or propositions cannot both be true.
- Falsifiability is the ultimate test of theory. The validity of an experiment can always be tested by replication.

All of the above assumptions, which were the foundations of conventional science have suffered much battering. They can no longer withstand the onslaught of contradictory evidence and argument. The scientific edifice on which they were built is tottering and needs to be replaced by a new paradigm.

These assumptions describe a circumscribed aspect of reality. They are still useful and will still serve science in its advance and in most scientific endeavors. But they describe limited linear aspects of the world and ignore nonlinearity. Relying only on them can lead humanity along a dangerous path. In science as well as in production, energy resources, and ecology mankind is entering the transition period between two eras.

The Control Model

With the close of the industrial era and the end of the ruling scientific paradigm, humanity is witnessing the undermining of the control, dominator model that was born from both of them. A basic element in the Western industrial paradigm was the belief in man's unbounded ability to control his environment and achieve unlimited material progress.

This meant that humanity was no more dependent on God but had the tools to take control of its own destiny. This is the mindset which allowed the development of the Industrial Revolution and the rise of capitalism and socialism. This view believed in the control of mankind's physical and human environment through the application of quantitive intellectual methods and saw nature as existing for humanity to exploit.

The basic themes of the Western industrial control paradigm are:

(1) The scientific method as the basic mode of research, with the purpose of prediction and control in order to manipulate the physical environment.
(2) Material progress as the major goal. This implies trust in man's expanding control over nature and his unlimited ability to understand the universe. Acquisitive materialism is a central operative value.
(3) Attaining the above through industrialization, subdividing work into smaller elements, specialization, and mechanization.

The scientific method, unlimited material progress, and industrialization, were major tenets of most modern countries, socialist or capitalist. The end of the industrial age marked by the breakdown of the current scientific paradigm, is also the final curtain of the control model. It is becoming increasingly clear that in a world of infinite, ever-growing complexity simplistic notions of man controlling the environment and dominating other people through science and technology cannot stand the test of experience and reality. David Peat (1991) writes that if we believe in the wholenes of nature, we will need a new ethic a radically different way for society to act. A radical transformation in our way of being is called for, one involving a totally new form of response in which we will no longer seek to control and exploit nature for our ends.

While most people cannot analyse the circumstances, they have lost their certainty about a future of infinite progress marshaled in by the march of science and technology. People's direct personal experience of the world wars and other wars, economic recessions, atomic threats and disasters, ecological menaces, the breakdown of governments, major institutions, and city managements, the spread of crime, the crises and closedowns in the organizations they work for or belong to, family difficulties, and personal anxiety and confusion--all stack up to undermine full assuredness in the blessings of industrialism, undisturbed continual progress of mankind, and man's ability to control the environment.

The Chasm between Societies

Two converging trends have accentuated the differences between the prosperous post-modern developed industrial societies and the poverty stricken underdeveloped preindustrial societies. The gap in standards of living, health, well-being, and longevity has widened far beyond the Feigenbaum Point. It is no more a matter of degree. It is a bifurcation into two causal basins, two worlds. In the advanced world the living standards, health care, educational opportunities, chances for professional advance, mobility, and freedom of movement, and recreational facilities of the majority of people are light years apart from all of these in the undeveloped societies.

The gap does not decrease but widens all the time, with the population growth rate, coupled with the devastation caused by the ravaging of the soil and forests and the mass migrations to disease ridden slums, all fanning the flames of misery, war, famine, hunger, unemployment, crime, family breakdown and helplessness. When natural disasters such as drought, floods, volcanic eruptions, and earthquakes add their contribution to the toll of misery, the conditions pass all limits of human description and comprehension.

The second trend is the growing awareness of the depth of this chasm. This awareness has been fed by the development of the media of communication--the worldwide satellite networks, the press, and the radio. The widening gap is accentuated by the communication flow; television, radio and newspapers sharpen the contrast.

There has always been a gap between the living standards of societies. But toward the end of the century two factors have brought this gap to a bifurcation point. One factor is the actual widening contrast between the two worlds. The second factor is growing awareness of the gap. In the past, suffering and misery have been accepted as part of man's lot and destiny in this world. When people become aware that this is not necessarily so and that in other societies many people live comfortable lives, the contrast deepens the misery.

Communication, information, and transportation break down the barriers that segregated different worlds. On the other side of the world in the undeveloped countries, movies, newspapers, television and radio show a different, more affluent world to the poverty-stricken masses. British television stations beam to the Far East through satellites "The Life Styles of the Rich and Famous." Migrant workers by the millions travel to the advanced countries to earn a living. In the process of doing this they become aware of the chasm widening between the conditions in their homeland and the conditions in the countries they work in. The widening gap between developed and developing societies coupled with growing awareness of the gap is creating a situation that is reaching its limits.

The danger signs of this situation deteriorating can be seen in the return to Muslemic fundamentalism and the unrest in the North African countries, the fanaticism of Khameini's Iran, the unrest in South America, the tragedy of Somalia, the proliferation of terrorism, the growth in strength of crime syndicates and the general increase in crime, the rise of illegal immigration to developed countries, the tragedy of the boat people from Vietnam trying to escape to Hong Kong, the Albanian stampede to Italy and the desperate Haitians trying to reach the United States.

The Autonomy of the Nation State

The former republics of the USSR rush to claim their national autonomy. The Kurds, the Armenians, the Azers, the Slovenians and Croatians, all are climbing onto the bandwagon. Each national identity is trying to differentiate itself, create a boundary around itself and integrate itself. These are still an expression of nations trying to get into the club of advanced industrial nations. The tendency toward higher levels of differentiation exemplifies the growth of complexity on an international scale. The drive for national self-differentiation, self-definition, autonomy, and independence is a characteristic of industrial civilization. It has accompanied the spread of the Industrial Revolution since its early stages. The rush for national independence, exemplified by the disintegration of the former colonial empires and the attainment of independence by the nations of Africa and Asia, has been a major trend in the last century.

The creation of the nation-state is a feature of the industrial era and is an expression of the need for both political and economic integration at the national level. Local economies had to be united into a single national economy for new technologies to be profitable. This entailed a national market for commodities and capital. Toward the end of the century another trend may be discerned. The advanced, industrial European nations are in the midst of the process of breaking down all kinds of boundaries among themselves, in trade, capital investment, banking, taxes, money, employment, travel, defense and international policy. The European Common Market and Gatt are examples of this trend..

The braiding together of large continental entities, consisting of many advanced industrial nations, is happening before our eyes. This is being accompanied by a shrinking of the national autonomy of those same nations. This is gradually but surely becoming a reality that can no longer be ignored. As in Europe, the advanced industrial nations in Southeast Asia, Japan, South Korea, Taiwan, and Singapore appear to be following the same pattern of increased cooperation and boundary lowering. The United States, Canada, and Mexico are also on the way to some kind of joint economic organization.

On the world level, international institutions of all kinds are taking an increasingly important role in world affairs. The United Nations, the World Bank, the International Monetary Fund, and many other international organizations are playing an expanding significant function in world affairs. At the same time there is a singular growth of all kinds of private corporations and political groups operating across international boundaries. Simultaneously there is a proliferation in the spread of globe-spanning associations of private citizens, involving people from every nation.

These trends of boundary breaking between nations and the growth in power of international organizations and boundary--spanning enterprises and associations--are an expression of the other face of complexity. Increased differentiation leads to growing interdependence and braidedness. Tightened economic linkages between nations make it almost impossible for any individual nation to manage its own economy independently.

Following the clamor for national identity grows the need for international cooperation. As the interdependence of nations in finance, production, trade, material resources, scientific and technological knowhow, and ecology continues to increase, their need for structures and institutions that ensure interdependence also grows. As the world becomes more and more complex, the autonomy and power of the national state is on the decrease. As world politics becomes more and more complex, the power of all states to achieve their purposes decreases.

At the beginning of the industrial era there was differentiation at the international level and integration at the national level. This led to the clamor for national identity and independence. As the industrial era draws to a close, there is the intrusion of the other side of complexity-increased interdependence and braidedness on the world level-pushing toward the shrinking of national autonomy and power.

Difficulties in Governing

Governments of nations are also inwardly losing their power. Because of the rise in complexity at the national level, the ability of governments to govern is diminishing rapidly. The dynamical complexity of national problems is so great that governmental policy and decision making is forever lagging and unable to deal with the problems.

The increasing differentiation, diversity, variety, and often conflicting interests of populations, regions, cities, age groups, ethnic groups, religous beliefs, interest groups, lobbies, power groups, classes, sectors, and professions-- has gone beyond the control of a central government. Toffler (1991) points out that the central government bureaucracies cannot handle growing internal diversity. National governments are finding it increasingly difficult to customize their policies. They are unable to treat each area, region, town, racial, religious, social, sexual, or ethnic group differently. As conditions diversify, the national governments remain ignorant of fast-changing local conditions and needs. When they attempt to identify these specialized needs, they end up swamped with undigestable data.

As the central government steadily loses its ability to integrate and address local problems and interests, a great deal of power is transferred to its periphery. The less central governments are able to address the problems of provinces, regions, and cities, the more the authority passes into the hands of local bodies or other organizations. Both society and polity abound in power centers that are outside of government.

In effect there is a breakdown of national government in all countries. In some countries, such as Italy, it is easier to follow. In other countries the contours of a breakdown are less discernible. Yet in every country the problems mount exponentially and governments steadily lose their ability to find answers to the multiplying problems and difficulties. Their inability and impotence in the face of the burgeoning issues discredits the governments and the people who govern. The word "politician" has already received an unsavory association.

Toward the end of the industrial era, there is also a breakdown of government and control at the regional, municipal, and institutional levels. The government and administrators of large metropolitan areas and big cities cannot deal with the exponentially growing complexity of the problems that bombard them daily. The nationwide institutions are in never-ending crisis, unable to give answers to the problems facing them. The growing complexity as the industrial era draws to its close, has bred the breakdown of the ability of human society to govern itself and is breeding rampant crises within the existing structure of society. One may persist in viewing each of these different crises as isolated events. They in fact are connected and are all tied with the process of the end of industrialism.

The Lost Individual

In premodern societies individuals did not face questions about identity that trouble modern man. The premodern mind had anchors everywhere, in religous institutions, in the myths that explained the universe, in the rituals and customs of society, in the statuses and roles of society. Today that has changed. People wander confused between the numerous identities they can choose from. They stray between lifestyles, ideologies, and religions. They have before them endless choices and variations. Throughout fast-changing life circumstances they wander from identity to identity.

Kenneth Gergen relates how chaos in the social environment leads to internal chaos. The individual loses his or her integrated identity in the maelstrom of floating pieces of identity absorbed from others. Gergen says that we "ingest myriad bits of other's being--values, attitudes, opinions, life-styles, personalities--synthesizing them and incorporating them into our own definition of self." As we do this, we find it more difficult to look inward to discover what we desire and believe in. To look inward, then, is to risk seeing a maelstrom of parts of ourselves in conflict. The endless changes in social patterns bring about a deep shift in our image of ourselves. "With social saturation, the traditional pattern is disrupted. One is increasingly thrust into new and different relationships--as the network of associates expands in the workplace, the neighbourhood is suffused with new and different voices, one visits and receives visitors from aboard. . . . The result is that one cannot depend on a solid confirmation of identity, nor on comfortable patterns of authentic action" (Gergen 1991:147).

With the breakdown of industrial civilization--the crises, crack-ups, turbulence and chaos in the environment, in society and other forms of human organization--exact their toll on the individual. The multiple pressures and the break down of the role structure lead to personality crisis. People search for their identities, They participate in group therapies, read self help books, change jobs, spouses, hobbies, styles and roles. "Rooting about in themselves for the source of their discomfort, they undergo agonies of unnecessary guilt. They seem blankly unaware that what they are feeling inside themselves is the subjective reflection of a much larger objective crisis: they are acting out an unwitting drama within a drama" (Toffler 1981:136).

Caught in a Turbulent Seam of History

Men living at the end of this century have the luck (or bad luck) to be living in a very eventful period of human history. They are living at the turning point, the period of transition between two major eras of human civilization. The present transition marks the end of the industrial era and heralds the coming of the post-industrial era. The transition period finds its expression in the breakdown and collapse of a number of basic interlocking complexes of human existence. In fractal form, the irregularity and degree of turbulence at the macro levels is copied and repeated throughout all levels down to the micro level of the human individual.

A number of these turbulent bifurcations have been described without attempting to cover all the areas of human existence that are falling before the onslaught of the beakdown of the industrial era.

9
The Adaptation Crisis

ESCALATING COMPLEXITY AND UNCERTAINTY

The human world is facing a tide of exploding uncertainty. It is in the throes of a chaotic transition between eras. At the close of an epoch, humanity seems to be riding a wild runaway horse. The world cannot be stopped to get off. As the industrial era draws to a close, growing complexity and periods of chaos at bifurcation points of complex human problems are accelerating.

The growth of complexity is the result of a number of interacting factors. It is the direction of evolution in the living world. It is the inevitable result of transformations in self-organizing systems. It is augmented by modern technology when this is not guided by a parallel development of a culture of mutual responsibility.

CRISES AND UNCERTAINTY

In the transition state between epochs, there is a rising level of stress and crisis as systems enter the chaotic stage before transformation to new orders. Societies, organizations, families, and individuals are being stressed beyond their limits. They are having problems transfiguring themselves and making the basic changes needed to continue developing in the accelerated, complex, uncertain circumstances of these times. They function in a world of growing uncertainty. When the crises affect a number of critical areas of their functioning, human systems reach the Feigenbaum Point and pass into a state of deep chaotic crisis, where they either deteriorate and breakdown or after a long, difficult chaotic transition transform themselves.

In our times, more and more human systems of all kinds are going through crisis and breaking down, or experiencing chaotic transitions from which they self-organize themselves and transform to a higher more complex level of existence (Levy and Merry 1986). We are at a point in history where human judgment and humanity's ability to deal with the consequences of its behavioral and social creations lag behind its ability to create behaviors and cultures to meet the needs of growing interdependence. The changes are too rapid and complex to allow regular, continuous biological or cultural evolutionary processes of adaptation without a parallel process of change to behaviors and relationships of mutual responsibility and cooperation.

The growing rate of chaotic crises in human systems of all kinds is creating a world that is becoming more stormy, turbulent and chaotic from day to day. The accelerating increase in crises in social forms of living and in individual lives is creating a human environment of increasing chaos.

In a complex, intermeshed world, whose components are tightly braided together in never-ending interdependencies and interactions, crisis breeds crisis both within and between human systems. As crisis breeds crisis, adaptation to the uncertain chaotic environment becomes more and more problematic. Rifkin summarizes thus:

Noting that the flow of energy through a dissipative structure causes fluctuation, Prigogine rightfully concludes that if the fluctuations become too great for the system to absorb, it will be forced to reorganize. Prigogine then asserts that the reorganization tends toward a higher order of complexity than the one preceding it, is even more vulnerable to fluctuations and reordering. Thus, complexity creates the condition for greater reordering and speedup of evolutionary development and energy flow-through.

No matter that this theory flies in the face of our everyday common sense. We experience a world where increasing complexity is narrowing our options, creating greater inflexibility, and increasing likelihood of collapse and fragmentation. (Rifkin 1981:241-42)

Crisis Breeds Crises

In complex intermeshed systems crisis in one part leads to crisis in other parts; it is "contagious". Never before, during the last few hundred years, have the various forms of human systems been passing through so many crises. In the present situation crisis breeds crisis, internally and externally. Uncertainty is outdistancing human adaptive capabilities. Humanity's evolutionary consciousness has not kept pace with the rate and magnitude of the changes and the degree of complexity in which it is immersed.

Television, radio and newspaper headlines carry stories of a new crisis or breakdown everyday. Both global and domestic affairs alike are destabilized. Crisis-laden events accelerate at a rate that is beyond human capacity to stay on top of them. Under these conditions, even the best bureaucracies totter, and critical problems are allowed to develop into stages of chaotic crises. The crises also affect the Westernized industrial nations. The Los Angeles riots were given much publicity as were the riots, rampages, property burning, and clashes with police in a number of towns in England in the early nineties. In Germany the skinheads burn down the homes of Turkish workers.

Writing about "the systems breakdowns in the contemporary world to which nonequilibrium or 'chaos' theory potentially relates," Loye and Eisler, refer to the crises that are affecting major parts of the world, the famines, financial, political, and military crises. Such crises and pressures drive the breakdown of systems that can lead to states of social chaos (1987: 53-54).

The problems proliferate when the crises breed and create other crises. Managers face decisions for which no former experience exists. The faster things change and crises proliferate the more decision makers face unique unprecedented situations. The Union Carbide tragedy that killed thousands in India and the oil spill in Alaska are extreme examples of these kinds of new unpredictable unique situations.

The rate of bankruptcies in most modern countries rises from year to year. Whole sectors of the economy break down. Over five hundred savings and loan banks in the United States got into financial trouble, necessitating government aid. The automobile industry went through a similar crisis requiring federal aid. The increase in the rate of organizational breakdown is especially prevalent among young organizations (Merry 1990). Industries are finding it compoundingly formidable to survive and flourish in an uncertain world that has become one market--where everyone can compete and copy everyone else; where new inventions, technologies, and materials come and go at dizzying rates; where firms cannot foresee and plan for the next development in their field; where giant concerns can oust small entrepreneurs and then themselves topple over; where specialization necessitates intricate coordination; where changing tastes and variety of needs outdistance production.

Therapy in all its forms, which deal with the stresses of individuals and families, is an expanding profession. Human systems of all kinds (e.g., organizations), are finding it difficult to adapt to a world of accelerated uncertainty. They are being stressed and stretched beyond their threshold of elasticity.

Crises rage in cities. Uncontrolled population growth, pollution, poverty, abandoned children and crime, are making Mexico City as well as other large growing urban complexes a difficult place to inhabit. The exploitation of new energy resources coupled with the growth of energy flow through resulting from increasing complexity, leads to an incredible explosion in urban life. Urban dwellers are becoming a majority of the world's population and this urban expansion increases pollution and health risks. The larger a city becomes the more energy input it requires. Rifkin notes that the greater the increase in energy use in cities, the greater the disorder. The more the disorder, the more is invested in institutions that have to deal with the various types of chaos (Rifkin:153-54).

Shorter Periods between Transformations

As complexity grows and more interlocked areas of human existence move closer to critical bifurcation points the periods of relative steadiness between discontinuous transformations appear to be becoming shorter. The human world is snowballing into states of greater turbulence and chaos at faster rates.

The average period of years of marriage becomes shorter as divorce becomes more prevalent. In the last 30 years schools have gone through many basic changes and upheavals. The major transformations in basic institutions come at a faster rate. It is almost impossible to find a single basic institution that has not gone through at least one major upheaval in our lifetime. All this is taking place, at ever-shortening time periods between each transformation.

For individuals, shorter periods between transformations mean that within their lifetimes they must handle transformations that were once dealt with by the next generations. Sons who took over from their fathers carried through major changes that their fathers had found too threatening. But in these times people can no longer delay the transformation until another generation takes over. People must deal with transformations themselves that were previously solved by a change of generations.

The Shorter Periods between Eras

The shortening period between eras is creating a future that might choke itself with rapidly following chaotic transitions. "Thus the seemingly aeons of time available to our distant forebears for reacting to and getting in synchrony with new developments and challenges are no longer available. The option of keeping one foot in the old and the other foot in the new has evaporated . . . the likelihood of stable--that is "flow"--periods of normality grows less and less" (Lynch and Kordis 1989:75).

The same authors describe a future of overlapping eras and compacted change, within each era:

With waves of change bursting forth on the scene every few years, we may soon face a spectacle of unprecedented global diversity in which perhaps as many as four, five, six, or even more "systems of ideas and beliefs"--worldviews--created by these waves of change are vying for dominance simultaneously.

Not only are the waves of change arriving more and more often, they are also arriving in a compacted state--that is, wihin the wave itself, developments are on a fast track. The computer system you bought nine months ago may already be obsolete. The "confidential" tip you received last week on an important business development in your industry was a headline in this morning's Wall Street Journal. The brainstorm you had yesterday for a new product or service has actually been under development in California, Sweden, or West Germany for several months. The market you were counting on to propel your company to its next phase of growth has been preempted--or eliminated. (p.75-76)

DIFFICULTIES OF ADAPTING

As more political systems, ideologies, cultures, nations, societies, governments, cities, towns, commmuities, institutions, organizations, families, and individuals become more complex and either breakdown or go through chaotic, turbulent transitions at a faster rate, the human world becomes more uncertain and more difficult to adapt to. Many signs indicate a sick society that is unable to function properly. This is a society in the midst of the chaotic stage of transformative change. "What is occurring now is not a crisis of capitalism, but of industrial society itself, regardless of its political form. We are simultaneously experiencing a youth revolution, a sexual revolution, a racial revolution, a colonial revolution, an economic revolution and the most rapid deep-going technological revolution in history. We are living through the general crisis of industrialism" (Toffler 1981:172).

This is a world that is more and more formidable to become a part of, join onto, adapt to, and live in. Morever, as crises proliferate they create an environment in which more forms of social living and human institutions are themselves pushed into crisis and then go through basic transformations or disintegrate.

THE CIRCLE CLOSES

This is a human world that is less and less predictable. People go to sleep at night never knowing what turn of events the morrow will bring that will affect their lives, The regularities of yesterday, and yesteryear are becoming increasingly disrupted. More and more randomness, uncertainty and unpredictability, stress and crisis, play a role in human life. This is a world abundant in butterfly effects; a world in which more often there is no proportion between cause and effect. In times of discontinuity, there are growing problems in generalizing from one case to another. Randomness is bursting into human lives with greater force and impact.

It is becoming more difficult to predict the future and thus to plan for it because in a time of discontinuous change the trajectories of the future have become increasingly incalculable. At this point, without seeing the whole pattern, the ability to control the future ahead of time is on the decline. It is only as we begin to discern the outlines of the patterns in the chaotic transitions that we return to human agency the ability to affect its future.

Trying More to Take Control

As the world becomes more uncertain, individual and social needs for order and regularity are threatened. The foundations of living in a world that has an underpinning of steadiness, regularity, stability, certainty, order, predictability, generalizability and controllability are shaken. Decrease in these characteristics and the growing prevalence of crisis and deep chaos arouse much stress, anxiety, and fear. They remove the assuredness of steady ground beneath humanity's feet.

Societies, organizations and individuals react to this threat with greater efforts to control. They attempt to re-create certainty and regularity by domination and control of the environment, both human and other, as well as their circumstances. They do this by the same means they have used in the past by trying to regain control with more structure and more technology.

Developing More Technology to Regain Control

As more efforts are exerted to control circumstances with the use of technology, the self-sustaining circle closes. Advancing technology leads to even more complexity, multiplying the rate of crisis and transformation, thus engendering more difficulties of adaptation, and making this a more uncertain world in which humanity invests even greater efforts to dominate with science and technology. Orenstein and Ehrlich (1990) write that each triumph of technology contains new kinds of threats. Rifkin says that each attempt at forcing order with new high energy technologies will only speed up the chaos. The more we apply technological solutions in the world, the more things seem to break down and disintegrate. "The world is becoming more disordered because each time we apply a new technological solution to a problem, it's like dousing a fire with gasoline. The whole process of increased complexity, increased problems, increased entropy, and increased disorder proceeds exponentially, and that's what makes the modern world crisis so frightening" (1981:82-83).

Thus toward the end of this century the circle is closing. Each trip around this vicious circle raises the level of uncertainty in human life and brings global society closer to its elastic limits. It seems that only a total transformation in worldwide society will allow humanity to escape out of the trap and deal with its complexes of metaproblems at a higher level of functioning.

The Dangers in the Transition

As the potential destructive power that can be unleashed during worldwide transformations and crises grows, the dangers in the coming transition become a mounting threat. The chaotic transitions of the past have been marked by turbulent times in which many people went through wars, conflict, economic catastrophes, breakdowns of institutions, and endless human suffering. With the dangers of mass-destruction weapons and the destruction of the ecology, the present transformation threatens the continued existence of humanity.

If transitions are delayed by attempts to stabilize the system and delay transformation, the situation is not easier. The compounding growth in complexity and energy-flow lead to the heightening and augmenting of the fluctuations. This makes the big caesuras of the transition more turbulent. Erich Jantsch describes it thus:

Does the complementary development of higher stability and ever-increasing fluctuations not lead into dangerous regions where destruction looms? Do the fluctuations which are potentially ready in the nuclear arsenals of the big powers not already threaten life on the whole earth? This is true, alas. If developments were to continue in the same ways, each quantum jump of evolution toward new social and cultural structures would potentially unleash such destructive forces that the substrate--the systems of the biosphere as well as the biological and socio-cultural experience stored in gene pools and libraries--would inevitably suffer. Are the ultimate limits to complexity reached here? (1980:256)

Ornstein and Ehrlich (1990) caution that the situation today is unprecedented. At no former time have people had the capacity to destroy their civilization in a few hours and to ruin much of the planet's life-support systems. Never before have humans been engaged in the process of destroying those systems wholesale in a manner that could complete the job in less than a century. Towards the end of their book, Prigogine and Stengers summarize the present predicament of humanity:

We know now that societies are immensely complex systems involving a potentially enormous number of bifurcations exemplified by the variety of cultures that have evolved in the relatively short span of human history. We know that such systems are highly sensitive to fluctuations. This leads both to hope and threat: hope, since even small fluctuations may grow and change the overall structure. As a result, individual activity is not doomed to insignificance. On the other hand, there is also a threat, since in our universe the security of stable, permanent rules seems gone forever. We are living in a dangerous and uncertain world that inspires no blind confidence. (1988:312-13)

The destructive capability of nuclear and biological weapons in the wrong hands is frightening to imagine, but it is a possibility. The world's brush with Saddam Hussein made this possibility more of a terrible reality than could ever be imagined. There is no guarantee that such situations will always end without mass-destruction weapons as did Desert Storm. The fate of nuclear weapons in many hands with the chaotic breakup and transition in the former Soviet Union (including the growth of extreme Russian nationalism) is a dangerous situation. North Korea and a fanatic Iran may soon threaten the world with nonconventional weapons. The present situation is one in which stability has ended. This can be a very dangerous time for mankind, one in which there can be many upheavals and extinctions. The period is one of punctuated equilibrium and discontinuous change in evolution.

THE INTENSIFICATION OF UNCERTAINTY

Taking a bird's-eye view of the four chapters in this section, it can be seen that mankind is facing an age of growing uncertainty.

Civilization is caught in the stormy, chaotic transition stage between two major eras in human history. Mankind is living in the chaotic, difficult times of the death throes of the Industrial Era before the consolidation of the new era that will follow it.

At this turning point in the history of civilization, interlocked complexes of basic problems facing humanity are reaching a bifurcation point and are stressed to their elastic limits, necessitating a discontinuous transformative break-through.

As the end of this era approaches, humanity is being whirled in the vortex of a spiral of ever growing complexity, which appears to be hastening the rate of chaotic transitions in human systems and intensifying uncertainty.

In the industrial era, humanity is ensnared in a vicious cycle of burgeoning technology, unbridled by values of mutual cooperation and responsibility, leading to greater complexity and to faster rates of transformational crises and chaos. These intensify the adaptation problems of human systems. As crisis generates crisis, and uncertainty proliferates, mankind attempts to overcome uncertainty by additional attempts to control it with more technology.

In this transformation of eras, with the unprecedented destructive capabilities in the hands of mankind, and the dangers looming ahead from the rape of the ecology--the transition is thwart with dangers to man's survival.

The combination and interactions of these trends together has led to an epoch of unprecedented turbulence, chaos and uncertainty.

III
COPING WITH UNCERTAINTY

10
Living with Uncertainty

This section of the book will examine if the New Sciences can give insights as to how to cope with the issues dealt with in the preceding section.

Maybe the anxiety involved in accepting a world careening wildly in the direction of growing uncertainty has pushed the situation below the level of collective conscious awareness and explicit recognition. As people have difficulty accepting the reality of the death of a loved one, so possibly humanity has refused to realize and accept the demise of the familiar industrial era of certainty and linear order.

Nevertheless, often without being fully aware of the growth of uncertainty, human systems as individuals, organizations, and societies have begun to react to the changing conditions. They try to find ways to coexist with uncertainty by developing behavioral and social systems that can deal and live with it. They may seek solace in the promises of the coming era that hopefully will diminish the severity of a number of problematic complexes that are bringing the industrial era to a breaking point. They may try to discern evolutionary trends that hold hope of ending or decreasing the dangers of the transition period.

Some are beginning to realize the critical part played in human evolution by the evolutionary competence, consciousness, learning, and design of human beings. They may attempt to derive policy and action implications as to how to midwife guided evolution in a nonlinear human world. They commence drawing the contours of a guiding image to draw humanity toward these ends. At the social level, they organize into worldwide movements to diminish the ecological consequences of intensifying entropy. They become conscious of the part played by human agency in forging its future. The final section of the book will try to make some of these trends explicit.

This chapter describes how people as individuals react to the stress of growing uncertainty in their lives. Different levels of behavior serve as a model to analyze the reactions. Together with dysfunctional reactions there are also attempts to adapt to growing uncertainty and turbulence without making basic changes in identity or personality. With the help of self-organization theory the forms of these adaptations are made explicit.

The following chapter clarifies the need for a simultaneous transformation, both at the individual and societal levels. It examines how individuals as complex adaptive systems are beginning to transform their identity and personality so as to continue functioning under conditions of growing uncertainty. It attempts to explicate some of the characteristics of people who can function effectively with evolutionary competence, at the edge of chaos.

Chapter 12 attempts to draw the contours of the coming era. and examine the possibility that the major trend of that era might alleviate the problems in basic areas of human concern that have reached a critical bifurcation point.

Chapter 13 clarifies new perspectives on evolution based on the marriage of natural selection with self-organization. It redefines the role of human beings as complex adaptive systems with the ability to be aware of and coevolve with evolutionary processes. It finds grounds for hope that there will be a transformational change in the basic rules of evolution itself. This may help in decreasing the dangers to mankind inherent in worldwide cataclyzmic shifts.

The final chapter discusses the place of human agency in transforming civilization hopefully toward a better future. It discusses the interplay of uncertainty and freedom. It clarifies the important role of evolutionary competence and learning, of creating a guiding image, and of developing evolutionary guidance and design systems.

STAGES OF DEALING WITH BASIC CHANGE

When individuals, organizations, and societies face uncertainty engendered by basic change in their environment they generally react to it in a number of ways.

These ways of reacting can be differentiated into the modes of behavior discerned in chapter 3:

A. Repeating former behavior over and over again
B. Varying behavior slightly and predictably
C. Adapting new behaviors
D. Transiting through a chaotic crisis
E. Transforming to a new more complex mode of functioning

Often these kinds of behavior follow each other in consecutive stages. When a human system faces a basic change in the environment it may react by attempting each of these modes in consecutive stages. The stages of reacting to basic change can be described as repetition, variation, adaptation, transition, and transformation. These are also the stages systems follow on their way from linear order through chaos to the emergence of a new, more complex level of behavior. That is from point attractors through increasingly nonlinear behavior to deep chaos and the emergence of new order, Feigenbaum provided numbers for these transitions.

REPETITION (A) is behavior structured by a point or limit cycle attractor. It is an attempt to deal with enviromental changes by doing more of the same. In its usual form it is repeating behavior that has been tried before. Industries often attempt to structure work roles in this mode treating employees as if they were components of a machine.

VARIATION (B) is changing behavior slightly within the confines of a torus attractor. It is reacting to change within the range of actions that are slightly different from but basically similar to behaviors the person has used in the past. An example of variation is always eating a similar lunch at noon. When a basic change has occurred this behavior may be dysfunctional. Like repetitive behavior, it can be metastable behavior if it resists necessary change. When a basic change has occurred in circumstances there is no recognition of it.

ADAPTATION (C) is trying out new behaviors within the confines of a strange attractor, but not beyond three bifurcation points. This is an intermix of predictability and unpredictability. The system is resilient and able to adapt new behaviors. This is a functional range of adaptive behaviors of most behavioral and social systems in the face of major changes. The change is recognized and the system displays the resilience needed to adapt new modes of behavior. These new behaviors do not include a basic transformative change in the person herself. An example of adaptation is developing new ways of behavior when immigrating to a new country. Both families and organizations display resilient adaptive behavior. Within this mode of behavior an adaptive system manuevers itself to function at the edge of chaos.

TRANSITION (D) is the the chaotic crisis-laden period before transformation. The system enters a state of deep chaos. Crisis often marks the deep chaotic transition stage out of which a new, higher level more complex order emerges. A person may go through a chaotic crisis when adaptation is unable to deal with basic changes that have taken place. What is needed is something qualitatively different--a transformative change in the person herself. Crisis is often the turbulent period between two ways of being--the way of the past and the yet unborn way of the future. The deep chaos of transition is the fertile void out of which is born the new way of being. An example of this is the confusion and loss of identity, as in adolescence, when roles and values of the past have lost their meaning, and a new identity has not yet formed. (Merry and Allerhand 1978)

TRANSFORMATION (E) is the emergence of a more complex, completely different higher level of functioning. It is Prigogine's "order out of chaos." It is the shift to a new way of being. It is a qualitative change in the person herself, in her personality and identity. Transformation is not acting or behaving differently it is being a different kind of person. It is changing identity in a way that allows the person to deal with the basic changes that have taken place. An example of transformation would be a religous conversion. Transformation takes place in societies, often in a revolutionary form, and in organizations as organizational transformation (Levy and Merry 1986).

The first three stages of change described above (A, B, and C) are analogous to many other change typologies such as that of Mark Michaels (1992). Michaels differentiates between equilibrium, near equilibrium, and far-from-equilibrium changes. Robert Marshak (1993) differentiates between three types of organizational change processes. These appear to be analogous to three stages (B, C, and E) in the above model. Developmental change builds on the past and leads to better performance over time, e.g., better teamwork. Transitional change involves a move from one state or condition to another, e.g., from manual to automated operations. Transformational change implies the transfiguration from one state of being to a fundamentally different state of being, e.g., from a regulated monopoly to a market-driven competitive business.

In terms of nonlinear dynamics, repetition is behavior formed by point and limit cycle attractors. Variation is structured by a torus attractor. Adaptation is assuming new behaviors within the confines of strange attractors while not exceeding the Feigenbaum Point. Transition is entering a deep chaotic state beyond the Feigenbaum Point. Transformation follows a period of deep chaos and is the emergence of a more complex, qualitatively different repertoire of behaviors within new basins of attraction.

Economizing in Change

Most people will not make a deeper kind of change if they can get by with a lighter change. They will first tend to try out behavior they are used to and create variations if circumstances demand it. They will adapt new behaviors only if old variations do not work. Only later if these are of no avail, will they try to transform themselves in line with the basic changes in circumstances. As a rule of thumb, if at all possible, they will not change to a new stage of behavior but will continue attempting to deal with the novel circumstances with behaviors they used in the past. People will try as much as they can to hold on to adaptive behavior without endangering themselves in the chaotic transition that can lead to either transformation or disintegration. They are aware that the chaotic transition may also lead to disintegration, in the form of breakdown of some kind.

Describing similar phenomena at the social level, Robert Artigiani of the U.S. Naval Academy writes: "All we can be sure of is that most members of a society will initially oppose evolutionary change, for emotional commitments will tie them to values encouraging conventional behaviors. Moreover unable to predict the future of a society in transition, most people seem reluctant to trade the devil they know for one of which they are ignorant . . . people will resist altering their cognitive maps even in unstable situations when their societies are falling apart" (1991: 152).

Individuals, families, organizations, societies or civilizations will not make a more basic change as long as they feel they can get by with less. They do not jump into major disruptive changes as long as they can get by with lighter changes, which will not upset the existing order (Merry 1990).

This principle is especially predominant in the passage from adaptation to transformation. The far-reaching consequences and the fear of the dangers of the unknown, and the chaotic transition period, tend to deter people and societies from making the quantum leap of a transformative change. Often they do not take this leap and attempt to continue as before. The result is disintegration in some form or another.

This principle of making the least disruptive change may possibly be the behavioral and social equivalent of Swenson's ordered flow (mentioned in chapter 4). Swenson states that in physical and chemical systems facing an energy gradient, the path the system will choose will be the path in which the energy flow has the fastest rate. As energy flows faster in an ordered flow this is the path it will choose. Choosing an ordered way of the past that people are accustomed to before venturing into unknown territory that will entail a major disruption might be the human equivalent of Swenson's "ordered flow."

The rest of this chapter will deal with the way people as individuals try to cope with the uncertain environment that has developed around them. This is often called "first order" change and includes the first three stages of coping with change--repetition, variation and adaptation This will be followed by a description of the predicament of people caught in a chaotic transition before making a basic transformation.

ADAPTATION TO UNCERTAINTY

The growth of uncertainty in the form of proliferation of crisis and multiplying chaotic periods, give rise to major changes in the human condition. Two of the reactions to these conditions--anxiety and stress--deserve special attention.

The increase of anxiety in everyday life is a reaction to the intensification of uncertainty in these times. The loss of the stable state and the destruction of the anchors of personal security have given rise to the widespread prevalence of anxiety as a regular feature of daily life. The American Psychiatric Association defines anxiety as apprehension, tension and uneasiness which stems from the anticipation of danger, the source of which is widely unknown or unrecognized. Anxiety is the fear of a nameless dread, a kind of floating fear unattached to a particular source. The emotional overload of dealing with too much uncertainty and too many unpredictable, threatening events may lead to a marked rise in the measure of anxiety in people's lives. At the level of individual lives, proliferating uncertainties overwhelm people. As T. R. Young (1994) points out, a person can generally manage with one uncertainty such as a health problem. Often two uncertainties, such as health and family problems can be dealt with. But if to these are added loss of job and economic insecurity together with the insecurity of living in a crime-ridden area, the uncertainties can be overburdening.

Living in a world that bombards people daily through the radio newspapers, and television with endless details of accidents, disasters, crises, criminal acts, wars and other tragedies, makes anxiety a constant companion. The constant growing uncertainty feeds fears and escalating apprehension of hidden, unidentified, and unexpected dangers that may befall loved ones or ourselves.

Stress in People's Lives

Stress is the adaptive reaction of the human body to anxiety and mounting emotional tensions. Hans Selye (1976), the pioneer of stress research, defined stress as the rate of wear and tear within the body. Stress is a natural integral element in the makeup of living things. Humans need a certain measure of stress for their conscious activity and for positive change. Positive occurrences, such as a marriage or birth, can also cause stress. Too much stress is dangerous to health and well-being.

Kenneth Pelletier of the Langley Porter Neuropsychiatric Institute points out that when major social change occurs, there is always stress on individual members of society. Writing about the combination of mounting change and the growth of the information media, he says that at all levels of society, people have to adapt to a changing world-view. This kind of evolution has occurred throughout history, but communication systems now propagate these ideas and attitudes at an unprecedented rate. Pelletier distinguishes between harmful and non harmful stress:

It is important to make a vital distinction between injurious and non-injurious stress responses. Obviously, not all stress can or should be avoided. A normal adaptive stress reaction occurs when the source of stress is identifiable and clear. When this particular challenge is met, an individual returns to a level of normal functioning relatively quickly. However, when the source of stress is ambiguous, undefined, or prolonged, or when several sources exist simultaneously, the individual does not return to a normal mental and physiological baseline as rapidly. He or she continues to manifest a potentially damaging stress reaction. This concept is fundamental to the understanding of psychosomatic disorders. (1977:5)

In these times, individuals are faced with conditions that are overburdening them with stress. Pelletier indicates that for people living in post-industrial Western cultures, the degree of stress has become excessive and deleterious. Modern man is subject to more and greater stresses than have been experienced at any other time in human history, and the effect is often devastating. In this chaotic transition stage, people have all the ingredients for continuing to "manifest a potentially damaging stress reaction." Personal sources of stress are intensified by the growth and spread of the media, especially the daily press, radio, and television. Humans are regularly subjected to sources of stress that are prolonged, ambiguous, and simultaneously coming from several sources.

The amplifying and intensification of internal stress in its psychological forms may be the parallel of internal gradients in chemical systems (in Prigogine's terms). With people the aggravation of external perturbations in the form of multiplying uncertainties aggravates internal insecurity and inflames the intensity of stress. Sometimes, the perturbations of stress snowball into proportions that can no longer be handled by the person's physical or psychological structure. He or she reaches a psychological bifurcation point that may lead to a breakdown.

Repetitions and Variations of More of the Same

The common adaptive reaction to uncertainty is to try to repeat with greater effort what has been tried before. This is doing more of the same (point, cycle and torus-like behavior). Accustomed to ways of thinking and behaving, most people have difficulties changing beliefs and assumptions developed throughout the industrial era. Many believe that dominating and controlling people and conditions will guard them from uncertainty so they try even more to control and dominate. They do more of the same. Afraid of the unexpected and unpredictable, people attempt to structure their daily lives. They follow fixed daily routines of repetitive behavior that provide a safe haven of certainty in the face of the growing uncertainty enfolding them. In order to attain control, some strive with greater efforts to attain power in some form, generally that of wealth. Wealth is seen by many as a means of gaining control over unpredictable circumstances and ensuring safety from life's uncertainties.

In their immediate environment such as family, workplace, leisure activies, people do all they can to build around themselves a cocoon of certainty in the form of repetitive or slightly variable (torus) behaviors. When they are troubled by changing circumstances they make every effort to return to their former regular, reliable ways of functioning. When the organizations they belong to are perturbed by fluctuations, people turn to stricter enforcement of rules, regulations, and norms of behavior.

Lifestyles of Escape

Many of the responses to the intensification of uncertainty and increase of internal stress do not confront the new situation but attempt to escape from it, deny it and become oblivious to it. Schon (1991) describes three of these responses. *Return* is a reaction against the intolerable present by returning to the last stable state. It is living in the past. *Revolt* is a kind of total rejection of all established institutions without an alternative ideal. This form of reaction is often found among younger people. The third response evades the new reality by not using mental functions. *Mindlessness* is an attempt to escape from uncertainty by evading reflective consciousness. This may be by achieved through drugs, routine, violence, or the like.

To Schon's list, it is possible to add other items such as faddish lifestyles, loss of commitment, hatred of strangers and neurotic behavior. Faddish lifestyles allow people to deny or repress awareness of the enfolding uncertainty and instability by losing themselves for a time in a certain fad. This leaves no energy to think of how to deal with uncertain reality and growing tensions. The fad can take hundreds of forms from total devotion and involvement in pop bands, or to a consumer lifestyle, an addiction to spectatorship of sport, or absolute loyalty to some new Moonie-like cult.

Loss of commitment is a common reaction to the breakdown and crises in values, institutions and ideologies. If everything is foredoomed to fail then nothing is worth allegiance. A kind of bored cynicism and disbelief in everything is one manifestation of this reaction. Flitting around like a butterfly, not settling anywhere or on anything is another expression of this unwillingness to commit or devote oneself to anything.

Sometimes economic stress coupled with anxiety and fear of the unknown and unexpected, lights the ugly fire of hate of the stranger. the others--of different color, religion, nationality, or culture--are seen as the source of all the difficulties and troubles and the growing anxiety, tension, stress, and fear is vented on them. Movements of racial hate and discrimination flourish in times of uncertainty.

In one of its most dysfunctional forms repetitive behavior is called neurotic behavior. Neurotic behavior is a repetitive pattern of dysfunctional behavior. Repetitive neurotic patterns of behavior may be found in individuals, families, and organizations. Individual therapy attempts to change such patterns. Systemic family therapy (e.g., the Milan school) attempts to break vicious repetitive cycles of behavior among family members. The same repetitive patterns of dysfunctional behavior may be found in organizations (Merry and Brown 1987).

All of these ways of escape from the intensification of uncertainty and rising levels of stress, do not confront reality. They do not solve a person's problems; they attempt to evade them. They are what was named in a former chapter "metastability" reactions to a changed situation. They are forms of clinging to old, dysfunctional ways of adaptation that are unsuitable to the changed circumstances. They do not provide personal solutions, they only try to deny, avoid, repress and escape the difficulties of adapting oneself to a turbulent, uncertain environment.

ADAPTATION TO THE STRESS OF UNCERTAINTY

When permanent, novel conditions develop in the environment, and regular everyday modes of adjustment are insufficient, people may adapt a new range of behaviors. In the stage of adaptation, they acclimatize themselves to some kind of permanent change, that has occurred. They adapt new patterns of behavior that open greater degrees of freedom in their choices of reacting to the new conditions. Thus persons partly regain some of the flexibility that decreased when they stressed themselves in dealing with the different circumstances. Adaptation is not a basic transformative change, but it is having a new range of possibilities. When people face growing uncertainty and stress, their resilience allows them to find novel forms of adaptation to the changing conditions.

In the stress evoking climate of the end of an era, a growing number of people are seeking ways to adapt themselves to the new conditions. They recognize that something basic has changed in the human condition and they attempt to habituate themselves to a range of new behaviors that will allow them to coexist with growing stress and uncertainty. They do not make the basic change in their identity and personality that the novel conditions demand, but instead develop a set of new behaviors that assist them either to reduce the amount of stress in their lives or to cope better with the stress they do experience. When they have at their disposal a wide range of novel behaviors and are able to utilize them to adapt effectively to changed circumstances, *they are functioning at the edge of chaos*. Three of these many ways people are adopting to deal with increasing stress are stress reduction, maintaining a healthy lifestyle, and creating new forms of relationship.

Stress Reduction

There are two kinds of stress reduction approaches: those that concentrate on relaxing the body, and those that are aimed at the mind. Progressive relaxation, breathing exercises, autogenic training and biofeedback are examples of stress reduction methods that calm the body mainly by releasing stress that has coagulated in the muscles. Releasing the muscular tension indirectly affects the level of mind and emotional tension and thus relieves the stress.

Visualization, meditation, self-hypnosis, witnessing, and thought-stopping focus mainly on the mind and emotions. They quiet the chattering mind or break its enslavement to troubling thoughts and concentrate the mind's focus on subjects that bring calm. Quieting the mind has a calming effect on the body.

The two types of approaches affect each other and the most efficient way to reduce stress is to combine both. Some methods do, in practice, combine both approaches and are aimed at working on both levels, that is, mind and body.

Maintaining a Healthy Lifestyle

Maintaining a healthy lifestyle includes a whole range of activities that in combination contribute to decreasing conditions or habits that raise the level of stress in one's life, or alternatively strengthen the person's ability to deal with them when they arise. Some methods work both ways.

Examples of means that contribute to decreasing stress factors are: healthy nutrition, stopping smoking, moderating alcohol, not using drugs, living in an ecologically safe area, reducing stress factors at work and home, finding meaningful work, finding a healthy balance between work and recreation, avoiding excessive medication, and limiting daily viewing or listening to the news. Some activities and conditions that contribute to a person's ability to deal with stress are: regular exercise, sports and other activities that contribute to health and weight control; actively experiencing and participating in activities that contribute to personal growth, such as learning in a variety of fields; sensitivity training, assertiveness, problem solving, and life-planning skills; personal horizon-widening activities, such as travel and reading; maintaining a healthy, loving, and warm family life; having someone close that can assist in coping with difficulties; and spending more time on creative activities and hobbies. In these turbulent times, functioning at the edge of chaos includes the ability to function daily maintaining a healthy life style through the ability to utilize a large range of these competencies.

Creating New Forms of Relationships

Networking refers to the ability to maintain ties and interact, with a range of people that can help, support, and assist in all of the above. These can be family, friends, associates, people with similar interests, or support groups. They may be far or close; the interactions with them may be regular or far apart. As a whole and in combination, they help a person in times of stress and provide a network of support that assists in dealing with difficulties.

Relationship patterns during times of unexpected, discontinuous, frequent change and turbulence assume a character of their own. The few steady relationships a person had with family and two or three friends are superseded by different kinds of ties. These new modes of relationship are the result of intensified change, which results in a person changing home, town, workplace, and career a number of times throughout his or her lifetime. Other facets of the post-industrial age--such as the growth of communication technology and transport facilities and the ease and widespread prevalence of travel beyond the immediate community--also effect the character of relationships. Kenneth Gergen (1991) has made a study of the changing patterns of relationships developing in the post-industrial era. In the past a person maintained a limited number of relationships that generally persisted throughout his life. The cast of others remained relatively stable. There were changes as a result of birth and death, but few people moved to a different town or country. But now things have changed. Relationships can continue over long periods even when people move away from each other. Cars, jet airplanes, telephones, fax machines, video cassettes, photos, and computers allow relationships to continue over distances. Formerly, time and distance between people typically meant loss. Now this has changed because time and distance are no longer serious threats to a relationship.

New kinds of relationships are developing. A person may maintain a plethora of relationships with family, television and radio personalities, fellow commuters, and work colleagues. Television expands the number of vicarious relationships. A person can identify with heroes of movies, television personalities, and athletes from around the world. The change in the mode of relationships is changing their form. They often change from the face-to-face relationships to relationships over distance.

There is an increase in the number of short, emotionally intense relationships. People express themselves more openly. The rate of creating relationships with others has accelerated. The pace of relationships is much more hurried. People develop and end relationships at a faster pace. Members of the same family have a variety of outside ties. In many families the ritual of dinner together is not an everyday event. The home is not a place one nests in but is more of a pit stop (Gergen 1991).

THE CHAOTIC TRANSITION

Crises in human and social systems are times of transition and have all the hallmarks of deep chaos. These take the form of randomness, uncertainty and unpredictability, unsteady relations between components, turbulence, sensitivity to small differences and greater degrees of freedom. The crisis in one part of the system spreads throughout the system and the system is besieged by an array of different crises in various subsystems.

The shake-up of the system brings together components that were far apart and flings apart elements that clung together. Relations of the past become irrelevant. The inner boundaries of the system are redefined. People realign themselves and redefine their loyalties (Merry 1990). An increase in energy intake adds to the turbulence and fluctuations. Chaotic uncertainty and confusion can be found at all levels. Glenn Perry describes a family crisis:

During the instability phase prior to transformation the principle of maximum entropy production holds. The system steps up its usual processes and attempts to accommodate the crisis from within its current structure. There is a maximum flow of energy through the system and maximum dissipation of entropy (waste) into the environment. An increase of entropy production equates to an intensification of the very process which produced the crisis, e.g., our pseudo-rational, counter-dependent male becomes even more critical, distancing, defensive and rigid, externalizing responsibility for the crisis onto his "sick" wife. (1993: 238)

People react to this chaotic crisis state in a variety of ways. Three of the common reactions are loss of security, letting go of the past, and loss of personal identity.

Loss of Security

Anxiety, impotency, helplessness, hopelessness, aloneness, loss of security, placelessness, being drawn into a vacuum, holding on to the familiar, turning inward, abandonment, conflict over boundaries, resistance, operating defense mechanisms, unpreparedness, seeking others, excitement, fantasy, resilience, creativity, intuition--these are expressions people gave to their feelings and actions in reaction to a growing state of chaotic crisis (Merry 1990). Most of the feelings have a negative connotation, a few are neutral, and some are positive. As a whole people's gut reaction tends to be more unfavorable than favorable. They are less aware of the important creative functions of chaotic confusion.

Turbulence and chaos in a time of transition are experienced as somewhat like the feeling of a person caught in an earthquake. The earth itself, the basis of all security and balance, is shaking under ones feet. The sudden explosion of many unpredictable events in a person's life and the exposure to a plethora of turbulent happenings tumbling capriciously and tempestuously into ones world is felt as a trembling of the very foundations of security, a loss of the stable state. The same emotions affect people in organizational crisis.

The passage through chaotic transition undermines the belief in the stable state and strikes at the very heart of people's feeling of constancy, steadiness, predictability, and security. The emptiness and void of the transition period deprives people of the anchors that gave stability and meaning to their lives. These anchors of values, belief systems, institutions, and roles that are sources of order, continuity, and meaning in life break down or are in crisis before the onslaught of the transition stage (Merry and Brown: 1987).

Letting Go of the Past

This is a time in which people need to let go of the past so as to open themselves to the new ways of the future. The old and familiar must be parted from before there is place for the new to enter. The "good old times" must be relinquished.

People sometimes attempt to disengage themselves from familiar places and faces of the past and break their identifications with past roles. They may become disenchanted and relinquish the innocence of belief in what the past world symbolized. People may become completely disoriented feeling they are in unfamiliar territory lacking direction to go. Behavior during this period is typified by growing detachment of the individual or the society from earlier fixed points and anchors of identity and all that was connected with them in roles, structures, and cultural conditions.

The Loss of Personal Identity

Losing the certainty of the stable state, deprived of the security of time-honoured social anchors--such as value systems, trusted institutions, and expected roles--people's sense of personal identity is undermined. With the shift in eras, anchors of security that were born in the industrial age have lost their meaning. Industriousness, loyalty to one's workplace, roots in one's hometown, the value of honest labor, the regular family form, and many other anchors of identity have been undermined. The coming era has not yet replaced them with alternatives. People are therefore wandering in the chaotic transition period, having lost the anchors of security of the past and not yet having a new set of anchors to fill their place. People are caught between the lost identity of the former age and yet without a new identity of the coming age. They are experiencing uncertainty as to who they are.

Add to this being daily bombarded through the media by never ending unpredicted happenings; experiencing visually and emotionally the trials, tribulations, tragedies, and dramas of others, throughout the world; receiving conflicting outlooks and messages from many different people and sources; having a boundless number of role models to emulate, it is no surprise that many lose their sense of coherent personal identity.

There is much emptiness, despair, and disintegration with the breakdown of life's certainties. Endless experiences and social contacts are introjected into peoples self-images and break up the coherence of their personal identity. Individuals must confront and negotiate, within themselves, the transformations that used to be handled by generational change. The undermining of the stability of most major institutions is also affecting people's sense of personal identity. People are losing their anchors for personal identity (Merry and Brown 1987).

BREAKDOWN

At a certain point, the futility of the old adaptation methods, the escape routes and avoidance tactics reach their elastic limits and a bifurcation point is met. Avoidance tactics and adaptations have their lifespans. In Prigogine's terms, the heightening internal fluctuations of intensifying cumulating stress break through and overpower the system. The existing structure gives way, and the avoidance and escape tactics or existing ways of adaptation cannot protect the individual any longer from the changed reality (Levy and Merry 1986).

The stress, tension, and anxiety that arise out of loss of personal identity cannot continue forever. If a person cannot center him- or herself on a healthy functional new identity, crisis deepens and opens the way to either a breakdown in some form or a transformation.

Crises involve positive feedback loops and morphogenetic processes which perturb the self system with destabilizing fluctuations. We can define crisis as an encounter with information which cannot readily be converted into habitual cognitive and behavioral patterns. . . anxiety accompanying this recognition is distressing and demands resolution. A cognitive reorganization to incorporate the new data brings a decrease in anxiety and leads to new, more functional alternatives of behavior. (Perry 1993:237)

If individuals after passing through a transition stage, have the ability to find ways of transformation to a higher state of functioning, that will enable them to live with a world that is more complex and uncertain. If they are unable to make the transition, they may fall victim to a breakdown.

Forms of Breakdown

Disintegration at the individual level often takes the form of a breakdown. Within the scope of this book, it is impossible to deal with breakdowns in detail.

They generally are a combination of two basic types; either physical or psychological.

Physical or psychological "breakdowns" in the form of an illness or a psychological disorder of some kind, such as neurotic behavior, or depression, are the common ways of reacting to accumulating stress. Many reactions are psychosomatic, that is, a combination of physical and psychological elements. Kenneth Pelletier describes how stress has become a dangerous phenomenon, with wide-ranging effects. Stress-related disorders have become a major problem. Stress-induced maladies have taken the place of epidemics of infectious diseases as today's major medical problem. Four disorders have become widespread in modern industrial nations. These are "cardiovascular disorders, cancer, arthritis, and respiratory diseases (including bronchitis and emphysema)." About 50 to 80 percent of all diseases are attributed to psychosomatic or stress-related sources.

Even the most conservative sources classify the following illnesses as psychosomatic: peptic ulcer, mucous colitis, ulcerative colitis, bronchial asthma, atopic dermatitis, urticaria and angioneurotic edema, hay fever, arthritis, Raynaud's disease, hypertension, hyperthyroidism, amenorrhea, enuresis, paroxysmal tachycardia, migraine headache, impotence, general sexual dysfunctions, sleep-onset, insomnia, alcoholism, and the whole range of neurotic and psychotic disorders. (1977:6-7)

The final stage of the disintegrative process can be both mental or physical and is most often a combination of both. Severe stress-induced physical illness may aggravate other physical and psychological systems leading to a state of a debilitating illness and an ambulatory invalid unable to take care of him- or herself. In extreme cases, mental illness in some severe forms can lead to almost complete loss of sanity and often demands physical segregation and hospitalization.

A combination of both physical and psychological disintegration can be seen in some of the dropouts of modern urban society roaming the streets without home or purpose. Drug addiction leading to crack-ups and suicides are also examples of the final stages of the disintegrative process.

TRANSFORMATIONAL CHANGE

Appropriate transformational changes in the identity and self of individuals might assist them in accepting uncertainty and coping with the stress of a world of intensifying insecurity. The self-organizing quality of the self enables it to transform itself when circumstances change so that a new self is needed (Levy and Merry 1986).

During years of growth and change throughout our life, the self satisfies our need for continuity and stability. Michael Schwalbe writes: "The real value of the self lies . . . in the stability and adaptability it gives us. It enables us to respond effectively to familiar and to new stimuli without undergoing radical changes, most of the time. The self thus enhances the autopoietic (i.e. self-renewing) capacities of the human organism. It does so by adaptively modulating our rhythms of energy dissipation" (1992:287). In Schwalbe's view, the self is a manifestation of energy-flows through the body and of information captured by these flows. The self continually renews itself and maintains what seems to be a steady state by managing the energy and information flow it draws from the environment.

The self, however also has the capacity to transform itself to higher, more complex forms. Glenn Perry describes "an inherent self-organizing tendency operative in the psyche which pushes it toward progressive differentiation and integration of system components; that is the psyche has an intrinsic need to evolve from states of lower to states of higher complexity" (1993:236). Schwalbe strengthens this point. He views the self as a nonlinear dynamical system, that can self-organize its own evolution and change dramatically. "This is not simply because new experiences, new imagery, and new grammars gradually alter the way the impulsive phase of the self is modulated. It is because the self acts iteratively on the information it generates, such that even minor changes, occurring at the right moment, can be amplified throughout the system and launch it into a qualitatively different state. Thus by virtue of its nature the self can sometimes radically transform itself" (1992:287).

Thus the circle is closed. Individuals facing the stresses of a chaotic transition era may self-organize their self and psyche to a higher more complex level of functioning and behavior.

11
Transforming Ourselves

THE PASSAGE TO THE NEW PERSON

The present stressful uncertain environment and the conditions of the coming era demand a new person. Moving toward a new era, novel ways of functioning may emerge predominantly among young people of new generations, born into and growing up in a world of intensified uncertainty and stress. This may happen less to generations that matured in the industrial era. They may be too attached to their old forms of being and conceptualizing. Individuals may come to novel ways of functioning after breakdowns and painful transitions or following and pursuing futile escape routes. They may transform their behavior after finding that ways of adaptation, such as stress reduction and healthy living, while helpful and positive, are alone insufficient to deal with the rising levels of uncertainty and stress they must face.

Personal transformations probably will not come all at once. Some people may change one aspect of their selves, others may experiment with another. Some attempts may be dead ends. But at some point the different elements will probably coalesce creating a variety of different types of people, whose personality makeups enable them to function in the uncertain environment and the coming era.

Co-transformation of Individuals and Society

The transformation of individuals and societies to higher, more complex ways of functioning will be a parallel interactive process between the social and individual level. Societies will self-organize themselves changing individuals and their relationships. Individuals will self-organize themselves into new identities and ways of relating and thus affect the cultures of their societies.

Chris Langton of the Santa Fe Institute describes the way in which the two levels affect one another: "From the interaction of the individual components . . . emerges some kind of global property . . . something you couldn't have predicted from what you know of the component parts. And the global property, this emergent behavior, feeds back to influence the behavior of the individuals . . . that produced it" (Lewin:1992:12-13). The two, society and individuals, will mutually affect one another, thus coevolving together. This is a process of co-transformation. Natural selection will encourage the growth and survival of societies where many individuals have self-organized themselves into higher, more complex ways of functioning. Societies that have developed cultures that are benevolent to the growth of these new ways of being, will both have higher survival rates and create the conditions that further encourage personal transformations that are more adaptive.

HUMAN SYSTEMS AS COMPLEX ADAPTIVE SYSTEMS

Individuals, organizations, societies and the global human society are what the Santa Fe Institute calls "complex adaptive systems." They are not only complex, but they are also adaptive systems. As adaptive systems they have an inherent ability to self-organize themselves into forms that can survive and develop in a changing environment. The new forms they self-organize themselves into have emergent properties that include the ability to anticipate the future based on internal models.

At the institute, biologists, anthropologists, computer scientists, economists and researchers from other sciences are working together to capture the essence of complex adaptive systems. They are building computer simulations, mathematical tools and theoretical models that try to clarify the principles that underlie the functioning of these systems. In doing this they are also beginning to develop a new understanding of evolution itself and within it the intertwining processes of emergence and adaption.

The Characteristics of Complex Adaptive Systems

Mitchell Waldrop reports of a lecture given by John Holland at the Santa Fe Institute. Holland describes complex adaptive systems as being everywhere in the world and including all kinds of systems from brains through ant colonies and human societies of all kinds.

Each of these systems consists of a network of component systems constantly mutually affecting each other. These systems consists of many agents acting together. They may be nerve cells in the brain or individuals in an economy. Each component continually affects and is affected by the others.

These mutually interacting agents are not centrally controlled; patterns arise from their interaction. There is no component that controls all other components. The coherent behavior of the system as a whole develops from the interactions of competition and cooperation between the components.

Each level serves as building blocks for the next level. Just as a group of cells will create a tissue, a group of workers will form a work team, and so on at all levels and in all kinds of complex adaptive systems.

A basic mechanism of adaption of these systems is that they are constantly reorganizing themselves. They are all the time reorganizing themselves into new patterns. Nations will constantly readjust their relations with other nations.

They anticipate the future. The anticipation of insecurity in an area may deter a person from taking a vacation there. All living creatures have such predictions encoded in their genes and in their brains.

The predictions are based on changing internal models. Internal models of what the world is like serve as a basis for prediction. These models are constantly being changed and modified as a result of experience.

New possibilities and opportunities are always being created by the system thus developing constant novelty. Each system is able to fill a variety of niches and there is place for all kinds of systems in this world. When niches are filled they create openings for other niches. Everything is in constant changing process. A final optimal state is never reached because this is always in relation to other systems that are in a permanent flux. (Waldrop 1992)

THE NEW SELF

With the characteristics of complex adaptive systems, societies and individuals have the capacity to transform themselves their behavior, and relationships so as to create the novelty needed for the changed conditions. Change will come. Yet, as in all transitions to a new transformative stage of complexity, it is impossible to predict what exact form the next stage will take. The future is open and on the way to a new era many unexpected things can happen and numerous unforeseen developments may emerge.

It is feasible, however, to try to begin to discern the vague outlines of some of the elements that might possibly interact to create the composition of the new person that cannot only cope with, but also thrive in a state of growing complexity and uncertainty. A number of elements that in some combination might be among the interacting building blocks of the new person would include: evolutionary consciosness, functioning at the edge of chaos, evolutionary learning, accepting uncertainty, constructing beliefs, creating ourselves, the mutable self, dis-identification, the observing self, and enhanced creativity. These elements attempt to discern the kinds of human personality traits and behaviors that might evolve out of the development of higher levels of evolutionary consciousness. The emergent properties of the whole that will arise from their interrelations cannot be forseen.

Evolutionary Consciousness

Evolutionary consciousness might be the binding pattern tying the various elements into one pattern. Evolutionary systems theory and the other New Sciences may provide individuals and societies with the consciousness needed for this stage of human interconnectedness. Individuals and societies in coevolution may self-create themselves into new forms that enable them to cope with the novel planetary conditions. They may become conscious of their mutual responsibility for human survival. "When translated into the context of a social system, self-organization implies that conscious learning on an individual and systems level can take place. Such coevolutionary learning can provide the conditions for the participants of the system to creatively help it evolve into new forms" (Bach 1993:108).

Evolutionary consciousness is born out of humans' ability to self-reflect and observe themselves. Human beings have a metability to be conscious of their consciousness, to be aware of their awareness, to learn about their learning, and to evolve their own evolution. These are metabilities in the sense that they are a higher level of functioning. Evolutionary consciousness will be returned to in the final chapter.

Functioning at the Edge of Chaos

Research going on at Santa Fe Institute by theoretical biologist Stuart Kauffman, artificial life researcher Chris Langton, and others focuses on the way complex adaptive systems function in the state called "the edge of chaos" mentioned in former chapters. The edge of chaos is at the transition phase of coupled systems between order and chaos. This is a phase, where on the one hand, the systems are not coupled together too tightly, and on the other hand, their coupling is not too weak. Numerous experiments with sandpiles or computer simulations of interactive changes of components of a system and coevolving interdependent species bring up the same findings.

When couplings between the components or between systems are too tight, any change in strategy of one system, or any outside perturbation can cascade the system into a random, dynamic, supercritical deeply chaotic state. On the other hand if the couplings are too weak and sparse, there will be little interdependence, no coevolution, and little change. This is an ordered static, subcritical state.

In an interview with Russell Ruthens, Kauffman claims that "It turns out that in a wide variety of coupled systems the highest mean fitness is at the phase transition. By selecting an appropriate strategy, organisms tune their coupling to their environment to whatever value suits them best." Kauffman says that "if they adjust the coupling to their own advantage . . . they will reach the boundary between order and randomness--the regime of peak average fitness. The bold hypothesis is that complex adaptive systems adapt to and on the edge of chaos." Kauffman declares that "It now begins to appear that systems in the complex regime can carry out and coordinate the most complex behavior, can adapt most readily and can build the most useful models of their environments" (1993: 117).

Kauffman gives an analogy of an ordered static state from human systems. It is as if everybody is caught in the foothills, and there is no possibility to get out in the direction of the crest. In organizations, it's like if the jobs are differentiated and specialized so that no one has any freedom beyond what he is told to do. If people were granted more latitude it would benefit both them and the organization. On the other hand if the people are together in an organization in a chaotic state each works at cross purposes with the others and the organization as a whole is not effective (Waldrop 1992).

Chris Langton says that the edge of chaos is where information gets the upper hand over energy. A system at the edge of chaos gains more control and it also obtains the possibility that information processing becomes an important feature of the system's dynamics (Waldrop 1992). In terms of behavioral and social science, the edge of chaos raises many intuitive associations and ideas of human systems that are not chaotic, yet are open, resilient, and creative to a degree that matches the constant novelty of their environment. This is the state where a person or an organization has a large range of behaviors to choose from in adapting to environmental variety and turbulence. It is a condition where the systems' components never quite settle into stability and also do not dissolve into a state of chaos and turbulence. It is the range where life has sufficient stability to maintain itself and also the degree of creativity and novelty to deserve being called life.

As suggested in a former chapter, in human systems, it might also be a state where a climate of mutual responsibility and cooperation matches the degree of interdependence and braidedness of the systems components or between systems. At the individual level, this is very much in accordance with Gestalt therapy

understanding of the need of components of the self to mutually accept one
another (Perls 1976).

Evolutionary Learning

An essential element of developing the competencies that enhance the ability
to evolve with the turbulent environment is evolutionary learning. Our present
form of learning is maintenance learning. Alfonso Montuori writes that
maintenance learning "is not self-reflective. It is incapable of questioning its
own assumptions and of engaging in change but 'more of the same.' Unable to
question its own origins and guiding framework, maintenance learning allows us
to learn only within a preestablished framework, but does not allow for free
enquiry" (1993:189). Comparing this to evolutionary learning: "Content and
storage are clearly the major issue for maintenance learning. . . . The focus of
our entire educational thrust shifts as we attempt to foster a capacity rather than
fill a container with information" (p.197).

Bela Banathy (1993) points out that evolutionary learning empowers us to
shape change. It assists us in overcoming our fears of uncertainty and in creating
our world. It allows us to reexamine and renew our viewpoints and enables us to
redesign our systems often at higher levels of complexity. Evolutionary learning
allows us to predict and deal with unexpected situations. It will further our
advance from adaptation to changes in the environment to conscious coevolution
with it. Banathy compares evolutionary learning to our current form of learning.
He points out that maintenance learning hinders the development of evolutionary
competence. Maintenance learning is dealing with fixed and known outlooks
and methods and maintaining the status quo. This kind of learning is necessary
to maintain society but is insufficient alone. "In times of rapid and massive
changes, turbulence and discontinuity--characteristic of our era--such learning
should be complemented by another type of learning, which is even more
important and essential at the current evolutionary stage of our society. We can
call this learning innovative and 'creating' learning or evolutionary
learning"(1993:76).

Banathy describes the possible curriculum of such learning as including
understanding and knowledge about evolution and the individual's role in it;
nurturing values such as cooperation, trust, benevolence, altruism, love, and
harmony; fostering self-realization, social, and ecological ethics; developing
cooperative group interaction skills; competence in systems thinking to be able
to work with complexity; and the nurturing of creativity and systems design.
Evolutionary learning is an important element in developing evolutionary
competence. In human systems, evolutionary learning might be an essential
element of functioning at the edge of chaos. It might be the foundation on which
human systems can develop the evolutionary competencies which enable them to
function effectively at the edge of chaos.

Accepting Uncertainty

The ability to function in a world that is full of surprises is enhanced by knowing it is so, accepting it as such, and also being aware of its positive contributions. The ability to accept uncertainty and tolerate ambiguity might become an essential aspect of a personality that has to deal with an unpredictable environment.

Seeking to ensure certainty in a world suffused with uncertainty is a hopeless undertaking. To be able to maintain their mental and emotional well-being, people will need to accept the reality of uncertainty, unpredictability, and the unexpected. Margeret Wheatley writes that "we must live with the strange and the bizarre, even as we climb stairs that we want to bring us to a clearer vantage point. Every step requires that we stay comfortable with uncertainty and confident of confusion's role" (1992:151).

Accepting uncertainty includes the ability to be in confusion and to accept that confusion as a necessary element in the process of interacting with a nonlinear world. This is not easy as people yearn for a measure of certainty in their ongoing relations with the ideas, people, and objects they interact with. As Margeret Wheatley writes: "I've become aware of how difficult it is not to be certain. I've encountered, in myself and others, a desire for these new understandings to translate quickly into reliable trusty tools and techniques. We are not comfortable with chaos, even in our thoughts, and we want to move out of confusion as quickly as possible" (p. 149). The chaos of confusion may be an essential stage on the way to new understandings, just as the transition phase of chaos is an inevitable bridge between the old order and the new.

Accepting uncertainty means learning to live in a world that is not clear-cut but suffused with ambiguity. Ambiguity is uncertainty of meaning. An ambiguous illustration is one that might mean either this or that. A nonlinear world is full of ambiguity as fractal objects can be seen in different ways. The doctor can also be acting in a parental manner. Is he or she now doctor or parent? Boundaries are not clear and objects can be viewed and understood from multiple viewpoints without one canceling the other out. Even polarities, such as attraction and repulsion, can coexist in relationships without one excluding the other.

Accepting uncertainty necessitates an ability to live with ambivalence such as having both negative and positive sentiments with regard to the same object. Ambivalence is uncertainty of value. People as a rule prefer a clear-cut attitude. Ambivalence may paralyze action because liking something leads to approaching it; disliking it leads to retreating. Living in a nonlinear world means that the same object may be felt or valued differently depending where it is on the route to chaos.

Accepting uncertainty entails giving up the hope of finding the final right answers. It is knowing that reality always changes and human beings take part in this changing which never ends. "I haven't stopped wanting someone, somewhere to return with the right answers. But I know that my hopes are old, based on a different universe. In this new world, you and I make it up as we go along, not because we lack expertise or planning skills, but because that is the nature of reality. Reality changes shape and meaning because of our activity. And it is constantly new. We are required to be there, as active participants (Wheatley 1992:151). This will not happen without us doing it and noone can do it instead of us.

Accepting uncertainty can be assisted by seeing uncertainty in a different light and by reframing uncertainty in a positive mode. A linearly ordered world is a world with no choices, and everything is predetermined. Nonlinearity and uncertainty open the gates to choice. Nonlinear dynamics are far more widespread and much more open to choice among uncertain futures. For many human goals and purposes varying degrees of nonlinearity are helpful.

Constructing Beliefs

An uncertain world is a world in which it is difficult to survive believing in one objective reality existing out there independently of people observing it. Sticking to irrefutable absolute beliefs is going to make life difficult in a world of relentless, discontinuous, unpredictable change. Living in a chaotic fractal world necessitates people recognizing the part they themselves play in constructing their own beliefs.

The length of England's coastline depends on the measuring instrument whether it is in units of miles or inches. Science has moved from an objective view of reality to a recognition of the place of the observer in creating that reality. A constructivist approach fits a world habitated by fractal forms that fill only a part of the space they occupy.

H. Anderson, H. Goolishian and L. Windermand (1986) of the Galveston Family Institute, write about the shift in thinking regarding the nature of reality that shakes our beliefs in the world as being composed of stable structures and properties existing independently of the observer. Our act of observing the world changes it. The world is no longer the world of observed systems. It has become the world of observing systems. This is a world in which the very act of observation itself changes that which is observed. We exist in a world where there is no distinction or separation betwen the observed and the observer.

Many scientific papers have been published lately which espouse "this growing position regarding the influence of the observing system in the creation of what is called knowledge, understanding, and reality. The basic constructivist position is that we do not discover reality or scientific fact. Thus, in the family therapy field we do not discover the structure or reality of families. Rather we invent the families we work with, just as we invent ourselves. We are, as they are, creatures of the mind" (p. 4).

A constructivist position shakes the belief in a world composed of stable properties existing independent from people's observations. There is no one single objective world out there independent of people knowing it. There are as many worlds as minds can create. "There is no single objective reality about a family and its problem waiting to be discovered. There are multiverses, each valid in its own right. None of these exists independent of the observer." We participate in the creation of all that we know. "The constructivist view holds that all knowledge, including scientific fact, is a construction of mind in the social domain" (Anderson et al. 1986:4). Psychologist George Kelly (1955) believed that there was nothing so obvious that its appearance was not altered when seen in a different light. Whatever exists can be reconstrued. We are not living in one universe, but in multiverses, each of which gives us a different angle from which to see things.

The major contention of constructivism is that our hypotheses about the world are not provable. Scientific hypotheses persist for two reasons: utility--we find them useful, and because no one has yet either disproved them or come up with a better hypothesis. Hypotheses that persist over time, are part of a temporarily acceptable working framework. Kelly said that none of today's constructions, which are our means of portraying reality, are perfect and, as the history of human thought repeatedly suggests, none is final.

The knowledge that human beings participate in creating their beliefs does not mean that anything goes. Belief constructions need to be tested by rubbing with reality, including other people's beliefs. We are not alone in this world and our shared beliefs and language distinctions with others are what become our realities.

The world that people create is created in language through which they communicate to others and themselves. Believing you are the pope is like ignoring a car that might run you over, because it is "a construction of your beliefs." This is a dangerous and misguided interpretation of the fact that people take part in constructing their realities through the social medium of language and there are many such realities, each of which might be as valid as the other.

One should not look for truth but for fit in our attempts to understand the world. From a constructivist view, it is not possible to match our perceptions with items in the environment; what is important is that they fit sufficiently to ensure our ongoing viability. Survival means the ability not to collide with the environment and to be able to elude its constraints. In order to be among the survivors, an adaptive system has to get by the constraints that the environment creates.

An uncertain, unpredictable environment is one to which a person must constantly find a fit. There are many ways to fit, none of which is the only one or the correct one. An uncertain universe is a fractal multiverse that can be seen and construed in many ways that may be equally valid because they are equally functional to human needs. Retaining a belief system in one immutable, objective reality, which is independent of people observing it, will make life an extremely hazardous undertaking in a world of growing unpredictability and fractal forms.

Creating Ourselves

To cope with uncertainty, paople will need to enhance their inherent self-creating nature. All living things by the very act of living are creatures that create themselves. As long as they are alive they are in a never-ending process of regeneration. They are continually replacing the cells in their body. They are physically not the same body they were a few years ago. The plant creates itself and builds itself from the seedling. This property of living things was named by the Chilean biologist, Humberto Maturana (1980) "autopoiesis" which means self creation. Working with Francisco Varela, Maturana wrote that this was a word without a history that described the organization of the living, without falling into the always-gapping trap of not saying anything new because the language does not permit it.

The materials of the physical world, machines and computers do not create themselves. Machines and computers are created by people; they are allopoietic--they are other created. They can do only what men planned and intended them to do. When they break down, people have to mend them; they cannot renew and create themselves. A living thing has the marvelous quality of continually creating its parts from the seed. It is always changing its elements, allowing itself to continually renew, heal, regenerate, and recreate itself.

Human beings are autopoietic entities whose behavior is structurally determined. All living (autopoietic) systems are structurally determined. This means that they can only do what their structure allows them to do. The structure means the components of the system and the interaction between them. Most birds are not structured to swim and cannot swim. The structure changes throughout the life span, and can continually enhance and change its capacities. Nevertheless the structure at a particular time fixes the limits of its possibilities. A washing machine cannot make toast.

People cannot learn in the sense of a teacher passing on to them packets of knowledge. A person's structure determines what he will learn and make a part of himself. After a series of experiments on perception that gained him worldwide recognition, Maturana argued against "the fallacy of instructive interaction." He showed that in people's interactions with the environment they do not acquire a direct representation of it; it is not mapped onto the nervous system.

Because human interaction is always through the activity of the entire nervous system, the representations of outer reality do not assume the nature of mapping. People can only hear sounds of an amplitude that their hearing and neuronal network, allows them to hear. All that humans observe depends upon their act of observation and the criteria that they put into use to distinguish those observations. Maturana and Valera's research strengthens the constructivist position of the impossibility of separating ourselves, the observers, from that which we observe. We participate in creating our reality. There is not one single reality, but as many realities as there are observers. Some may be more functional for their observers than others.

A living system is autonomous in the sense of self law. It maintains its identity, that is, its wholeness, and its ability for renewal under conditions of never-ending change. It is affected by outside perturbations to the degree that its structure determines. The autonomous system organizes itself and renews itself; it constantly self-produces itself. It retains its identity in the face of constant environmental change through its flexibility, mobility and ability to learn. It can and does change its measurable properties while maintaining its identity and autonomy.

The evolutionary principle of self-organization embodies two key ideas: the idea of a consistent identity and the idea of dynamic variations essential for its continuous viability. These two aspects of systemic behavior are entirely compatible, expressing the facts that notions of stability and adaptive behavior revolve around maintaining a balance between constancy and steady state on the one hand and between change and variability and reorganizaton on the other. (Wailand 1993:145)

Autopoiesis enables the individual to maintain his identity over time while changing and transforming himself to adapt to the changing environment. While human beings are by their very biologic nature autonomous and self-creating, they are generally not aware of this and do not invest themselves in enhancing this in their belief system, their basic view of the world, and in their behavior and the social systems they create. Their growth and capacity to deal with turbulent change depends on people's freedom to act unchained by belief in an objective, independent reality.

Maturana sees the shift to a position in which people put objectivity in parenthesis as not a mere shift of emphasis, but as a change that involves a fundamental change in human responsibility. Believing in an objective reality without parenthesis may lie at the very foundation of a domination/control attitude to one's environment.

Maturana writes that the operating rule of modern human societies is the concession of power under the assumption that he or she who has knowledge of an objective independent reality has an intrinsic right to it. If we believe that we can characterise things as they intrinsically are, because we are viewing them objectively, then we have the right to correct the other for his errors, or to punish, control and dominate him.

The Mutable Self

Chaos in the external world can lead to internal chaos. The individual may lose his own integrated identity in the maelstrom of floating pieces of identity which he absorbs from others. The person's belief in himself as a singular integrated autonomous identity may break down under the stress of aggravating internal conflicts. Facing the acceleration of change, proliferation of uncertainty and rise in stress levels, the individual is driven to changing the basic conception of his self. The self, which is the bedrock that absorbs all these changes may itself go through a transformation to seeing itself as in constant process.

One can see one's self as something stable or as in constant change. Louis Zurcher of the University of Texas writes that accelerated sociocultural change can influence modification in the self-concept of adapting individuals. This modification is a shift from orientation toward stability of self in terms of seeing the self as an object to orientation, toward seeing the self as a process. Zurcher regards the centrality of change (process) within the adapting individual's personality as the basis for a new kind of self, that he calls the *mutable self.*

Zurcher conducted long-term research in the United States and points out that "dissatisfaction with self as object is increasing among people in contemporary American society. Societal changes are accelerating, including changes in social structures, to the point where people cannot successfully identify fully with them, since the structures themselves are unstable. Consequently, in such cases self as object is not adaptive; self as process is, with certain qualifications" (1977:27-28).

The mutable self is a self view which affords the individual full recognition of the different components or aspects of his self; an openness to "the widest possible experience of self"; the flexibility to move between different components of the self; the ability to integrate the different components of the self and "to accept the productive dialectic among them"; and "the ability to accommodate, control, or resist rapid sociocultural change and its concomitants, without the necessity for affecting defensive stances in, or denial of any of the . . . components of the self" (1977:35-36).

Summarizing the characterization of the twenty-first century in literature prepared by futurists, Zurcher enumerates its components in terms of impermanence, transcience, ephemerality, marginality, instability, novelty, and value-conflict. He suggests that in the midst of this vortex of changes, the individual will organize his life around transcience, to have the ability to endure discontinuities and disjunctions, and to be able to withstand ego-flooding from an environment exploding with sensory stimulation. His personality will have begun to become change-oriented. The twenty-first century individual will live in an uncertain environment not being rendered ineffective by rapid change. Transition, ambiguity, or uncertainty can be tolerated, accepted, accomodated, modified, or controlled as the person best sees fit.

Kenneth Gergen (1991) describes a similar phenomena as a "populating of the self, the acquisition of multiple and disparate potentials for being." The chaotic environment, which Gergen sees as processes of social saturation, exposes people to a wide range of persons, new forms of relationships, unique circumstances and opportunities, and intensities of emotion. With social saturation, each of us comes to harbor a vast potential of hidden potentials, disparate aspects of ourselves that we can assume as our identity.

Zurcher sees the capacity to express manifold competing potentials as contributing to adaptation. He suggests that orientation to change and the ability to shift among self concepts is typical of the mutable self. Nevertheless, people who manifest mutability paradoxically also manifest stability, consistency, and adaptation. A person's self-perception rises to a level of abstraction that includes the physical, social, and other functions of self. The person is aware that it is he who is experiencing each different mode. This kind of self seems to have remarkable freedom together with great adaptability.

Dis-Identification

The stable, consistent, adaptive aspect of the mutable self may be enhanced by the ability to disidentify. Identifying oneself completely with one's role as a General Motors assembly engineer can cause deep trouble if General Motors closes plants and lays off many employees, you included. In times of an accelerating rate of unpredictable discontinuous changes throughout a person's lifetime, being totally identified with a sub-personality, a role, an occupation, a way of life, an emotion, or an aspect of identity can be a heavy burden. The same may be said of complete unknowing identification with something exterior, such as a person, an organization, a value system, or an ideology. Identification of this nature makes something exterior a part of oneself without a person's full awareness.

Piero Ferrucci, of the Psychosynthesis Institute of Florence, Italy, describes the difficult side of identification; people identify with feelings, desires, opinions, roles, and body. If a person identifies himself with an idea which he particularly cherishes and then that idea is proved to be wrong, the person feels that he is wrong. If you equate identity with the role of a businessperson, then when that role ceases to be, you may feel that your sense of being is diminished or annulled.

Since all the contents of consciousness change and at some moment inevitably cease to be, identification with any of them inevitably leads to death of some kind. . . . As long as we are identified with sensations, feelings, desires, thoughts, it is as if our sense of being were sewed onto them, and therefore they can submerge us, control us, limit our perception of the world, and block the availability of all other feelings, sensations, desires, and opinions. (1982:62)

Ferrucci does not suggest that people should not identify with what they awaringly wish to identify with. He warns about unawaring identification. He suggests practicing dis-identification which is to detach our consciousness from the states that mold it. He writes that people have a tendency to identify with a subpersonality and come to believe that they are it. Dis-identification consists of pulling oneself out of this illusion. People can then awaringly make choices with what and when to identify; "dis-identification does not prevent us from subsequently identifying with any aspect of ourselves, if we so choose. On the contrary, this ability is expanded. What we want to avoid is a continual, unknowing identification with any random process of our personality. This latter kind of identification always brings a thickening or freezing of some sort" (p. 63).

Describing the process of dis-identification, clinical psychologist and author Frances Vaughan writes that if a person is disidentified from emotions, she is no longer the victim of emotions beyond control. "This does not mean one does not have emotions. On the contrary, the more one is willing to be fully aware of subjective experience the better one can see how it is actively created. When one is relatively unconscious and unaware of inner experiences, then thoughts, feelings, and sensations seem to just happen" (1985:44).

Vaughan suggests that dis-identification gives persons access to a large range of possibilities. "Healthy dis-identification implies mastery, in contrast to dissociation, wherein the range of available experiences is diminished and one remains confined to a very restricted portion of potential being, out of touch with both subjective and objective reality" (p. 44). Psychiatrist R. Assiogli (1973) notes that we are dominated by every thing with which we become identified. We can have some control over everything from which we disidentify.

A self-identity, which is built on the basis of strong, unconscious identifications with a small number of select characters or roles, is going to have major difficulties, in turbulent times of growing uncertainty that demand the ability to frequently change roles and character and activate different subpersonalities. Fritz Perls (1976), the father of Gestalt therapy, says that the ego becomes pathological if its identifications are permanent ones instead of having the ability to function according to the requirements of different situations. The ability to disidentify may be an essential ingredient of a person's ability to function effectively at the edge of chaos. The ability to disidentify allows a person to escape bondage to one set of behaviors and gives him the freedom of choice of a variety of behavioral options.

The Observing Self

A mutable self and dis-identification are enhanced by the ability to create a calm center and develop an observing self. Ferrucci speaks about the ability to be centered like a flame which is not blown out or like a place which remains quiet while outside it is very noisy. From this center it is possible to disidentify and make choices. From this center, we can choose to be in this subpersonality or that. We need to attain flexibility so as not to be dominated by subpersonalities while not suffocating their expression and ignoring their needs.

When you drive your car you do so unconsciously, most of the time hardly aware of what you are doing. When you eat a meal and your mind wanders away to thoughts about your work or some problem that is bothering you, you completely forget that you are eating. You may be watching a drama on television and be totally involved in the narrative. In all of these cases you were not aware of what you were doing. You had lost yourself, your center.

It is natural that internal functions such as the flow of the blood through the body should go on automatically, without awareness. But most of people's everyday behavior is also performed automatically, without their being aware of what they are doing and without their being aware of themselves. When you are doing something like taking a walk in a park or in nature, you probably will be thinking about something else that concerns you. You will have lost the enjoyment of walking among the trees and flowers and will have lost awareness of yourself. This level of consciousness may be sufficient for functioning in a slowly changing, predictable environment. When regularity, steadiness, and stability are predominant, people may possibly get by at this level of awareness.

An environment of turbulence and discontinuous change may necessitate functioning at a higher level of awareness. Humans may need to accustom themselves to everyday functioning at a level of consciousness that is suited to an uncertain environment. This would necessitate their being able to maintain a state of consciousness of being fully aware of what they are engaged in within the environment together with a hold on their self as the focal point from which to decide in what to engage. This entails awareness of awareness and also enables both dis-identication and conscious identification and adaptability of the self.

Being fully aware entails maintaining consciousness focused awaringly in two directions simultaneously: on what one is engaged in with the environment and on the self that is observing the activity. When eating one is focused on the activity of eating and not being preoccupied by something else. At the same time one is keeping a part of consciousness aware of the self who is observing what one is doing.

Writing on evolutionary design, Judy Bach (1993) states that the inward shift happens as the knower becomes aware of himself in the act of knowing. Human beings are the only creatures who have this ability. When a person is unawaringly completely immersed in what he is doing and not aware of himself, he is in a state of consciousness that may be called "waking sleep." Most people are in this state of consciousness a great part of their waking life and they see it as natural.

A student immersed in her studies is lost in the task. The student lacks the separated awareness, the sense of two, of observer and observed. The everyday state of "waking sleep" can be contrasted to a higher level of consciousness in which a person maintains awareness of what she is doing and of herself. This state of maintaining a part of consciousness observing the activity one is engaged in with the environment is sometimes called "The Witness." It is that which is capable of observing the flow of what is without interfering with it, reacting to it, or manipulating it. The Witness quietly observes the stream of events inside and outside the mind and the body in a detached manner. The Witness can watch any content of a person's psyche or any activity he is engaged in without being caught up in its atmosphere, feeling tone, stress, tension, and problems.

As the human world moves into a period of transition and uncertainty typified by chaos and aggravated stress, people may have no option other than to acquire the ability to center themselves by maintaining a focal part of themselves separated from the turbulence around them and remain capable of inner quiet. From this part they may observe the tumult around them accepting what is, without getting caught up in the confusion and uncertainty that rages. At the same time they may awaringly choose what they wish to do and engage in that with full awareness.

Enhanced Creativity

Times of transition and chaos are times of predominance of novelty over confirmation. New conditions, unfamiliar situations, unexpected events are often the rule and not the exception. In regular times there is a measure of balance between novelty and confirmation. In periods of intensifying uncertainty, novelty gains the upper hand. People are faced with an endless succession of new situations to which they are not accustomed and for which they may have no ready response or solution.

Complex adaptive systems have the ability to create perpetual novelty. To enhance this ability humanity will need to learn more about the relationship between chaos and creativity in the human brain. Both chaos and creativity appear to have common roots. Creativity is often the result of the juxtaposition of two completely foreign frames of reference. Arthur Koestler (1979) sees the creative act as selecting, reshuffling, combining, synthesizing "already existing facts, ideas, faculties, skills." It is often the result of bringing together two or more completely distinct and separate contexts or frames of reference. Chaos flings together existing components that were far apart to create a new state.

W. Freeman of Berkeley University, and C. Skarda, of the Polytechnical School in Paris research the relationship between the brain and chaos. They say that chaos provides us with a state of not knowing in which new activity patterns can be generated. When the brain is in a chaotic state, it is more easily able to switch patterns. The chaotic background state provides the system with openness and readiness to respond to novel as well as familiar inputs. The normal background neural activity of the brain is chaotic and chaos keeps the brain in a ready state, so as to be able to accept new inputs (Bower 1988).

Neuroscientist Paul Rapp has reported that the brain functions normally and at its best in a chaotic state. He has come to the conclusion that chaos may actually be most beneficial during problem solving. A person may want to be able to scan as wide a range of solutions as possible and avoid locking on to a suboptimal solution early on. Rapp says that one way to do this is to have a certain amount of disorderliness, or turbulence, in the search. The randomness of the brain's activity taps the sources of creative ability (McAuliffe 1990).

These are times that call for man's most creative potential. Increasing novelty necessitates enhanced creativity. The measure of human creative ability must fit the degree of increasing novelty in the environment. At the moment it appears to be lagging. Orenstein and Ehrlich (1990) estimate that "human judgement and humanity's ability to deal with the consequences of its creations lags behind its ability to create." At the end of the industrial age, there is a mismatch between the human mind and the real world. The mismatch interferes both with the relationships of people to each other and their relationship with their environment.

An age of chaos demands the release of the hidden reserves of creativity lying untapped within mankind. Most estimates are that people utilize no more than 5 percent of their creative potential. Human beings have unbounded creative resources within them that can still be marshaled to meet the challenge of unprecedented novelty and growing uncertainty.

Transformations in Organizations and Communities

Uncertainty is bringing people to create new kinds of organizations and communities. Novel forms of organization, different organizational cultures, and new ways of leadership are developing to cope with a world of accelerating change complexity, and uncertainty.

Organizations are moving away from:

- rigid structures to changing structures
- one right way of organizing to many varied forms of organization
- sharply defined boundaries to fractal changing boundaries

- defined forms of membership to different ways of connection
- hierarchies to networks
- central control to semi-autonomous units
- competitiveness or cooperation to new combinations of both
- a control dominator approach to a self-organizing approach
- management by authority to associative management
- directing employees to empowering autonomous creative individuals and teams
- the orderly management of change to building changeability in the organization
- indifference to coevolution with the social and natural environment
- always maintaining linear order to knowing when to encourage fluctuations and transformations
- preserving regularity and certainty to encouraging nonlinear forms of creativity and novelty
- striving to maintain linear stability to functioning at the edge of chaos
- organizational maintenance learning to inbuilt evolutionary learning
- strategic planning to evolutionary system design
- striving to attain objectives and goals to creating an evolutionary vision of the future
- male dominance to cocreation
- seeing people only as serving organizational purposes to forms of relationship that encourage mutual aid and caring
- extremities in differences of status to differentiated but less polarized status differences
- focusing on economic competence to focusing on evolutionary competence.

All of the above and many other new developments in organizations and communities deserve a wide and more thorough treatment that is beyond the scope of this book. Appropriate changes in the identity and self of individuals will assist them in coping with uncertainty and the stress of a world of intensifying crises and problems. Possibly, however, the coming era may ease the tensions and stress by dampening the severity of some of the major issues that are creating turbulence at the end of this century. The following chapter will examine this possibility.

12
The Coming Era

EXPECTATIONS OF THE COMING ERA

Chapter 8 dealt with humanity's present predicament of being caught in the chaotic transition period between two eras. Based on a Prigoginian viewpoint, our times were described as being a turbulent turning point in the transformation of civilization on the threshold of a new age. The coming era was depicted as certainly more complex but with having the potential of resolving some of the pathologies that led to the breakdown of the existing era. The transition period might not be short and easy. Like other chaotic shifts of eras in the history of mankind, it will probably be arduous, difficult, and painful. But this time it is also dangerous.

What Is Desirable Is Not Inevitable

There can be no assurance that the coming era will fulfill the hopes of an optimistic humanistic viewpoint. There have been a number of books describing the characteristics of the coming era in terms of a better world people would all wish to live in. But one must be careful not to confuse human wishes and goals with what may happen in reality.

Despite an urgent need, change in a humanly desirable direction may not be taking place at all, or may be taking place at such a rate so as to be irrelevant. Mankind's belief in its happening may lead into complacent inactive passivity. People need hope, but making an ideology of social change taking a benevolent direction deflects energy from what needs to be done. Hopefully the coming era will ease some of humanity's problems. But one should heed the warning not to confuse the desirable with the inevitable.

Possibilities but Not Certainties

There have been a number of books and much research done on the coming age. Despite the scholarly work and intellectual effort, the human race cannot know for sure what the future holds for much of the picture is still hidden in the mist of chaos. At points of bifurcation, prediction is basically impossible. What is possible, is to attempt to discern some of the elements of the future, knowing that their integration into a new composite unity will yield an emergent novel quality to the coming era. The elements themselves are possibilities and not certainties. They are educated guesses, often based on observing developing trends and the desire to alleviate pressing problems.

At the Santa Fe Institute, speaking about some of the needed transitions to a more "sustainable" world, Nobel Laureate Murray Gell-Mann with R. A. Millikan and R. Maxwell (1990) make the point that to understand the needed transitions it is necessary to treat the subjects as strongly interconnected. In dealing with a complex nonlinear dynamical system, one cannot describe the behavior of the system by putting together its separate pieces. One needs to take a look at the whole pattern, while taking into account the interactions among its various parts.

Therefore together with a short summary of areas of concern it is worth attempting to take a look at the whole picture--that is the underlying basic pattern binding all the various elements together. From that viewpoint we can examine the possibility that the coming era will be able to alleviate some of the present metaproblems.

THE ERAS OF HUMAN HISTORY

As mentioned previously, humanity is in the transition period between the third and the fourth era in history. It is in the midst of chaotic transformation of the third major epoch of human civilization into its fourth epoch.

The major sources of energy of the industrialized era were the natural deposits of energy such as coal and oil. The industrial era is an era of unprecedented use of energy. It might also be named the high energy industrial era. But as noted before, the intensified use of these limited deposits is leading to their depletion within the foreseeable future. The high energy industrial era is drawing to a close. About 40 or 50 years ago, after the Second World War, the industrial nations of the world began the first steps in the painful transition to the next epoch in human history--the fourth era.

At the turn of the century mankind in the modern world is in the midst of the transition to the fourth era. It is a chaotic, wild, stormy transition that is causing havoc in social and individual lives. It is creating uncertainty in all the domains of human life. We may assume that we are the final generation of an old era and still not yet the first generation of a new era. Much of our personal stress, confusion, crises, uncertainties, and difficulties are connected to this conflict within us. The same conditions exist in our political, social, educational, and other institutions. They are caught between the disintegrating industrial age and the coming era that will replace it.

Mode of Production as the Integrating Base of Each Era

Hunting, gathering, foraging, and fishing were the modes of production on which the first era was based. Agriculture was the basic mode of production of the second era. High energy industry is the basic mode of production of the present era that is drawing to a close. Each era with its different sources of energy, means of communication, bases of power, ways of government, forms of organization, scientific know-how, technological level, value systems, cultural forms, family frameworks, and individual identity coalesced around a basic mode of production. The question is what is the basic mode of production of the coming era? If that can be defined, all of the above listed features should fit with the production mode.

It is therefore necessary to observe the characteristics of the developing production modes and to attempt to distill their basic integrating feature. When the pattern of the integrating principle is discerned, it can then be possible to examine if the civilization it promises harbors any solutions to problems troubling society in this era.

THE KNOWLEDGE ERA

There is a movement in all areas of human production to activities based on a much higher level of knowledge, information, and communication. With the end of the smoke-stack age, knowledge, information, and communication industries may become the foremost vital section of industry, and they will become the critical factors in every industry.

The ever-growing services sector of the workforce is assuming a much more important role in the economy, exceeding already the percentage of people employed in industry and agriculture. Many of these services, such as, health, social welfare and culture facilities, necessitate a horde of new professionals on whose knowledge and know-how the service depends.

Whole new areas of production develop around the knowledge gained by crossfertilization of new sciences, such as biotechnology, genetic engineering, and research on new materials from space. Production moves from standard mass production to catering to a variety of different needs and even custom-built products. Computers, automatization, and robotics based on new knowledge change the ways of production.

Nations are moving from a society of blue-collared workers in industry to a society of "gold-collared" knowledge workers. This is the end of an era in which smokestack, high energy industry was the major occupation of people. Industries have moved from machines to automatization and robotics. They have moved from the worker who replaced the machine to the knowledge worker who supervises many machines that run themselves. Manufacturing is withdrawing from the preeminence of mass production to custom-made products which suit the variety of consumer needs. Post-modern nations are changing from a society dominated by heavy industries symbolized by steel mills, coal mines, and sweat-shop industries to industries based on knowledge, information, and scientific breakthroughs.

The basis of industries is moving from the dominance of physics to the ascendancy of the biologic sciences and materials science. The biological sciences are replacing the physical sciences as the major industries of the future. Cellular biology, molecular biology and ecology are advancing into experimental techniques on the way to understanding the basic processes of life. Cross-fertilization between the biological sciences added to scientific and technological advances in other sciences are pushing forward in a variety of areas such as medicine and agriculture. They can create special drugs to conquer specific diseases, create plants that are weather resistant and program bacteria to clean up pollutants.

New knowledge gained from the information sciences and technologies are taking their place at the center of industrial development. This includes the gathering of information through new techniques such as imaging and sensors; the storage and processing of information by computers, microfilm and so forth; and the transmission through satellites, faxing, and computer networks.

Materials science is becoming another major center of revolutionary industrial development. Research is developing new materials with special properties based on progressions in the knowledge of solid state physics. This allows great strides forward in areas such as superconducters, fiber optics, semiconductors for computer chips, lightweight construction materials, materials for magnetic storage of information, and fiber optics for speedy communication. The major advances in production are less within the scope of the inventive tinkerer, but now, more and more, necessitate the knowledge gained by costly interdisciplinary research projects and large-scale technology.

The entire foundation of industry is changing before humanity's eyes. Societies are transforming the basis of their production centers from mechanical centered industries to knowledge-based service, information, bioscience and new materials industries. This fundamental conversion in the basis and foundation of production is a turning point in human history of no less importance and repercussions than the move from agriculture to industry. Humanity is now in the throes of the chaotic transition to the knowledge era.

The Knowledge Base

The thread tying all the major changes in modes of human production and wealth creation together is the quantum leap in the importance of the knowledge component. The high energy industrial age is drawing to a close and trends ushering in the coming knowledge era are becoming more pronounced.

It helps to differentiate between data, information and knowledge. *Data* generally refers to raw facts, such as unconnected bits of information. *Information* is used to decribe organized data, such as being divided into categories. Gregory Bateson (1972) described information as "a difference that makes a difference." *Knowledge* can be understood as a body of organized information in a particular area. Knowledge, therefore subsumes and contains both information and data.

The passage to each era in the past always involved an increase in human knowledge. The coming era does not only entail a quantum leap in human knowledge, but, also builds its mode of production first and foremost around knowledge. The smokestack, mechanical, high energy industries give up their primate before new modes of production in which knowledge is the prime factor. Novel areas of production in agriculture, industry, and the services evolve out of new knowledge, are based on knowledge, and dependent on the growing number of knowledge workers.

Toffler (1991) writes that the new system for wealth creation more and more depends on the exchange of data, information, and knowledge. In this sense it is super-symbolic; if knowledge is not exchanged, wealth is not created. The new money takes the form of electronic exchanges of information. The knowledge gained from science has become a major factor in the advancement of all forms of production and is a trailblazer in opening up new, major fields of production. New knowledge is the bedrock of the breakthroughs in novel lines of industry in the areas of biology, materials and information, transportation, and communication. Knowledge gained from genetic engineering is beginning to create a revolution in medicine and agriculture.

The Power Shift

There are three major resources that control of which gives people power over others. These three resources are violence, money, and knowledge. The control of a combination of all three resources gives greater power. In different historical eras one of the three has been the basic source of power, and control of it generally led to command of the other resources (Toffler 1991).

During the agricultural era the basic source of power over people was probably that of force, muscle, or violence. While wealth and knowledge gave power, force was the foundation of social control. Social order and change were in the hands of those who had at their disposal the greatest resources of physical force, such as soldiers and their weaponry. They also held sway over wealth and knowledge and those who had them.

During the industrial era, force, in the form of armies and police, still played a major role but the basic source of power moved to wealth, money, or capital. Wealth could mobilize behind it the power of force and knowledge. Social order and control were in the hands of those who had wealth and could mobilize resources of wealth. Those who had wealth had power and they could acquire resources of force and knowledge. In his book (*The Power Shift* 1991), Toffler has documented the shift in power. He writes that in the past the battle for the control of the future made use of violence, wealth, and knowledge. Today the changes we see in business, the economy, politics and at the global level "are only the first skirmishes of the far bigger power struggles to come." We are at the edge of the greatest power shift in human history.

The coming era will lead to a major shift in the primary source of power over people. Knowledge is becoming the major source of power and will supplant both force and wealth as the basic resource of power. Those who have knowledge will be able to mobilize both force and money. Toffler believes that the control of knowledge will be the focus of future global struggles for power in every field of human endeavor. The clash between forces favoring the new base of wealth creation and the defenders of the old industrial money-powered system is the major conflict of these times.

The shift to power based on knowledge is causing an upheaval in the economic, financial, and industrial world. The movement from an industrial economy to one based on computers and knowledge necessitates enormous transfers of power, and helps business people understand the crises, reorganizations, mergers, and other forms of financial and industrial restructuring that have been occurring in industry and business.

Expressions of the Knowledge Era

The advent of the knowledge era comes to expression in a variety of ways:

- The advance of human knowledge in the last few decades of this century has outstripped all the combined discoveries and advances of human knowledge throughout history.

- Production based mainly on knowledge and information is becoming the major source of human wealth.

- The development and advance of new directions of production (e.g., biotechnical or new materials) depends most on their knowledge base.

- The knowledge element becomes the crucial factor in the advance and success of agriculture, services, and industry.

- Knowledge ("gold-collar") workers become a growing important, essential element of the workforce.

- Power shifts into the hands of those who have control over knowledge. They also control resources of force and wealth.

- With the rise in centrality of knowledge and information comes the growing importance of the media and others who handle and direct the flow of information.

- Wealth loses its material form of money and takes an informational nonmaterial form of numbers stored in the memories and transferred by computers.

- The success of an enterprise depends increasingly on the quality of people, the level of knowledge, information, and know-how at their disposal.

- Societies with a greater and faster ability to acquire knowledge and information advance more and outstrip other societies.

- Knowledge is substituting saving and replacing other resources such as energy, materials, warehouse facilities and transportation.

- The free flow of knowledge, information, and immediate internal and external feedback and sensors are becoming critical factors in the successful running of an enterprise.

- Knowledge is becoming the key factor in global power struggles replacing power conflicts over material and energy resources.

AREAS OF CONCERN AND THE KNOWLEDGE ERA

It is impossible to foretell to what degree the knowledge era will be able to supply solutions to areas of human concern, such as old problems that have troubled humanity for ages and metaproblems that are intensifying in the last century. Knowledge itself is neutral and can be put to use both for human development and annihilation.

It is, however, possible to point out possibilities and opportunities. In other words it is possible to dileneate transitions that must be made and areas of concern for which the knowledge era may create openings. These are potentials and openings that may not of necessity come about.

World Macro Problems

The major areas of human concern and in dire need of a major transformation have been given different names such as "metaproblems," "transformations that must take place," and "world macroproblems". Willis Harman (1988), president of the Institute of Noetic Sciences, sees the world's macroproblem in the interrelationship among three of its chief aspects: widespread poverty and hunger, environmental degradation, and nuclear weapons.

As reported by Prof. Murray Gell-Mann et al., discussions at the World Resources Institute about global sustainability crystallized around the idea of a set of basic transitions that must take place early in the next century if human society is to approach sustainability. Gell-Mann et al. list the following:

1) the demographic transition to roughly stable populations across the world;

2) the technological transition to a situation where the environmental impact per person and per unit of conventional material prosperity is reduced as much as possible;

3) the economic transition to a world in which serious attempts are made to charge real costs, so that there are incentives for the world economy to be based on nature's "income" rather than depletion of its "capital";

4) the social transition to a broader sharing of that income, with the generation of relatively nondestructive employment for the poor families of the world;

5) the institutional transition to a situation in which global cooperation to solve planetary problems is facilitated and in which the various aspects of policy are integrated with one another, in recognition of their actual interdependence; and

6) the informational transition to a world in which scientific research, education, and the perfection of indicators permit large numbers of people to understand the nature of the challenges they face. (1990:7-8)

NECESSARY TRANSITIONS AND THE KNOWLEDGE ERA

Taking the approach of a set of transitions that needs to take place if human society is to approach sustainability it is possible to examine which of these transitions seem likely to be made in the coming knowledge era.

Curbing World Population Growth

Gell-Mann et al.'s list begins with the problem of demography--curbing the growth of the world's population. Putting a stop to the overcrowding of the earth beyond its carrying capacity. Keeping the number of people within bounds that are relative to the resources that are needed to be able to maintain them and the capacity of the environment to imbibe and recycle the refuse of human civilization.

So far in human history a rise in the standard of education and knowledge of masses of people in a country has almost inevitably been accompanied by a decrease in the average number of children in a family. Hunting and gathering and primitive agriculture societies, such as still exist in parts of Africa, necessitated a large number of children so that some could still survive to support their parents. The birthrates in advanced countries with large sectors of educated populations is far below that of developing countries in Africa or Asia that consist of a large majority of illiterate or poorly educated populations.

The information about, knowledge of, and accessibility to birth-control methods in countries such as India, Bangladesh, Egypt, and the nations of Africa is meager and insufficient to curb the population explosion in those countries. If the knowledge era signifies the acquisition of information, education, and knowledge not only by a priveleged minority, but also its spread, dissemination, and diffusion among the large masses of the peoples of the world, then the knowledge era will also usher in the era of population control. The knowledge era has the potential to put a stop to the explosion of the world's population beyond the earth's carrying capacity. A recent research by B. Robey, S. Rutstein and L. Morris (1993) has shown that birthrates can fall without economic improvement. Greater access to contraception devices along with changes in cultural values and education are decreasing birthrates in Third World Nations.

Depletion of Energy and Natural Resources

This is the problem of the depletion of the world's energy and natural resources. This means reducing the level of energy flow and exploitation of nonrenewable natural resources to as low a point as possible so that we may be able to sustain human life on this planet as far into the future as possible. This means using natural resources and creating an economy and forms of production and consumption within bounds that allow the earth to renew its resources.

The shift from a technology of high energy industry to the knowledge era is a shift in the technology of energy and materials consumption. In contrast to former smokestack industries that were high energy guzzlers, the new modes of production demand far less energy and less non-renewable material resources.

Industries based on information science, biosciences, materials sciences, and services are, as a whole, lower consumers of energy than the typical smokestack, mechanical heavy industries. Comparing a new industrial area developed close to the knowledge base of a University, such as the Boston strip, with a typical industrial area town such as Liverpool, makes this point very clear.

Knowledge substitutes for resources such as materials and transportation and the same is true for energy. Breakthroughs in superconductivity will decrease the amount of energy that must now be transmitted for each unit of output. Up to 15 percent of electricity generated in the United States is lost in moving it to where it is needed because copper wires are not the most efficient carriers. Superconductivity can decrease this loss immensely (Toffler 1991).

Umberto Colombo, Chairmen of EC's committee on science and technology, says that in today's advanced and affluent nations, each successive growth in per capita income is linked to an ever-smaller rise in the quantity of raw materials and energy used. Japan in 1984 used only 60 percent of the raw materials it needed for the same volume of industrial output in 1973 (Toffler 1991). The knowledge era has the potential of changing the trend of the escalating depletion of the earth's natural resources.

The Ecological Problem

This is the problem of dealing with the ecological threats and environmental deterioration, such as: the ozone layer, the greenhouse effect; the poisoning and contamination of rivers, seas, forests, and the air in cities; the destruction of forests; the extermination of wildlife species; the proliferation of harmful foodstuffs; and the dangers of nuclear power stations and waste.

Low energy knowledge industries spew less fumes. The less coal and oil burned, the less poisonous the air people will breath. The areas around heavy industrial sites in many countries are rapidly becoming uninhabitable. The rise in cancer, lung sickness, and other diseases connected with the dangerous residues pumped into the air in such areas may be arrested. The decrease in smokestack industries and the rise in the knowledge industries may have an effect on the ecology.

Less trees cut to supply fuel and less use of raw materials means less harm to the ecological balance built on the oxygen created by the world's great forests. If fewer trees are cut down there may be an end to the steady decrease in arable land brought about by the depletion of the forests.

The advent of the knowledge era may lead to the introduction of new clean energy sources for transportation. This could be an enormous contribution to decreasing the amounts of toxic fumes from the emission of vehicles that are poisoning the atmosphere and killing the forests of central Europe.

Information about ecological matters brought daily into people's homes daily by the mass media such as the British Sky Satellite television broadcasts will increase ecological awareness. Growing ecological awareness among millions of people might become a force that will affect the readiness and willingness of those in power to take practical steps and enforce regulations to decrease ecological degradation.

The knowledge era may put at man's disposal alternatives to the spray materials and refrigerator chemicals that are now causing the growing hole in the ozone layer. New materials that disintegrate might replace the plastic bags, wrappings and other products that last endlessly.

Doing Away with Extremes of Poverty and Deprivation

This is the problem of poverty, starvation and unemployment. This means closing the gap between the "haves" and the "have-nots" by helping the underdeveloped nations of the world attain a basic standard of living and development for their peoples; ending the extremes of poverty, degradation, disease, homelessness, and hopelessness among the deprived sections of the population in the developed countries; and ensuring some form of basic social security for all. This is also the problem of discrimination, whether racial, religious, national, or sexual. This means putting an end to ill treatment, unequal opportunity and deprivation of rights based on people's origin, color, sex, or beliefs and doing away with hatred and conflict based on others being different and unlike us.

The general trend in countries with higher levels of education, literacy and knowledge is in the direction of a broader sharing of income and a decrease in gross inequalities, extreme poverty and mass unemployment. Together with a higher level of education among a country's masses comes a tendency to do away with gross manifestations of discrimination based on racial, religious, or other dfferences. While there are exceptions such as in Nazi Germany, in most cases higher education of the majority of a people, combined with economic well-being, has a positive affect on tolerance of difference. Many advanced nations make actions and manifestations of economic or other forms of discrimination a criminal act punishable by the law of the state.

The higher educated and economically advanced countries such as the Scandinavian nations and Holland have already made these trends a matter of public policy. Free education for all, employment and social security are building blocks of the social policy of these nations.

International Cooperation

As has been noted previously government, authority and power are moving from their present base, practically a monopoly at the national level, in two directions. With a government incapable of managing centrally the growing complexity of human affairs, authority and power are moving down from the national governmental level to lower levels, such as regions, districts, cities, communities, and local authorities as well as to interest groups and organizations of all kinds both formal and voluntary.

t the same time the increasing interdependence and interconnectedness of the world's economy, ecology, and other lifelines, brings a flow of power and authority from the national level to higher more encompassing levels. Regional organizations--such as the European Common Market, and North American Free Trade Agreement, military alliances such as Nato, international organizations such as the UN, Unesco, the World Bank, gigantic international economic concerns such as Sony or IBM--all take a bite out of the resources of power and authority formerly vested in the national governments. These trends may enable the development of societies that can govern themselves with fewer crises, breakdowns and disintegrations. The present concentration of authority in the hands of national governments is no longer capable of functioning effectively in a world of ever-growing complexity.

On the one hand the passage of authority and decision making to local bodies that are more in direct contact with issues and the coordination and integration of the ever-growing interdependencies that crisscross the national levels holds hope for structures that will be better able to deal with human issues. On the other hand the growing interdependence between nations in all fields--such as economy, science, ecology, communication, natural resources, energy, military conflict --makes the creation of world-wide regulatory bodies that can deal with these issues an absolute essential feature of the coming decades. The actions of the UN with regard to South Africa, Iraq, and even the feeble efforts in Yugoslavia and Somalia are all expressions of this trend. The international conference of world leaders on ecology, even though its results were meager, also signifies this trend.

The development of these trends is more and more reaching the awareness of the rulers of nations. There are occasionally backlashes of demand for total national independence and resistance to forms of international or regional integration and regulation. But for all their seeming strength these are all manifestations of skirmishes of a vanquished retreating trend. The knowledge era does hold hope for the widening of international organization and cooperation in dealing with planetary problems.

THE DIFFUSION OF KNOWLEDGE

In the knowledge era, the source and substratum of power that in the industrial age was based mainly on money and force, now moves to knowledge. The knowledge, information, and scientific elements in all areas of human activity become the primary wellspring of power. Divisions between and within societies align themselves more and more around these sources of power.

The question is if the power shift to a knowledge base is the privilege of a small minority or the natural right of all. Hopefully in the coming era more education and the diffusion of knowledge will encompass larger sections of the world population. The trend can already be discerned at the end of this century and all signs point in the direction of it continuing into the future.

This greater dissemination of education and knowledge among the uneducated sections of the population of advanced countries is a feature of modern life. Simultaneously as more developing countries pass through the industrial era they will of necessity invest more in education and science gradually increasing, year by year, the educated sector of their populations.

Educated workers are an essential feature of the era of knowledge. Illiterate, unskilled workers could replace machines on the production lines of the industrial age. The knowledge era demands a new breed of knowledge workers in all fields. Post-modern production necessitates not that people replace machines but that people have the knowledge to supervise and deal with the problems of complex technology. The need for knowledge workers in all fields of production and the decreasing need for illiterate, unskilled labor are possibly the strongest incentive and major assurance that the knowledge era holds promise for the diffusion of higher levels of knowledge among wider stratums of population.

Many of the advances in communication technology, such as radio, television, satellites, and easy travel possibilities are serving as catalyzers to further this process. Worldwide efforts to raise the standard of education and living in undeveloped regions are also playing a part in hurrying this development

Maximizing the Acquisition of Knowledge

The possibility of dealing with the major concerns described above depends on knowledge being at the disposal of large majorities of the people rather than in the hands of a privileged few. The bifurcation in the possession of knowledge is like other resources. Inequality in its distribution among people is inevitable, necessary and natural. But deep, extreme, polarized inequalities and monopolies in the possession of knowledge--among sectors of a society or between societies can cascade the societies past the Feigenbaum Point into chaos.

An increasingly nonlinear, complex, interdependent human environment creates a condition that puts much power in the hands of small groups, for better or for worse. The butterfly effect of the actions of an autocratic ruler or a small group of fanatics can undermine democracy and cause worldwide disasters. A power- hungry dictator or a small group of extremists in the instability period before a major bifurcation can set history back for ages. The takeover of Iran by the Ayatollah Khomeini or the Iraqi invasion of Kuwait illustrate this point.

When knowledge is sparsely spread among populations this danger is greater. When ever-higher levels of education become the natural birthright of most people these dangers decrease. As with the other resources, the relatively just and humane distribution of knowledge is a major force in the maintenance of a measure of stability in human relations.

Knowlege Not for Domination

Knowledge as an instrument of control is harmful. When knowledge becomes a resource to control others, society meets the same fate as when it applies other forms of control. Hopefully those who with knowledge will acquire the wisdom to understand that if it remains their monopoly and becomes in their hands an instrument of domination, it also foretells their doom.

There is a very clear message coming from Chaos theory. That message is that for its own good, humanity must give up its desire for control, manipulation, and domination. D. F. Peat (1991) writes that Chaos theory alerts us to the sensitivity within nature's systems and shows us the futility of trying to control and manipulate the world.

From an evolutionary systems perspective, Riane Eisler (1991) writes about a necessary change in values from a (male) dominator model of society to an affiliative-nurturance (female) partnership model. This demands a shift from competition to cooperation, from chronic warfare to peaceful coexistence, from selfism to mutualism, from aggression to compassion, from exploitation to empathy, from isolation to connectedness, from hierarchy to heterarchy, and from domination to creativity and caring.

Current Knowledge

A third factor affecting the diffusion of knowledge to alleviate problems is the currency of that knowledge. The change-over rate in knowledge in all areas of human endeavor increases yearly at an exponential rate. Most of the data and information that served as the basis for this book was from the last few years, especially the 1990s. While the book was being written some of its ideas became outdated by new discoveries and explanations. This is happening in all areas of life. Referring to business, Toffler (1991) points out that the acceleration of change makes knowledge-about technology, markets, and all other business factors perishable.

People organize information into categories that were suitable at a certain time, but soon these categories and the information they contained become outdated. The problem will be to keep knowledge current among the majority of the population of societies. Dealing with a nonlinear human world with knowledge born out of linear science only exacerbates the problems. Living in knowledge of the past in a world that is bursting into a nonlinear future contains a threat.

Knowledge means current and ever-changing knowledge, not outdated knowledge. If the present is constantly born anew, then the knowledge process will never be completed. "And so we try to steer the course of our evolving future and control a creative, living nature by operating from what has ceased to be" (David Peat 1991). Outdated knowledge can be worse than ignorance. At least with ignorance a person knows that he does not know. A person holding on to outdated knowledge can arrest progress in the name of a science that is no longer relevant. The knowledge era does hold promise for the diffusion of science, education and knowledge among large and growing sectors of the world population. Hopefully this will assist them to understand the nature of the challenges they face. Possibly the main hope in dealing with evolutionary metaproblems of complexity and uncertainty will be a level beyond the context of the coming era, and more within the province of evolutionary trends as a whole. That will be discussed in the next chapter.

13
The Self-Organizing Universe

RETHINKING EVOLUTIONARY TRENDS

The growing difficulties tensions, and dangers facing us as individuals and as societies demand that we take a fresh look at evolutionary processes and what we thought were immutable laws guiding them. In Darwin's time self-organization and emergence were unknown. Mutation created variety and evolution was a matter of competition between species in which the fit survived. Self-organization and emergence add new dimensions and understanding to evolutionary processes that could not be attained before.

Stuart Kauffman says that Darwinian selection is not the whole story. Darwin did not know about self-organization and that it applied to living systems. The evolution of life is not only chance, but also the tale of order and creativity that are a natural part of existence (Waldrop 1992). Self-organization adds new dimensions to evolution. A characteristic of complex systems is their ability to reorganize themselves. Self-organization addresses the self-organization dynamics of complex systems that evolve through a sequence of structures and maintain their integrity as a system.

The system itself, and not some outside force restructures itself into a completely new order and creates the form of its own future. Self-organization is a process of spontaneous structuration, of self-determination and self-renewal. It is the ordering principle that guides the evolution and development of all complex systems, including living and social structures. Contrasting self-organization with the Newtonian worldview, Paul Davies (1990) points out that the paradigm of self-organization recognizes that physical systems can display new and unpredictable behaviors that are not part of the Newtonian and thermodynamic approaches. In self-organization, systems spontaneously change into more elaborate forms. The new forms they take are more complex, they entail cooperative behavior and global coherence and their final forms are unpredictable.

Self Renewal and Self-Transcendence

In the Darwinian view, mutation served evolution by allowing new forms to come into being. But mutation was not enough. It is now possible to understand how living and social structures both change and evolve at the same time. Each system in its history passes through critical bifurcation points, where, when unable to contain the increasing fluctuations anymore, the system reorganizes itself on a higher level of complexity creating new forms. This continues throughout the system's history, with each new order persisting for some time until once again the system self-organizes itself.

Thus, self-organization fulfills two basic functions: self-renewal and self-transcendence. Through self-renewal, by changing its structure, the system is able to continue to maintain itself as a coherent whole under changing conditions. It need not disintegrate; it has the option of renewing itself in the form of a new structure. Capra (1983) calls this function "self-maintenance" which includes the processes of "self-renewal, healing, homeostasis, and adaption."

The second function of self-organization is that of self- transcendence. The system is able to go beyond its former self and create something new. Life has the ability to reach out beyond itself to create new structures and behavioral patterns. This creation of novelty brings forth orders of greater complexity.

Emergence and Evolution

Self-organization is a process whereby, in effect, components at one level interact and amalgamate to create a structure at a higher level. Components at that higher level interact and combine to again create an even higher level. This is found in all complex systems like teams creating departments and departments becoming a company. The richness of the interactions allows the system as a whole to go through spontaneous self-organization. To satisfy their material needs, people organize themselves into an economy through the interactions of many individual acts of buying and selling (Waldrop).

In self-transcendence, a system displays emergence. New properties and novel characteristics emerge that were nonexistent in the previous form of the system. This means that at each different scale and level of organization, new types of behavior develop. These could never have been predicted from an analysis of the lower-level components. Professor Robert Artigiani of the US Naval Academy describes the property of emergence in self-organizing structures:

When a dissipative structure evolves, a new level of reality may emerge. Emergence means qualitatively new behaviors appear in association with components whose attributes are changed by reason of their participation in a self-organized whole. The emergence of a new level of reality must be understood holistically, and that requires non-linear logic. The emergence of a new whole cannot be predicted on the basis of attributes of its components or of their separate histories. Something is present in an emergent dissipative structure that was not present--or even implied--prior to its existence . . . components constituting an emergent whole are mutually captured and capturing. They do things and display qualities as members of a whole they did not do or possess independently. Each component regulates the behavior of the others, and the whole regulates the behavior of all. (1991b:103)

The property of emergence is the basis of the creation of new species of life on earth, new civilizations, new cultures, new forms of human organization, and new laws of nature. Emergence born out of the self-organization of open dissipative, far-from-equilibrium structures is also the building block of evolution. Emergence is the principal message of the New Science of Complexity. It will bring about a reformulation of Darwinian evolutionary theory.

Coevolution

Systems are connected to and coevolve with other systems. They are like the patterns in a kaleidoscope that all change together. You cannot separate between species, or organisms and their environments. They are not isolated from each other. They are connected and change together. They survive together in coevolution.

An animal species that survives by eating all the grass that feeds it will become extinct. The unit that survives is the organism in its environment. If a species takes care only of its own survival, in the process of doing this it can destroy its environment. When it destroys its environment it removes the possibility of its own survival.

Roger Lewin points out that the coevolutionary model builds the ties between species. Connectedness is necessary if the system is to function as a whole, and not as separate entities. Connectedness is also necessary if perturbations are to spread throughout the system, producing in their wake avalanches of speciation and extinction.

Coevolution takes place not only between species and their environments, but also at other levels. In the history of life, the coevolution of microcosm and macrocosm is of special importance. Most accounts of the evolution of life describe microevolution and not macroevolution. But the two complement each other in evolution. Microscopic life "creates the macroscopic conditions for its further evolution" and the macroscopic environment creates the conditions for the evolution of microscopic life. Complexity develops from the "coevolution of organism and environment at all systems levels" (Capra 1983).

Jantsch (1980) traces this coevolution of the micro forms of single-celled life forms together with their macro environment from about four billion years ago until today. At each step in the evolutionary ladder the micro forms of life created the macro conditions for their survival and the macro conditions supported the sustenance and survival of the new micro forms.

A coevolutionary approach might hold a ray of hope for man's ablity to coexist with a world of growing complexity and uncertainty. Coevolution opens the door to the scenario that man might develop the ability to coevolve with the uncertainty and turbulence of the macroworld of his environment. Simultaneously the enviromental macro world, affected by human agency, might coevolve within the constraints of humankind's potential to adapt within certain limits of complexity and uncertainty.

This is not a mystical belief in some kind of benevolent hidden hand that will intervene to save mankind from the dangers it faces. Coevolution does not separate mankind and its environment into self-contained separate categories each evolving in its own orbit. It sees them and their evolutionary paths as intertwined and interdependent. Coevolution necessitates active human agency in directions that ensure the survival of both the environment and man. This may necessitate a change in orientation to cooperation and mutual responsibility.

Competition and Cooperation

Out of the interaction of interdependent entities comes the creation of new entities. The forms the interaction takes are both of cooperation and competition. Darwinian theory stressed only the latter. Complexity points to the important part played in evolution by cooperation. In the evolutionary process, cooperation and competition complement each other. Whereas biologists overlooked cooperation and sought competition everywhere, as Willis Harman suggests:

the biological world abounds with symbiotic relationships, some of which are not relationship of prey to predator or parasite to host, but genuinely appear to be cooperative, driven by something more and different from the survival instinct. As bioligist Lewis Thomas says, "The urge to form partnerships; to link up in collaborative arrangement, is perhaps the oldest strongest and most fundamental force in nature." Yet this picture endures, of nature darkened by brutal competition, whereas with different eyes the central interdependence and cooperation would be obvious. (1991:73)

S. Goerner strengthens this viewpoint, "Ecologism's other clear message is that . . . cooperation is the more likely route to massive increases in efficiency than competition (particularly internal competition)." And "there are signs that cooperation is being forced into being by the increasing speed and complexity of the modern world" (1992:11-8).

Emergence, connectivity and coevolution are processes which contain strong elements of cooperation. Doyne Farmer of Santa Fe Institute says that organisms cooperate and compete in coevolution, and in this way become "an exquisitely tuned ecosystem." Atoms join together to create molecules. Human beings try to satisfy their needs through economic relationships with each other and in this way create a market. By acting in a mode of mutual accommodation, groups of agents "transcend themselves and become something more" (Waldrop 1992).

John Holland, from the same institute, indicates the complementary nature of competition and cooperation. He says that competition can create the incentive for cooperation as agents build alliances and relationships with each other for mutual aid. It happens everywhere in biological, economic and political systems. Competition and cooperation may appear to be in conflict, but in fact they complement each other (Waldrop 1992).

Complexity and Evolution

Out of cooperative and competitive forms of interaction emerge self-organization processes that lead to more and ever-more complex systems. We live in a universe driven by evolutionary forces to the emergence of systems that are always more complex than those that created them. Laszlo (1991) describes the trend in which evolution creates first relatively simpler dynamical systems at a particular level of organization. Evolution leads to increasing complexity of these systems and finally to the development of simpler systems on the next higher organizational level. At this higher level the process of complexification begins again. In this way evolution moves "from the simpler to the more complex, and from the lower to the higher level of organization."

Evolution is a never-ending story of punctuated equilibriums where both the world and human societies within it evolve to levels of greater and greater complexity. This process of punctuated discontinuous change is a natural aspect of evolution. In the history of all complex systems, periods of relative stasis (balance) are followed by a shorter stage of major qualitative transformation, which is in its turn followed by another more complex period of relative stasis. Referring to the social level, Laszlo says that the New Sciences suggest that complex nonequilibrium systems evolve through discontinuous jumps toward societies of growing size and complexity, of increasingly higher and more levels of organization, of more dynamism, and stronger interaction with the environment.

The process of the evolutionary cycle is strongly nonlinear. There are many changes and times of fluctuations and reversals, punctuated with times of stagnation. "Major perturbations, such as wars and social, political, and technological revolutions, rock and ultimately destabilize societies. Governments fall, systems of law and order are overthrown, new movements and ideas surface and gain momentum. This is a period of chaos as new orders take shape. But new orders do arise, and history sets forth its jagged course from the Stone Age to the Modern Age--and then beyond" (Laszlo 1991:49).

The Gaia Hypothesis

Can our global system be functioning as a complex self-organizing adaptive system? Many astronauts, viewing the earth from outer space, as one whole blue-white globe, have been profoundly moved and some of them have since said that it was a deep spiritual experience that changed their relationship to the earth. Might not the planet earth itself be a whole system based on the same self-organization, emergent, and growing complexity principles? Is its history one of dynamic self-regulating regimes, each following the other in greater forms of complexity and creating new self-regulating structures with emergent properties that are able to contain the fluctuations that disrupted the former structure? The British chemist James Lovelock and the American microbiologist Lynn Margulis have proposed that this is exactly what has happened and is still happening. Their basic idea has been named The Gaia hypothesis, in honour of the earth mother in Greek mythology. It is gaining more support from a growing number of scientists from a variety of disciplines.

The Gaia hypothesis states that planet earth, like other nonequilibrium, nonlinear systems, functions as a self- organizing system. The earth is not only full of life but appears to be like a living being. Life and all the forms of matter on earth create together one whole complex self-organizing system. As Capra puts it: "It persists in a remarkable state of chemical and thermodynamical nonequilibrium and is able, through a huge variety of processes, to regulate the planetory environment so that optimum conditions for the evolution of life are maintained" Capra 1983:284).

With changes taking place all the time, as in outer space, in the degree of the sun's radiation; or on the planet, with the appearance of plants and life the earth has always found a way to self-organize itself. During the planet's history the sun's radiation has increased by at least 30 percent. Yet somehow throughout time the earth's temperature has been regulated and, as Capra points out, the planet maintains a fairly constant surface temperature throughout the evolution of life. This is similar to the way our body maintains a regular body temperature notwithstanding changing conditions. Paul Davies describes how the primeval atmosphere contained immense quantities of carbon dioxide, which was a blanket to keep the earth warm in the weak sunlight of that time. The carbon dioxide cover was gradually eaten away by life as the sun grew hotter. Oxygen was released and the carbon was synthesized into living material. "The oxygen produced an ozone layer in the upper atmosphere that blocked out the dangerous ultra-violet rays. . . . The fact that life acted in such a way as to maintain the conditions needed for its own survival and progress is a beautiful example of self regulation" (1988:132).

Capra writes that similar patterns of self-regulation can be found in the environment, in the chemical composition of the earth's atmosphere, in the concentration of salt in the oceans, and in the distribution of trace elements among animals and plants. All these are organized into complex cooperative networks that show the properties of self-organizing systems.

The Gaia hypothesis which describes the earth as one whole self-organizing system means in fact that the earth as a whole passes through different stages in its evolution. It survives these changes by self-organizing itself into new structures. When new exigencies arise, such as the change in temperature, they may cause fluctuations that cannot be absorbed by the existing structure of relations between the living and inanimate components of the earth. The earth overcomes these perturbations by transforming itself into a new structure that is able to deal with and contain the new conditions.

If there is no discontinuity, the Gaia hypothesis holds some hope for mankind. The globe as a self-regulating system, which includes the active agency of humanity, might transform itself into new structures that will allow mankind to survive and maintain itself. The self-organizing and self- regulating properties of the earth have so far created the optimal conditions for the evolution of life. Hopefully, if mankind does not botch them up they will continue doing so in the future. An optimistic stance would anticipate an evolution of evolution itself.

THE EVOLUTION OF EVOLUTION

The former chapters of the book on the intensification of chaos and complexity discussed the increasing stress and the growing dangers to mankind developing from the complexity spiral, the control trap, and the transition period to a new era. This raised the issue of mankind's survival through the transition stage.

With the growing power of destruction in human hands and the havoc humanity is wrecking in its natural environment, the specter of the human race destroying itself by its own hands steps out of science fiction pages and becomes a fearsome reality. "Now, as before, the human future remains inscrutable, and we do not know if we are heading for a nobler future or toward unavoidable self-destruction" (Ruelle 1991).

Jantsch (1980) discusses the dilemma in which the human world finds itself. With flexible coupling of the subsystems, due to the development of communication and transport technology, political, social, and economic structures become even more metastable. This, however, means increasing danger that the global fluctuations get bigger and bigger and become disastrous. Mankind has prepared fluctuations of potentially destructive force, such as nuclear weapons.

Mankind faces questions that entail the continued existence of life in this world. Jantsch believes that society needs to ask how evolution is to continue? Is humanity caught in a net of factors in which it is becoming ever more inextricably entangled with every motion? "Is the evolution of man coming to its end--or is even the evolution of life on earth coming to its end with man?"

The self-organizing, self-regulating capabilities of the earth, as expressed through the Gaia hypothesis, give a ray of hope and a basis to believe that with all the dangers, mankind can believe in a positive future. In the face of the present dangerous fluctuations, the world in coevolution with the creative abilities of man, will, it is hoped, self-organize itself into structures that will avert the impending dangers. Jantsch believed that with man's anticipatory ability this is possible. Humanity for the first time in its evolution can be aware of evolution and act accordingly to guide itself on a less dangerous path.

From a global viewpoint, mankind gets further away from equilibrium and seems to demand a new structure which may only be reached after a major chaotic instability. There is no lack of fluctuations (wars, oil crisis, recession) or autocatalytic reactions in the form of escalation of tensions between nations. But it is the potentially strongest autocatalytic factors, such as the preparation of a huge arsenal of nuclear weapons and fears of mutual strikes, which may also act in a strongly inhibiting way (Jantsch 1980).

Fluctuations that threaten systems' boundaries and continued existence may also be dampened by the system in an anticipatory way. This is definitely possible with the excessive exploitation of nonrenewable resources. The dangers can be decreased because they can be anticipated. This anticipatory capability is the difference between adaptive self-reflexive complex systems and merely physical autopoietic structures.

The Laws of Nature Also Change

There are no ironclad laws of nature or evolution that determine our future. One of the eye-opening insights that come from the nonlinear sciences is that the laws of nature are not fixed, but they themselves also change. We have grown up with a world-view based on the assumption that the basic laws of science are immutable and will hold forever.

It is difficult to accept the fact that things are just not so. The basic fundamental laws of science and nature are themselves not impervious to change. People need to begin thinking in terms of laws that hold for certain periods and circumstances, at certain levels, and then themselves go through a transformation.

Prigogine saw the laws of nature as emerging, developing, and changing throughout time. They were not fixed at the moment of creation to remain immutable forever. They themselves are emergent phenomena and as the universe develops and becomes more complex, out of its fluctuations and transformations new laws come into being. There could be no laws of biology before there were living systems. The laws of the motions of the planets could emerge only when the planets were formed.

There is no hierarchy of laws with the laws of physics at their base. No discipline is more fundamental than the other. The laws of different disciplines are connected together as if in a web, not linearly and not hierarchially, and are ever-changing.

Young (1994) points out that axiomatic theorems and universal theory itself are inappropriate to the ontology of the cosmos revealed by chaos researchers. Young draws attention to a useful distinction between social theory as a social narrative and sociological theory. Social narrative helps an age understand its own dynamics. Sociological theory attempts to attain a grand unified theory that aims to reveal a universal language which subsumes all social life. The science of Chaos makes it clear that there is no purpose in searching for grand unifying theories. They do not exist; they themselves change with time and circumstances. Wheatley describes the feelings that develop from this. In the past the tradition was to work on something and then generalize it into answers and solutions that would be widely transferred. But now this has changed. We can no longer expect to receive answers. Solutions are temporary events suited to specific circumstances. We will have no more patrons, expecting our return, just more searchers and explorers venturing out by themselves.

It is not only the world that is undergoing constant change. It is also the laws of nature that govern the world that are changing. But even more than that, it is not only the laws of nature that are changing it is the way they change that is also changing.

Evolution Is Open

Evolution is not fixed by immutable laws but is open. Evolution itself is also subject to change. The form that evolution takes was not created once and for all with the birth of the universe. Evolution itself evolves and it evolves in a way that was not determined before. It is open. As different circumstances develop new principles of evolution emerge.

Paul Davies (1988) points out that in the new paradigm determinism is irrelevant. We inhabit a universe that is intrinsically unpredictable. There is a certain freedom of choice that is not in accord with the conventional worldview. Conditions develop in which many possible paths are open within the laws of physics. In this way there arises "an element of novelty and creativity, but also of uncertainty."

This might frighten some people who crave greater certainty in the future. "This may seem like cosmic anarchy. Some people are happy to leave it that way, to let the universe explore its potentialities unhindered. A more satisfactory picture, might be to suppose that the 'choices' occur at critical points. . . . where new principles are free to come into play, encouraging the development of even more organized complex states" (1988:200).

The future trends of evolution are not fixed by laws laid down by Darwin, Lamarck, or any other great genius. The laws themselves will evolve. Evolution is not heading on a predetermined path but is open. The complementarity between micro and macro evolution reveals an open indeterminate evolution with ever-new dimensions of novelty and exchange with the environment (Jantsch 1980).

Capra writes that evolution is basically open and indeterminate. It has no goal or purpose, but does have a pattern of development. "The details of this pattern are unpredictable because of the autonomy living systems possess in their evolution as in other aspects of their organization" (1983:288).

Prigogine sees the future as open and undetermined. He wrote about a new uncertainty principle, in a universe governed by fluctuations, bifurcations, randomness, and transformations where complexity ever grows. The openness of evolution and the possibility of changes in the basic laws of nature open the possibility of an evolution in the laws of evolution, themselves.

A Gliding Evolution

Humanity's great concern is with the cataclysmic, catastrophic, dangerous transitions between orders of human civilizations. How can man create a world order that, if a major transition takes place, the whole world does not blow up in the process? An intriguing possibility is a change in the way things change. This can be possible if the way that evolution works itself changes. There can be an evolution of evolution itself. Like other systems evolution may self-organize itself into a different order. Evolution itself is open not only with respect to its products, but also with regard to the rules that govern it. The result of this openness is an evolution in evolution itself, its mechanisms and principles, the self-transcendence of evolution in a "metaevolution" (Jantsch 1980).

So far, in history, the move from one era to another has taken the form of a big step. It had the form of an entire civilization changing together as a whole. The sociocultural system as a single unity self-organized itself into a new order. The self-reinforcement of fluctuations led to a transition period of chaos, until a new order of civilization took over. This was the way the Roman civilization, which was built on slave labor, broke down, followed by a long period of chaos until gradually the feudal system took over. In a similar manner the Industrial Revolution gained ascendance. These gigantic moves of entire civilizations covered all aspects of their existence, political, social, economic, and technological. The entire process involved decades of chaotic transition until finally the new order took root.

This form of evolution may itself change "from quantum jumps to gliding evolution." Instead of the replacement of one entire civilization by another, there may be a wide range of changes in different areas of existence over a prolonged period of time. The process may be so dispersed and so gradual that it would *not* take the form of a major shift in civilizations following a period of chaos.

Waddington suggests a musical analogy as not wanting to listen to the confrontation of extremely different themes as in one of Wagner's operas, but to the running through of themes as in Bach or boogie-woogie. The posibility emerges that:

it is no longer whole structural platforms, whole civilizations, societal systems, art and life styles which must jump into a new structure. A pluralism emerges in which many dynamic structures penetrate each other at the same level. In such a pluralism, there is no longer the familiar evolution in big step functions. Change, increasingly in an absolute measure, occurs not only vertically, in historical time, but also horizontally, in a multitude of simultaneous processes, none of which necessarily has to assume destructive dimensions. The reality of the human world becomes dissolved into many realities, its evolution into a multitude of horizontally linked evolutions. (Jantsch 1980:256)

The shift in civilizations in ancient times meant the complete replacement of the old by the new. Not very much remains from the ancient civilizations except archaeological ruins. The shifts in the last millennium have been less destructive and complete than the shifts in ancient times. Much of the former civilization remained in the new one. The Christian civilization took over many of the elements of the Roman and Greek civilizations, in political philosophy, culture, sports, theater and other fields. The movement from one era to another might be evolving into a new form that is less abrupt, drastic, enfolding, catastrophic and dangerous.

Can this be a sign that an evolution of evolution is developing? Is it possible, that the move from one civilization to another will be less drastic and total? Does a "gliding" evolution in which many partial processes and changes replace restructuration in one big jump, open up opportunity for imminent restructurations, not only in Western society, but in the whole world? Jantsch believed that this may be happening and that the massive restructuration in discontinuous quantum leaps of social and cultural organization might be changed at our level of complexity, which includes the human capability for self-reflection and anticipation. A monolithic form of culture might dissolve into cultural pluralism that may allow smoother or gliding transformations.

This new form of evolution might diffuse the dangers inherent in the turbulent quantum leaps of the past. Man's capabilities of self-reflection, anticipation, and creativity are coevolving with increasing complexity and can play a part in diffusing the dangers. Can mankind still find an optimistic scenario in its future? Possibly so, if there is substance to the theories described in this chapter: the role of cooperation in evolution; the coevolutionary nature of evolution; the ability of complex adaptive systems to tune themselves and balance themselves at the edge of chaos; the self-organizing and self-regulating nature of the planet as in the Gaia hypothesis; the openness of evolution; the evolution of evolution itself into a gliding evolution; and (as discussed in the next chapter), the part played by human agency and creativity in evolution.

14
Human Agency in Evolution

HUMAN SYSTEMS AS COMPLEX ADAPTIVE SYSTEMS

Human beings and societies are not only complex systems they are also complex adaptive systems. They are not confined in their choice of behaviors to a limited number of attractors. They have before them many choices they can make to better adapt to changing turbulent circumstances. They also have countless variables they can manipulate to make these choices.

Complex adaptive systems are all the time gathering information about their environment while sifting the information to choose what is relevant from what is just noise. From the information they devise hypotheses and models and use these to guide their behavior. When reality in the form of new information clashes with their models, they modify the models.

Human beings have foresight and they learn from experience. Their behavior is not only reactive, they can also anticipate events and display proactive behavior. They have the freedom of choice to use behaviors they find suitable to the changed circumstances. These allow them to both anticipate and react to change. They have the ability to alter their reactions in ways that reflect their new knowledge of the environment and themselves.

P. Malaska (1991), a systems theorist, sees the basic difference between chemical, biological, ecological, and human systems in that in human systems the impulses which cause the primary fluctuations are initiated consciously by man himself and not by chance. These sources can include both learning and innovation, and war and environmental destruction. Goerner (1992) says that evolution forms the context that shapes individuals and events. At the same time individuals and events change the shape and context of evolution.

It would be unwise to ignore the place of human agency and human creativity in channeling the flow of evolution. Human consciousness begins to be a major causal reality in shaping the future. Jantsch (1980) points out that humans are not only capable of much faster learning processes and thus of quicker adaptation to environmental changes but they are also shaped by evolution for an existence of great uncertainty and the absorption of much novelty. Organisms that developed earlier in evolution were generally highly specialized, for example, in eating one or only a few types of food, or in the ways they acquire the food, in how they communicated or defended hemselves. Humans in contrast, are extremely versatile. It is only technology whch leads them to forgetting and unlearning this.

Attaining Evolutionary Consciousness

Human nature has emergent properties that differeniate it from the rest of the world. Whereas before man, novelty arose by chance, now man has the ability to create novelty by deciding to do so. Humans are able to see what is happening to their societies and civilizations and take action to avert the dangers. As self-reflective systems, they may anticipate the dangers ahead and act so as to defuse the fluctuations. E. Laszlo (1991) says that humanity can achieve a large degree of control over the evolution of its societies at the time that such control is needed. Eisler (1991) believes that a notable aspect of evolution is the movement to ever-greater levels of complexity, which offers progressively more choice and flexibility. With the emergence of the human species, choice takes on a whole new dimension. It is not only the ability to choose among existing realities, but also the capability to create entirely new realities.

At the end of this era, man both becomes aware of evolutionary processes and acquires the competence to awaringly guide them. Goerner points out that "We get the Ecological Transformation at this juncture in history in part because generations of standing 'on others' shoulders' has allowed us to reach a level of complexity that can deal with greater complexity in the world. We also get it because the modern world's level of complexity--its pace of change, level of economic interconnectedness and skyrocketing increase in knowledge--forces a crisis" (1992:11-12).

Man has the ability to become aware and conscious of evolutionary processes. He can attain evolutionary consciousness and use it to create a conscious evolution. System's scientist Bela Banathy (1993) notes that in evolution the most advanced state of existence is human consciousness. And the highest form of human consciousness is evolutionary consciousness.

Evolutionary consciousness allows us to cooperate actively with the evolutionary process and use the creative powers of our minds to guide human systems and societies toward the fulfillment of their potentials. Evolutionary consciousness can recruit human action toward conscious evolution, through which man can guide his future, if he has a vision of what he wishes to achieve.

Man's abilities of self-reflection and anticipation may allow him to play a major role in determining the future of evolution. Man can look backward at his past and see how it evolved into the present. He may use this experience to partially guide him in evolving the future. Jantsch believed that sociocultural man in coevolution with himself can create the conditions for further evolution, in the same way that life has always created the condition for its evolution toward higher complexity.

Banathy proposes that, by purposeful action, humanity can take charge of its future and guide its evolution, also the evolution of the various systems to which people belong, and the evolution of society. Humanity has greatly affected the evolutionary process. Man's unlimited ability to learn and the acceleration of knowledge production together with the human capacity to design systems--have had an enormous impact on societal evolution.

Taking Responsibility for Guided Evolution

Evolutionary consciousness brings to man's awareness that he lives in a coevolutionary network of mutual relations both with all other human beings and with his environment. With evolutionary consciousness comes the full awareness that we inhabit one Global Village and are all interrelated and interconnected with each other and with nature.   There has never before been a time when the human beings' responsibility for the planetary process has been greater. "Never before have we gained power of such magnitude over the primordial issues of life and death. The density and intimacy of the global village, along with the staggering consequences of our new knowledge and technologies, make us directors of a world that, up to now, has mostly directed us" (Jean Houston 1982:213).

As the worldwide crises deepen and the survival and ecological threats loom more closely and frighteningly on the human horizon, awareness grows. More people, governments, and international bodies are beginning to realize that humanity is responsible for its future and can play a major role in shaping it. Man is seen less as being at the mercy of blind forces of history, or destiny, or evolution. Human beings are gradually beginning to realize that they are responsible for the problems they face and that they are also the lords of their own futures. They will be the ones to decide which directions the future will take.

Young writes that "if we have learned anything from the many contributions to the knowledge process in the past 2,500 years; in the past 400 years, in the past 15 years, it is that there has been a great increase in human agency; whatever now goes wrong or right is, increasingly, our own responsibility." It may have been different in earlier periods of human history, but now human society bears the brunt of the responsibility. "There may have been a time when we were innocent, when events were beyond the reach of human agency; but now, with knowledge or cunning, technology or tactic, wisdom or greed, compassion or contempt, we have the capacity to intervene in those historical processes which, over that history, have swept the world and turned it inside out" (1992:4).

Humans have always been the most adaptable creatures in the world, and they should be able to design a new direction for themselves. There are early signs of growing awareness and the beginning of evolutionary consciousnesss. There is a developing awareness of the need for international cooperation that is taking a number of directions. There are initial steps being taken throughout the world and by the UN to decrease the dangers of environmental pollution, the greenhouse effect and the disintegration of the ozone layer. The international and bloc agreements aimed at decreasing stockpiles of nuclear weapons and the policy of limiting the proliferation of mass weapons of destruction are actions in the same direction.

The growth and worldwide efforts of the ecological forces in the advanced countries, the activities in effect in many places for recycling materials, the constrictions being placed on industrial pollution, the move to lower energy consumption industries, the major attempts to stop deforestation, the curbs on population growth in China are all signs of man making the first steps to begin to take responsibility for his future on this planet.

EVOLUTIONARY COMPETENCE

Human beings are also in need of the competencies to guide evolution. Banathy (1993) has expanded knowledge on evolutionary competence. In Banathy's view, evolution may be guided under four conditions. The first condition is to develop evolutionary consciousness. The second condition is to create guiding images of the future. The third condition is to create the evolutionary competencies needed to bring reality closer to the vision. The fourth is to use the competencies to design and create the systems in the form depicted by the vision. Some applied scientists (e.g., Frantz and Miller [1993] for families and Judy Bach [1993] for organizations) have made interventions in smaller systems using the guidelines of Banathy's evolutionary competence model.

Sally Goerner (1993) stresses the following elements of developing evolutionary competence: First a realizatioon of our connectedness in an unfolding process that directs us and in which we also play an important role. Second the fostering of difference, variety, and uniqueness and a valuation of diversity and experimentation. Third is the development of structurally sound energy flows in which the development of fine-grained close synergetic relations between all parts of the system is a crucial element. Fourth is the ability of people to adapt to accelerating change by building their identity around being a learning system. Fifth is the ability of human systems to move easily between forms and create within themselves the structures that attend to the continual change of form and structure as the conditions demand. Alfonso Montuori (1992) has noted the crucial importance of societal and individual change from maintenance learning, which deals with content and storage, to evolutionary learning, which is a self-reflective process that tries to foster capacity instead of trying to fill a container with information.

System theorists and futurists are beginning to grapple with the issue of which competencies human systems will need to cope with uncertainty and hectic discontinuous change, while being able to function effectively. Some of the elements for furthering evolutionary competence may possibly be:

- Creating guided images of the future
- Developing a new value system
- Evolutionary learning
- Designing and improving systems

CREATING GUIDED IMAGES OF THE FUTURE

Our behaviors depend on images we hold in our heads. Our environment, including society, constantly sculptures the images we have and the images we hold in turn mold the environment and society. The way people see themselves, their self-image, decides how they behave and present themselves to others. If I see myself as a powerful person I will behave accordingly. Whether the United States sees itself as responsible for maintaining order in the world affects its policies and actions. Our images of ourselves and outside reality and moreover our images of a desired reality are critical forces in our behavior and ability to guide evolution.

When we continue to use old images in a new reality we create a gap that leads to deepening problems. If we are able to become aware of evolutionary trends and are capable of creating positive guiding images of the future based on these, we have begun to take the first steps toward creating a conscious evolution.

Banathy (1993) sees the creation of guiding images as the first stage of attaining evolutionary competence. This is a process wherein human systems of all levels--individuals, organizations and societies--develop a representation first of current reality as they see it, and then of a future reality they wish to attain. This evolutionary image of the future is a guiding vision that motivates, affects, and canalizes behavior.

In Banathy's view the guiding image should be built around a number of basic values. The values he suggests are universal values that have been part of various cultures throughout history and include, among others, such values as harmony and balance and the unlimited ability to develop human potential.

Most societies today are motivated and guided only by their past and not by visions of the future. They get bogged down with the immensity of their problems with no guiding light as to how to create a better future. Having a positive image of the future built on values, that transcend self-interest, is the bedrock of being able to deal with problems of the present. Societies that have not built positive images of the future based on the realities of evolution may face a problem of disintegration.

Human systems at all levels are in need not only of guiding images of the future but should also have the ability to change such an image with the acquisition of new knowledge. The world may change and societies may go beyond the stage where the former image was adequate. Policies based on a dominant image that is outdated become faulty and counterproductive leading to a stage of disruption and social crisis, wherein the stage is set for the development of a new image.

DEVELOPING A NEW VALUE SYSTEM

Evolutionary consciousness needs to be joined to a guiding image that is articulated through values that provide direction to personal and social endeavor. The coming era necessitates a new value system for mankind. Banathy (1993) proposes what he calls an evolutionary guidance system, which can be a guiding image for the evolution of social and societal systems. Banathy believes that such a system must include all the dimensions of our experiential reality. He suggests a framework of essential values in most basic areas of social reality, focusing on these dimensions:

SOCIAL ACTION--cooperation and integration of societal systems.
ECONOMIC--economic justice, integrated and indigenous development.
MORAL--self-realization, social, and ecological ethics.

WELLNESS--individual/societal physical, mental, emotional, and spiritual health.
HUMAN DEVELOPMENT--learning and development of individual and social potential.
SCIENTIFIC--for human and social betterment.
TECHNOLOGICAL--in the service of enhancing the quality of life.
AESTHETIC--pursuit of beauty and cultural values and inner enrichment.
GOVERNANCE--self-determination, peaceful resolution of conflicts, peace, and goodwill.

From Domination to Partnership

Many system thinkers (e.g., Eisler, Wailand) stress the crucial importance of replacing the dominator culture of former eras with a partnership, a collaborative and cooperative culture. Connectedness through partnership and cooperation is viewed as the essence of the new evolutionary ethic. This may require that we overcome or sublimate our tendency to dominate and excell over our rivals. At an earlier period in human history these drives may have been adaptive, but now they are a hindrance.

Eisler (1991) traces the history of cultures throughout human civilization. She differentiates between cultures that were built on the basis of domination and cultures that were built on the ethic of partnership. The dominator model is built on the principle of ranking, whether male over female or vice versa. Generally most cultures were based on male predominance. The other model, that of partnership, is based on the principle of linking without ranking, where difference is not equated with superiority or inferiority. Examples of the dominator male model are Khomeini's regime and Nazi Germany.

In societes that are based on the partnership model, feministic stereotyped values are central. These can be values such as cooperation, peaceful coexistence, mutualism, compassion, empathy, connectedness, heterarchy, creativity, and caring. The industrial era was suffused with the male dominator model. To ensure sustainability, global society in the coming era will have to embrace a partnership model based on the above values.

The new values will also evolve with time and other values will become central. As Montuori notes "evolutionary values are values in process, lived in a world that is process. A static conception of justice reflects the maintenance learning of responding to preexisting problems and situations. Given our increasing globalization, complexification, and interdependence, we must learn to think on our feet, and when preexisting schemata fail in the light of the new, of 'Other,' be able to care" (1992:200).

As was discussed in former chapters, inevitable growing complexity that involves increasing connectedness and interdependence leads to intensifying uncertainty, unless it is matched with a culture based on values and relationships of mutual responsibility, compassion and cooperation.

EVOLUTIONARY LEARNING

Transformation to a new era necessitates a transformation in learning. The current mode of learning is maintenance learning. Maintenance learning "involves the acquisition of fixed outlooks and methods and rules that deal with known events and recurring situations, which promote already established ways of working in our systems and institutions, and aim at the maintenance of status-quo" (Banathy 1993:76). In Banathy's view maintenance learning should be complemented by evolutionary learning, which is a form of creative, innovative learning that is essential to the present predicament of mankind. Evolutionary learning allows us not only to deal with change but also to shape it. It assists us in dealing with uncertainty. It helps us suspend old assumptions, and create new perspectives. This form of learning allow us to redesign and transform our systems often "at higher levels of complexity (which is a mark of evolution)" (1993:76-77). Banathy believes that evolutionary learning will allow us to anticipate and be prepared for unexpected situations. It will assist us to coevolve with our environment and increase our competence in managing change.

An Evolutionary Learning Agenda

Banathy suggests an evolutionary learning agenda that includes among other subjects: knowledge about evolutionary processes, appreciation of the domains of our experiental existence, evolutionary values, self-realization ethics, cooperative interaction skills, systems thinking and practice and the nurturing of creativity and problem management.

Montuori (1992) accentuates the following aspects of evolutionary learning: Its constant questioning of existing assumptions and ways of doing things, and reorganizing the way we do these at a higher level of systemic complexity and organization; development of entirely new creative systemic ways of learning; emphasis on systemic and holistic approaches to learning versus the present form of compartmentalized knowledge and overspecialization; finally, the emphasis on cooperation as a way and method of learning, together with developing competence in group interaction skills needed for this kind of learning.

Knowledge of the New Sciences

A general understanding of the New Sciences and their global, social, and conceptual implications is an essential feature of evolutionary learning. The New Sciences are an instrument of evolutionary learning. They help us to understand the role of human agency in forging our future. They put a way of seeing and understanding reality in the hands of humanity that can assist us in midwifing changes in directions that are congenial to our future.

Young (1994) notes that chaos theory offers insight into a theory of human agency which was not possible in a god-hewn world or a world that was tightly governed "by 'iron laws' of nature and society." There are both regions of order and regions of uncertainty. Of these regions of order, "some are of an impersonal structural nature and some are decidedly human in origin." Some regions of disorder may increase human choice and agency, while some regions permit little rationality in terms of probability of achieving a goal or plan.

The New Sciences put in man's hands the first glimpse of understanding of the nonlinear world he lives in. They help him understand the interplay of order and chaos in the functioning of the human and non-human world. They point out the inevitable growth of complexity. They help man accept the necessary evolution of all systems through periods of chaos out of which are born new orders.

The New Sciences throw light on the fractal nonobjective nature of reality. They offer possibilities of understanding the intensification of chaos in human affairs, especially at the end of this century. They create a new paradigm in science that opens endless vistas for discovery in all fields of human knowledge. They point to the ways of enhancing human creativity. They show the futility of the dominator/control paradigm born in the industrial era. They give hope to the possibility of human agency creating humanity's future.

Loye and Eisler (1987) point to the value of Chaos theory in human efforts to take possession of human evolution. The significance of Chaos theory is that it is the first time in the evolution of man that humanity is starting to develop a way to scientifically understand not only the return to forms of systemic equilibrium, but also to break out of our social and evolutionary stalemate into a world of unbelievable possibilities. This new breakthrough of the human mind is sure to renew and revitalize humanity's vision of the future and remotivate achievement of new goals.

Nonlinear Science and Learning

The knowledge era holds promise in science for a movement away from the traditional, industrial age paradigm of linearity and equilibrium that emphasized order, stability, and uniformity to a science based on the nonlinear, far-from-equilibrium reality of today. A science is developing that has place for the disorderly, irregular, turbulent, discontinuous, disequilibrium chaotic reality that encompasses us.

Possibly, we are on the threshold of a new science of the universe. "It reveals a vision in which mind and matter, subjectivity and objectivity, are unified into a single whole in which every cell and atom within our bodies can participate in the same creative process as the human mind and spirit. It argues that the universe is, at every level endlessly complex and that its subtlety can never be explained fully, by any theory or system of scientific investigation" (Peat 1991:1).

This approach might lead to the flowering of interdisciplinary sciences, hybrids of integrating sciences that were once far apart, assisted by the ever-growing possibilities given by the computer. There will be further development of the meta-sciences of Complexity, Self-organization, and Chaos and their application to all areas of scientific endeavor, on the macro level of the origins of our universe to the micro level of neurobiology; from the exact sciences of physics and chemistry, to the human sciences of sociology and psychology.

Accompanying the exponential growth, diversity, and variety of scientific knowledge and information, there might be a growing importance in learning how to learn, being creative, learning from practical and inner experience that transcends present limitations, and a flowering of unorthodox ways of thinking and learning. Learning and personal development may be accepted as a lifelong process. All of these trends that possibly will develop in the knowledge era hold hope for a humanity that will know more about, and be better able to deal with complexity, and to cope with uncertainty. The leap to a higher level of diversity, speed, and complexity requires a corresponding leap to higher, more sophisticated forms of integration. In turn, this demands radically higher levels of knowledge processing.

The progress in the New Sciences, of which this book is a part, combined with the enormous advances in the information and computer sciences may hold hope for a humanity that will be able to use that knowledge to deal with the growth of complexity and the intensification of uncertainty. The sciences of Chaos, Self-organization, and Complexity along with evolution are just beginning to put at mankind's disposal the insights and understanding that may be the base of evolutionary learning and strengthening human agency in self-organizing a more livable world.

DESIGNING AND DEVELOPING SYSTEMS

There is need for a process that turns images into reality. Evolutionary system design attempts to translate the vision into policies and activities that advance human systems closer to their future vision. System design is different from former approaches that dealt with complex problems to attain desired future states. This was done by breaking the problems up into manageable pieces and dealing separately with the solution to each piece.

In system design the different pieces of the problem are seen as interacting, interdependent components. Dealing with change depends on dealing with them as such and changing the patterns of relationship between them to create a new pattern. The system to be designed must be designed as a whole. Pieces cannot be broken off to be dealt with separately. The quality of the part is dependent on its relationship to the whole. The design needs to focus on interactions and interrelations of all the components of the system.

System design tries to draw alternative images of a desired future. It also develops criteria that allow evaluation of the alternatives and choice of that alternative which appears the most suitable. Finally it involves working on a plan to develop the chosen alternative (Banathy:77).

System design is not a one shot affair. The design is continually changed during implementation, based on the learnings of those who are attempting to realize it. The theories used in system design are not exploited as a form of control but as suggestions and springboards to move in the direction of the future vision.

Designing through Dialogue

Wailand (1993) proposes that system design empowers those who engage in it. It moves their focus from looking at the past to looking to the future. Much emphasis is placed on the importance of process in system design. Participation of all those concerned with the design is essential. Careful thought must be given to the processes by which systems are designed. A centralized hierarchical process of laying down the design from above without involving most stakeholders in the design process might be doomed to failure. It has been suggested that the design be created in a continuous process of dialogue between all stakeholders.

Dialogue, as suggested by David Bohm, Peter Senge, and others, differs from discussion and debate. Dialogue is approached in a climate of inquiry. Ideas are put forward not to win support, but in the spirit of investigation. The participants are not encouraged to debate the relative merits of the ideas. There is respect for differences and acknowledgment of each speaker's contribution. Judgments are suspended so as to be open to new and different perspectives of reality. Effective listening skills are encouraged and blocks to listening are explored.

The group encourages its members to attend to and be aware of their feelings and thoughts. This means encouraging inner awareness and mindfulness. There is a process of emptying oneself for receiving the ideas of others. There is also a climate of suspension of ideas in the sense of holding them lightly and not being attached to their rightness or wrongness. People share their intuitions and ideas without attempting to impress and without fear of rejection.

People listen to each other with selfless receptivity, thus opening themselves to create a common understanding. Mental models are made explicit and cultural assumptions that may be behind differences in perception and opinion are surfaced. The structure of the deep, underlying assumptions of the group are examined and an attempt is made to uncover meanings shared by all the group members. Different views are encouraged and developed so that the deeper meanings will emerge. The focus is on learning and inquiry so as to collectively reach deeper, more complex levels of understanding and unveil hidden patterns.

As a result of sustained inquiry in dialogue, a group can achieve a state of shared meanings, collective intelligence, and deep understanding. Dialogue is a move away from a linear analytic approach to team work in a nonlinear, systemic, holistic approach. It creates the conditions that allow the discovery of the deep patterns underlying the complexities of human problems and the search for system parameters that shape the patterns.

Application to Present Meta Problems

A number of attempts have been made to draw an outline of the major strategies needed to implement a systems design that will address humanity's present metaproblems. Most suggestions emphasize a movement from a culture of domination to one of international cooperation. Challenging humanity's metaproblems will demand higher levels of cooperation between peoples and nations to avert the dangers threatening mankind. Lynn Margulis, one of the creators of the Gaia hypothesis, stresses the need for new kinds of unifying cooperative ventures to allow mankind to survive the crises facing it.

Briggs and Peat write that at this time in history, caught in the chaotic conditions we have created, to continue as the individuals we have become "we will have to couple on a worldwide scale with each other and with the environment. In their own way, the early bacteria facing the oxygen crisis 'realized' the same thing: Cooperate or perish. But this time, if it occurred, the global cooperation would have the added dimension of becoming aware of itself through billions of autonomous human brains" (1989:156).

Erwin Laszlo (1991) has suggested four major objectives of a strategy to deal with present-day global meta-problems: (1) Restrain the power of the nation-state. This would include downward transfer of authority at all levels from large powers to their constituent states, from cities to smaller communities and so on. (2) Restrain the power of politicians and limit it, encouraging democracy and creating conditions to eliminate power abuse. (3) Create voluntary concluded agreements between societies for defense cooperation. These could be used to bring about cessation of hostilities. (4) Create voluntary concluded agreements to cooperate in dealing with environmental problems. These would regulate the exploitation of natural resources and safeguard the balance and regenerative cycles of nature.

GUIDELINES IN SYSTEM DESIGNING

Each human system, at its own level, needs to involve its members in a dialog of system designing and developing. The designs of different systems will be different and the design of the same system may be different at different points in its development and under dissimilar environmental conditions.

While there will be differences, there may be a number of guidelines that can assist those attempting, in these times, to create a design and develop it. At our present state of knowledge, some of these guidelines might possibly be:

- Balancing at the edge of chaos
- Creating an identity of a learning system
- Taking a coherent part in the network of ecological processes. Encouraging variety and diversity
- Learning to manage chaos
- Coevolvement of the outer and the inner world

Balancing at the Edge of Chaos

We will need to learn how to design human systems that have the ability to balance themselves at the edge of chaos. Being at the edge of chaos is where information gets the upper hand over energy, and information processing becomes an important part of the system. Computation, which is a basic characteristic of complex adaptive systems, is at an optimum at the edge of chaos. Complex adaptive systems, in a never ending process of adaptation and coevolution, through emergence and natural selection, bring themselves to the edge of chaos. This is where complex behaviors assume a lifelike character. It is where complex adaptive systems try to be.

Being poised at the edge of chaos means not being straitjacket in an unresilient structure of too much order. It also means not passing a critical bifurcation into too much irregularity, disorder, and anarchy. It means being poised in a dynamic balance with sufficient nonlinear freedom to enhance creativity, novelty, entrepreneurship, risk taking, experimentation, and discontinuous change while not drowning in totally chaotic confusion and uncertainty.

A system designed to balance at the edge of chaos centers its identity around being a learning, changing system. It knows that all structure-dependent solutions to problems are short-lived, it is oriented to continuous accelerating rates of inexorable change. It cherishes variety and diversity. It encourages uniqueness and nonconformity. It is open to the new and the novel. It takes risks and encourages risk taking.

While maintaining this climate it is careful to remain dedicated to its vision and evolutionary mission as long as they are still meaningful, and to redefine them when they do not reflect the changed reality. The regularity and order within it are maintained not so much by outside penalties, structure and constrictions but mainly by inner-conviction in the values and vision of the system. Learning to design systems with the characteristics described above is a major guideline for evolutionary design.

There is evidence to suggest that achieving a balance at the edge of chaos can be better attained by tuning a number of key parameters such as: The degree of internal complexity needs to match external complexity. The degree and quality of external communication and relationships needs to match the level of mutual interdependence. The measure of component autonomy needs to match the level of complexity of the system. The degree and quality of internal communication needs to match the degree of internal complexity. The quality of mutual responsibility and cooperation needs to match the degree of interdependence. Resource schisms should be maintained below the Feigenbaum Point.

Creating an Identity as a Learning System

Having an image as a learning system means that the system never sees itself as static but as constantly changing with every new learning. Learning and changing complement each other as part of the identity of the system. No structure is seen as final and the only way to survive is to be able to move through different forms. Moving through different forms entails the ability to be self-reflectively aware of the processes of change the system is going through and use the advances of the New Sciences to attain this consciousness.

Goerner (1992) believes that all solutions that are dependent on structure are sure to fail. To meet the challenge of accelerated change is to acquire the ability to move easily through forms. Structures that have the ability to change form will be able to survive. Consciousness and science have this ability to change their form; they are able to learn.

Contributing to Evolutionary Processes

In attempting to design a healthy system there needs to be awareness of its role in the wider developmental processes taking place around it. Fitness is also taking a coherent part in evolutionary processes. Fitness is the ability of a species to participate in the evolution of ecological processes. Goerner stresses our need to understand that the world ecology is not only our responsibility, but also our origin and it will create our future. We are not only interconnected, but our interconnection and existence are part of an evolving process that we take part in and to which we contribute. Through this process we were born, and through it we can end.

There is no sense in attempting to evaluate the fitness of a system on its own. Fitness only has meaning in terms of a coevolutionary context. Every system is connected to other systems in evolutionary developments. It affects other systems and they affect it. Together in their interactions they contribute to wider developmental processes and the latter in its turn affects them.

It is impossible to design social systems at the end of this century, without taking into account their changing contexts within the era of bifurcation, and the part the system plays in these processes. Defining the system's specific contribution to these processes is part of its vision and gives meaning and purpose to its existence.

Encouraging Variety and Diversity

An important factor in a system's viability is its ability to match external variety with internal variety. As the world becomes more complex, it also becomes more differentiated and varied. To be able to function in such a world the system needs the capability of matching its environmental diversity with internal diversity. It is internal differences in energy gradients that catalyse the self-organization of dissipative structures. And richness of the ties between diversified internal components contributes to a systems viability.

A certain measure of internal economic diversification appears to be a precondition of economic growth. As they do not reach this degree of internal economic variety and complexity, even with large investments banana republics do not reach the takeoff line. "Inhomogeneity is a necessity of growth. Our differences, those random uniquenesses are critically important. The image of cherishing the maverick, the odd-ball, the non-conformist, is well founded. Difference is the seed of change and growth. Evolutionary competence must include improved valuing of diversity and experimentation" (Goerner 1993:177).

Managing Chaos

Systems functioning in an age of intensified chaos may necessitate the ability to manage chaos. The New Sciences are just taking the first steps in advancing mankind's knowledge of how to manage chaos. In a recent article, W. Ditto and L. Pecora (1993) describe methods of mastering chaos. They describe how engineers use chaos to stabilize lasers. They relate how the motions of metallic ribbons swaying chaotically in a magnetic field can be transformed by making slight changes in the field. A team at the Naval Research Laboratory has developed a new approach to managing chaos called tracking which compensates for parameters that change as the system ages. This extends the range over which the control of chaos can be maintained.

A team at the medical school of UCLA has developed a technique for controlling chaos in biological systems. They have been able to stabilize a rabbit's chaotic heartbeat by stimulating it using seemingly random electric signals. Using a similar approach research is going on to control chaotic seizures in the human heart.

A. Hubler (1992) of the Beckman Institute and S. Guastello (1992) of Marquette University have addressed the Chaos Network on managing chaos in natural and social systems. The strategy is described as first determining the systems dominant chaotic regime and then adding sufficient matching chaos so as to keep a desired balance between disorder and order. In short this means using chaos to cope with chaos. Guastello describes how he used this process in the area of population dynamics and workforce productivity. As a whole, research in the area of managing chaos is just beginning and holds hope for a future of coping with chaos in human systems.

Coevolution of Outer and Inner Worlds

In designing new human systems care should be taken to ensure coevolvement of the inner and the outer world. The industrial era has channeled human energy into controlling the outer world. All of its efforts and resources have gone toward the development of technology to conquer the environment and put it in the service of man's needs.

Possibly the time has come to channel far more energy to cultivate the inner world. Industrial civilization has focused on the outer path. At this bifurcation point in human history, for the first time, we may choose a symbiosis in the complementarity of both paths (Jantsch 1980).

There is need for a movement from a point of reference focused only on the outer world to a focus also on the inner world. The shift to this perspective comes about when people become aware of themselves in the act of knowing. Differing from other creatures, humans are able to do this. In doing this, as Bach suggests, man joins together the outer and inner worlds. "As an organism, he is a biological being. As a self aware organism, he is a member of the socio-cultural world. And to the degree that he is a super conscious being, he inhabits the universal world" (1993:111).

Willis Harman (1991) discusses how the Western neglect of subjective experience has created a confusion about values. It is in the realm of the subjective, the transcendent, and the spiritual that societies have found the basis for their sense of meaning and deep value commitments.

The coevolution of both worlds, inner and outer, becomes a guideline for designing human systems. Humans have utilized, so far, a tiny part of the vast resources of their inner potential. Almost unlimited horizons are open before them in developing their creativity and in utilizing the possibilities of levels of inner awareness, intuition, consciousness, and transcendental ideals.

It seems, as Jantsch suggests that the most important task today is that the openness of the inner world be matched to the openness of the outer world. Jean Houston sums this up:

We find ourselves in a time in which extremely limited consciousness has the powers once accorded to the gods. Extremely limited consciousness can launch a nuclear holocaust with the single push of a button. Extremely limited consciousness can and does intervene directly in the genetic code, interferes with the complex patterns of life in the sea, and pours its wastes into the protective ozone layers that encircle the earth. Extremely limited consciousness is about to create a whole new energy base linking together computers, electronics, new materials from outer space, biofacture, and genetic engineering which in turn will release a flood of innovation and external power unlike anything seen before in human history. In short, extremely limited consciousness is accruing to itself the powers of Second Genesis. And this with an ethic that is more Faustian than godlike.

We must therefore begin to do what has never been done before. We must assume the Imago Dei and humbly but tenaciosly educate ourselves for sacred stewardship, acquiring the inner capacity to match our outer powers. We must seek and find those physical, mental, and spiritual resources that will enable us to partner the planet. (1982:213)

Thus we begin the journey into a new era, wherein humanity first becomes aware of its place in evolution and takes responsibility in designing its path into the future. Together with the intensification of uncertainty and man's capability to destroy life on earth is born the human ability to become aware of evolutionary processes, to attain evolutionary consciousness, and to apply human agency in designing and creating a better world.

References

Anderson, H., H. Goolishian, and L. Widermand. "Problem Determined Systems." *Journal of Strategic & Family Therapy* 5 (1986):1-13.

Artigiani, Robert. "Post Modernism and Social Evolution: An Inquiry." *World Futures* 30 (1991a):149-161.

---. "Model of Societal Self-Organization." In *Time, Rhythms and Chaos in the New Dialogue with Nature*, edited by George Scott, 101-116. Ames: Iowa State Uiversity Press, 1991b.

Assiogli, Robert. *The Act of Will*. New York: Viking, 1973.

Bach, Judy I. "Evolutionary Guidance System in Organizational Design." *World Futures* 36 (1993):107-127.

Banathy, Bela, H. "From Evolutionary Consciousness to Guided Evolution."*World Futures* 36 (1993):73-79.

Bateson, Gregory. *Steps to an Ecology of the Mind*. New York: Random House, 1972.

Bower, Bruce. "Chaotic connections." *Science News* (Jan. 1988):58-59.

Briggs, John, and David F. Peat. *Turbulent Mirror*. New York: Harper & Row, 1989.

Capra, Fritjof. *The Turning Point*. New York: Bantam, 1983.

Crutchfield, James P., J. D. Farmer, N. H. Packard, and R. S. Shaw. "Chaos." *Scientific American* (Dec, 1986):46-57

Davies, Paul. *The Cosmic Blueprint*. New York: Simon & Schuster, 1988.

---. "Chaos Frees the Universe." *New Science* (Oct. 1990).

Dell, Paul. "Beyond Homeostasis: Toward a Concept of Coherence." *Family Process* (1982).

Dell, Paul and H. Goolishian. "An Evolutionary Epistemology for Cohesive Phenomena." *Family Dynamics* 6 (1981).

Dertouzos, Michael L. "Communication, Computers and Networks." *Scientific American* (May 1991).

Ditto, William L. and L. M. Pecora. "Mastering Chaos." *Scientific American* 269 (Aug. 1993):62-69.

Dooley, Kevin. "Chaos and the Deming Management Method." Proceedings of the First Annual Chaos Network Conference. Urbana Il: People Technologies, 1991.

Eisler, Riane. "Cultural Evolution: Social Shifts and Phase Changes." In *The New Evolutionary Paradigm*, edited by Ervin Laszlo. Reading, UK: Gordon and Breach, 1991.

Elkaim, Mony. "Chance and Change in Family Therapy." *Journal of Marital and Family Therapy* (July 1981).

Ferguson, Marilyn. *The Acquarian Conspiracy*. Los Angeles: Tarcher, 1980.

Ferrucci, Piero. *What We May Be*. Los Angeles: Tarcher, 1982.

Frantz, Tad G. and Curtis Miller. "Evolutionary Competence in the Postmodern Family: An Idealized Design Approach." *World Futures* 36 (1983):83-105.

Gell-Mann, Murray, R.A. Millikan, and R. Maxwell. "Visions of a Sustainable World, " Working paper, Santa Fe Institute, 1990.

Gergen, Kenneth. *The Saturated Self*. New York: Harper & Collins, 1991.

Gleick, James. *Chaos: Making a New Science*. New York: Penguin Books, 1987.

Goerner, Sally J. *Chaos and Its Implications for Psychology; Science and the Dynamical World Vision*. San Francisco: Saybrook Institute Mimeograph, 1991.

---. Chaos and the Evolving Ecological Universe: A Study in the Science and Human Implications of a New World Hypothesis. Mimeograph, 1992. Reading, UK: Gordon and Breach, forthcoming.

---. "Reconciling physics and the Order-Producing Universe: Evolutionary Competence and the New Vision of the Second Law." *World Futures* 36 (1993):167-179.

Goldstein, Jeffrey. "Predictability and Planned Change in Organizations:Linear and Nonlinear Perspectives." Proceedings of the Organizational Development Annual Conference, 1991.

Guastello, Stephen. "Population Dynamics and Workforce Productivity." Proceedings of the Second Annual Chaos Network Conference, 1992.

Harman, Willis. *Global Mind Change*. New York: Warner Books, 1988.

---. "The Emerging Wholeness Worldview and its Probable Impact on Cooperation." *World Futures* 31 (1991):73-83.

Hawking, Stephen. *A Brief History of Time: From the Big Bang to Black Holes*. New York: Bantam Books, 1988.

Houston, Jean. *The Possible Human*. Los Angeles: Tarcher, 1982.

Hubler, A. "Modelling and Control of Complex Systems." Proceedings of the Second Annual Chaos Conference, 1992.

Jantsch, Erich. *The Self Organizing Universe: Scientific and Human Implications of the Emerging Paradigm of Evolution*. New York: Pergamon Press, 1980.

Keller, Kenneth. "Managing the Innovation Explosion." *Foreign Affairs* (Fall 1990).

Kelly, George. *The Psychology of Personal Constructs*. New York: Norton, 1955.

Koestler, Arthur. *The Act of Creation*. London: Pan, 1977.

Kuhn, Thomas. *The Structure of Scientific Revolutions*. Chicago: University of Chicago Press, 1970.

Laszlo, Ervin. *The Age of Bifurcation: Understanding the Changing World*. Reading UK: Gordon and Breach, 1991.

Leonard, George. *The Transformation*. Los Angeles: Tarcher, 1972.

Levy, Amir and Uri Merry. *Organizational Transformation: Approaches, Strategies, Theories*. New York: Praeger Publishers, 1986.

Lewin, Roger. *Complexity: Life at the Edge of Chaos*. New York: Macmillan. 1992.

Lukas, Mary. "The World According to Ilya Prigogine."_*Quest* (Dec. 1980).

Loye, David and R. Eisler. "Chaos and transformation." *Behavioral Science* 32 (1987).

Lynch, Dudley and Paul L. Kordis. *Strategy of The Dolphin*. New York: William Morrow & Co., 1989.

Mandelbrot, Benoit. *The Fractal Geometry of Nature*. New York: Freeman, 1983.

Malaska, Pennti. "Economics and Social Evolution: The Transformational Dynamics Approach." In *The New Evolutionary Paradigm*, edited by Ervin Laszlo. Reading, UK: Gordon and Breach, 1991.

Marshak, Robert. "Managing the Metaphors of Change." *Organizational Dynamics* (Summer 1993).

Marshall, Lisa and Mark Michaels. "The Chaos Paradigm." *Proceedings of the First Annual Chaos Network Conference.* Urbana IL: People Technologies, 1991.

Maturana, H. and F. Varela. *Autopoiesis and Cognition: The Realization of the Living*. Holland: Reidel, 1980.

McAuliffe, Kathleen. "Get Smart: Controlling Chaos." *Omni* 12 (1990).

McCartney, Scott. "Thinkers Ponder Perplexing Problems." *Wisconsin State Journal* (May 19, 1990).

Merry, Uri. *Coping With Crisis*. (Hebrew) Tel-Aviv: Cherikover, 1990.

Merry, Uri, and Melvyn Allerhand. *Developing Teams and Organizations*. Reading, MA: Addison Wesley, 1978.

Merry, Uri, and George Brown. *The Neurotic Behavior of Organizations*. Cleveland: The Gestalt Institute of Cleveland Press, 1987.

Meyer, Leroy N. "Nonlinear Self-Organization and Non-Reductive Unification of Science." In *Time, Rhythms, and Chaos in the New Dialogue with Nature*, edited by G. Scott, 285-304. Ames: Iowa State University Press, 1991.

Michael, Mark. *The Chaos Paradigm*. Video Cassette of workshop. 1992.

Miller, Eric. Chaos, *Creativity and Containment*. Lecture at The Israeli OD Network Conference, 1992.

Montuori, Alfonso. "Evolutionary Learning." *World Futures* 36 (1993).

Murray, Carl. "Is the Solar System Stable?" *New Scientist* (Nov. 1989):60-63.

Ornstein, Robert and Paul Ehrlich. *New World New Mind*. New York: Simon and Schuster, 1990.

Pagels, Heinz R. *Dreams of Reason: The Computer and the Rise of the Science of Complexity*. New York: Bantam Books, 1989.

Peat, David F. *The Philosophers Stone*. New York: Bantam Books, 1991.

Pelletier, Kenneth R. *Mind as Healer Mind as Slayer*. New York: Delta Books, 1977.

Perls, Fritz. *Ego Hunger and Aggression*. New York: Random House, 1969.

---. *Gestalt Therapy Verbatim*. New York: Bantam, 1976.

Perry, Glen A." The Evolution of the Psyche." *World Futures* 36 (1993).

Prigogine, Ilya and I. Stengers. *Order Out of Chaos: Man's New Dialogue with Nature*. New York: Bantam Books, 1988.

Rifkin, Jeremy. *Entropy: A New World View*. New York: Bantam Books, 1981.

Robey, Bryant, S.O. Rutstein, and L. Morris. "The Fertility Decline in Developing Countries." *Scientific American* (Dec. 1993).

Ruelle, David. *Chance and Chaos*. Princeton, N.J: Princeton University Press, 1991.

Ruthen, Russell. "Adapting to Complexity." *Scientific American* (Jan. 1993).

Schon, Donald A. *Beyond the Stable State*. New York: W. W. Norton, 1971.

Schwalbe, Michael L. "The Autogenesis of the Self." *Journal for the Theory of Social Behavior* 21 (1992):270-293.

Scott, George, ed. *Time Rhythm and Chaos: In the New Dialogue with Nature.* Ames: Iowa State University Press, 1991.

Selye, Hans. *Stress in Health and Disease.* Boston: Butterworths, 1976.

Stein, Daniel L., ed. *Lectures in the Science of Complexity.* Reading MA: Addison Wesley, 1989.

Stewart, Ian. "Portraits of Chaos." *New Scientist* (Nov. 1989):42-47.

Swenson, R. "Emergent Attractors and the Law of Maximum Entropy Production: Foundations to a Theory of General Evolution."*Systems Research* 6 (1989):187-197.

Toffler, Alvin. *Future Shock.* New York: Bantam Books, 1971.

---. *The Third Wave.* London: Pan Books, 1981.

---. Introduction to *Order Out of Chaos*, by Prigogine,I. and I. Stengers. New York: Bantam Books, 1988.

---. *The Power Shift.* New York: Bantam Books, 1991.

Vaughan, Frances. *The Inward Arc.* Boston: New Science, 1985.

Waddington, C. H. *Tools for Thought.* London: Jonathan Cape, 1977.

Wailand, Christine B. "Evolutionary Systems Management." *World Futures* 36 (1993).

Waldrop, M. Mitchell. *Complexity: The Emerging Science at the Edge of Order and Chaos.* New York: Simon and Schuster, 1992.

Wertheim, Margaret. "The Nature of Chaos." *Simple Living* (1990):49-57.

Wheatley, Margeret. *Leadership and the New Science.* San Francisco: Berrett-Koehler, 1992.

Wysocki, B. "Santa Fe Institute Engages in Research with Profit Potential." *Wall Street Journal*, 8 May, 1990.

Young. T. R. "A Metaphysics for the Post-Modern." *The Social Dynamicist* 2,2 (1991): 5-7.

---. "Chaos and Crime: Explorations in Post-Modern Science." *Transforming Sociology Series.* Weidman: 1992.

---. *Chaos Theory and the Drama of Social Change: Essays in Postmodern Philosophy of Science.* Forthcoming.

Zurcher, Louis A. *The Mutable Self.* Beverly Hills: Sage, 1977.

Index

About the Author

URI MERRY holds a Ph.D. from the University of California at Santa Barbara, where he has taught in the Graduate School of Education. He is the author or coauthor of four books, including *Organizational Transformation* (Praeger, 1986).

ISBN 0-275-94910-9

EAN

HARDCOVER BAR CODE